A Life in Nature

A Life in Nature

At Home and Abroad

Napier Shelton

Nᴀᴘ NEW ACADEMIA
PUBLISHING

Washington DC

Library of Congress Control Number: 2019933431
ISBN 978-1-7326988-2-6 paperback (alk. paper)

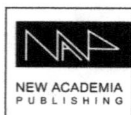

NEW ACADEMIA
PUBLISHING

4401-A Connecticut Ave., NW #236 - Washington DC 20008
info@newacademia.com - www.newacademia.com

To my father, Frederick DeWitt Shelton,
who I suspect gave me nature-loving and writing genes,
and supported me in all my interests.

Contents

List of Illustrations

Preface

Over the years, I've written books about various natural places. The present book is an attempt to be more fundamental, exploring the evolution, meaning, and importance of relationships with nature throughout one's life.

Part I, Growing Up Green in a Green City, explores my developing childhood interest in nature and adolescent involvement with people and organizations that furthered that interest and instilled a conservation commitment. It also tells my experiences at school and around the country, and what Washingtonians did to preserve nature in their city—places that offered close-at-hand communion with the natural world.

Part II, Speaking for Nature, describes my work as a writer/editor for the National Park Service and writing books about national parks and other natural areas.

Part III, Living Abroad, follows my investigations of natural history and conservation in Malaysia, Nigeria, Turkey, and Azerbaijan, thanks to my wife's career as a diplomat.

Part IV, Concluding Thoughts, considers the range of relationships that people have with nature and the increasing importance for conservation as we go up the list. It ends with the need to instill in children a bond with nature strong enough to deal with the threats to our Earth in their adult years.

Now let us think about what is at stake here, and how a close relationship of children with nature can grow.

For a long time, we inhabitants of the earth have been facing a crucial choice: live within the earth's physical limits as responsible members of a natural community, or continue on our present path toward sick environments, impoverished natural resources, and unbridled conflict over what remains.

Unfortunately, the consequences of making the wrong choice become more dire with each passing year. A still-increasing and more affluent population, with expanding needs and wants, operating within an economic system that takes insufficient account of its environmental costs, tightens the screws on our earth home, in proportion to our numbers and our increasing ability to inflict damage. Climate change, water shortages, pressure on food supplies, and diminished biological diversity are just a few of the results.

The choice is made individually and collectively. Three emotions, I suggest—fear, love, and guilt—could push the individuals making up cities, nations, and the world toward the saving choice. Fear that continued degradation of our earth will harm us physically, economically, socially, and politically. (This fear will only increase in the next generations if enough progress is not made by those in power now.) Love of living things and their environments that will move us to protect them. And guilt over destroying those things, a moral awareness that that destruction is simply wrong.

Those emotions with respect to nature begin forming in childhood and, if blended into an intellectual framework, can lead to adult caring about, understanding the need for, and actions toward creating sustainable societies—societies that live within the earth's limits.

Besides a transformed economic system, this will require an expanded ethic, one envisioned so intelligently and clearly by Aldo Leopold in the 1940s:

"All ethics so far evolved rest upon a single premise: that the individual is a member of a community of interdependent parts. His instincts prompt him to compete for his place in that community, but his ethics prompt him also to cooperate (perhaps in order that there may be a place to compete for).

"The land ethic simply enlarges the boundaries of the community to include soils, waters, plants, and animals, or collectively, the land....a land ethic changes the role of *Homo sapiens* from conqueror of the land-community to plain member and citizen of it."[1] (Aldo Leopold was a forester and ecologist who developed wildlife management into a science and whose *Sand County Almanac* became the most influential book in modern conservation.)

Aldo Leopold

Such a citizen can be formed more easily if the process begins in childhood, when one is open to all sorts of possibilities. A considerable literature explores human relationships with nature, some of it focusing on childhood experiences. The Harvard biologist E.O. Wilson hypothesizes the existence of "biophilia" in humans—"the innately emotional affiliation of human beings to other living organisms. Innate means hereditary and hence part of ultimate human nature."[2] (Many scientists think Wilson is too bio-driven vs. culturally-influenced, but I lay it out here as an interesting idea that seems plausible. I assume it can't be proved or disproved.) Evidence for the hereditary aspect includes the attraction of people to savanna-like landscapes—open areas with scattered trees—the environment in which our species evolved, and the impulse to bring living things into artificial environments, such as potted plants in high-rise offices. One might call the "bug" phase that many or most children go through another bit of evidence.

E.O. Wilson

But if that affiliation is buried in our genes, it comes from a long time ago, when we were hunters and gatherers, a time when such an affiliation was necessary for survival. But now, as Gary Paul Nabhan and Sara St. Antoine ask, "if...biophilia is the *genetic* affinity for other life, why is it expressed in some people and cultures more than others?....[a] possibility, which we believe is consistent with Wilson's original hypothesis, is that a child's learning environment greatly conditions the expression of any genetic basis for biophilia. Unless the appropriate environmental triggers are present in a certain cultural/environmental context, biophilia is unlikely to be fully expressed."[3] Thus we see a deep respect for other life in an Inuit hunting society in northern Alaska and usually little of that in poor urban neighborhoods.

So, if children are to develop a love and understanding of nature, we must make it possible for them, preserving and even creating natural spaces in and around cities, and giving them time and safe conditions in which to explore those places. Parents and mentors who can communicate their love of nature offer powerful competition to the computers and other electronic attractions that keep so many kids out of the woods. One might hope that biophilia exists in humans, but if it does not, that is all the more reason to bring children close to nature.

There are other reasons for encouraging children's contact with nature besides starting them on the road to constructive environmentalism. That is the benefits children gain from that contact. There is, of course, the physical exercise involved in exploring nature, and associated with that the discovery of one's abilities and limits: can I jump across that stream, can I climb that tree or rock face? Further, as Richard Louv expresses it in his important book, *Last Child in the Woods*, "Nature offers healing for a child living in a destructive family or neighborhood. It serves as a blank slate upon which a child draws and reinterprets the culture's fantasies. Nature inspires creativity in a child by demanding visualization and the full use of the senses....Nature can frighten a child, too, and this fright serves a purpose. In nature, a child finds freedom, fantasy, and privacy: a place distant from the adult world, a separate peace."[4]

Lack of contact with nature, for which Louv coined the term "nature-deficit disorder," is harmful. "Nature-deficit disorder describes the human costs of alienation from nature, among them: diminished use of the senses, attention difficulties, and higher rates of physical and emotional illnesses."[5]

Stephen Kellert, a professor at the Yale School of Forestry and Environmental Studies, studied human relations with nature for over 20 years. He found that "our inclination to connect with nature [addresses needs beyond the materialistic]: intellectual capacity, emotional bonding, aesthetic attraction, creativity and imagination, even the recognition of a just and purposeful existence."[6]

There is a progression in the ways "people perceive and process their understanding of nature....Sometimes we view nature with fear, desire, or need. At more complex levels of experience, we reveal interest, fascination, curiosity, imagination. At even more sophisticated planes of perception, we form attitudes, judgments, and beliefs."[7]

Looking specifically at children's formation of attitudes toward nature, he found a similar progression. "The preschool period from four to six years of age marks the time when children largely express feelings toward nature and animals—particularly desire, attraction, fear, and aversion....The next stage, usually from six to nine years of age, involves a greater appreciation of the feelings and needs of other creatures....The stage that follows—the middle school years—marks the time when children reveal a dramatic increase in knowledge, interest, and curiosity about nature and life.... Finally, in late adolescence children express more abstract and conceptual orientations to life and nature, becoming much bolder and more exploratory in their experience of the natural world. Children at this stage form ecological and moral judgments about nature, as well as views about human responsibilities and ethical obligations." [8]

The bottom line for Kellert and many other students of this subject is that contact with nature is very important, even necessary, for physical, emotional, intellectual, and spiritual growth.

In this book I relive my own experiences in nature during childhood and adolescence and try to discern whether and how they reflect the ideas presented above. I explore the possible role of heredity in these experiences, the influence of my parents, mentors, and other people and organizations in supporting and guiding my affinity with nature, and the many natural environments of Washington, D.C. that offered me outdoor adventures. At times we move beyond Washington as my geographic universe expanded, but Washington has been my home from birth to early adulthood and much of the time after that.

Washington, D.C. was a good place for someone interested in nature to grow up in during the 1930s and '40s. Some residential areas, including my own, were still emerging from a rural past, with grassy fields and patches of woods; traffic outside the downtown was light; and in much of the city kids could roam without fear. It was also the site of many institutions and organizations devoted to the study and welfare of nature and natural resources, such as the Smithsonian Institution, the Fish and Wildlife Service, the National Park Service, the Audubon Society of the District of Columbia (now the Audubon Naturalist Society), the Wilderness Society, and Defenders of Wildlife. Some of these were second homes for me. Thus, Washington was both physically and institutionally green.

We had many people who were prominent in the conservation efforts of that day, such as Rachel Carson and Roger Tory Peterson, and many others less prominent but equally dedicated. Even the Congress, pushed by Franklin Roosevelt, got involved in conservation, at least in the 1930s, before war commanded national attention. All these, too, had an influence on me.

Though some elements are common to the stories of most people who grew up "green," each story, as any person's life, is essentially unique and worth telling. Mine was fun, exciting, perhaps idyllic.

I hope it will inspire others to find the health and strength nature offers, and to lead children along that path. Luckily, my father persuaded me to begin keeping a journal when I was nine, and I have continued it to the present day. Quotes from it make more real and objective my evolving relationships with nature and correct some of the inaccuracies of memory.

As stated at the beginning of this preface, I take my story beyond adolescence through the succeeding years of my life. During those years I shared my love and understanding of nature primarily through writing. Now in my 80s I increasingly see nature as something that must be protected for practical reasons, and for all it gives us, but also because I see it as sacred.

PART I

Growing Up Green
in a Green City

1

Three to Five

Before I was old enough to remember anything, my parents took me, their only child, from a Georgetown apartment to a rambling frame house in Chevy Chase, Maryland, just outside the D.C. My father had joined Willard Kiplinger in the recently formed Kiplinger Washington Agency in 1931. Success of the Kiplinger Letter, a short, snappy, weekly analysis of probable effects of Congressional and Administration decisions on business, sheltered us economically from the deepening depression of the 1930s. My only awareness of hard times was aroused by "hobos" asking for food at our kitchen door.

His job enabled my father to buy that house with a spacious yard, dotted with trees, that sloped down to a small, square pond edged with flagstone. Four memories remain from our short time there: sledding down our street with my mother; standing on a limb in our apple tree making a speech that got no further than "ladies and gentlemen," riding tricycles with my neighbor, Robert Whitmore; and a misadventure at the pond.

The last event raised, however dimly, a moral question in my childish mind about our relations with other forms of life. Robert and I had been stalking the frogs that lived in the pond and I actually managed to spear one before it could leap into the water. Then, somewhat sorry I had extinguished its life, I began running around the flagstones bordering the pond. At one corner I tried to jump across and fell into the pond. Sinking, I saw bubbles rising above me. Then the hand of my father, who fortunately had been working in the yard, grabbed me. He carried me, coughing and spluttering, into the house, where I eventually calmed down. But the fright lingered. Somehow I associated killing the frog with my supposed near-drowning—a case of crime and punishment. I had followed an impulse to hunt frogs, but perhaps, I thought, it was wrong to

Father and son raking at the home in Chevy Chase, Maryland

kill them. The morality of hunting and killing would come to mind more sharply when I was old enough to own a bee-bee gun.

Later that year, 1935, we moved to a new home near Foxhall and Reservoir roads, in northwest Washington. It was in a new subdivision called Colony Hill. Our white, brick house, built to my parents' specifications, sat on one-half acre. Beyond the back yard a steep slope led down to another level, where my father put in a rose garden. Our side yard was populated with black cherry trees and later a sycamore and a holly. Beyond the rose garden lay a vacant lot where rabbits roamed. Across graveled Hadfield Lane, atop steep banks, a patch of woods beckoned.

At first my territory didn't extend beyond Colony Hill, in its early days of development. Bounded by Foxhall and Reservoir roads and the quieter Hoban Road, it consisted of a few houses, many vacant lots, and the woods across Hadfield Lane. American elms had been planted along some of the streets. The woods offered the most adventure. I would climb the steep bank across from our house and into the mid-sized trees. It was a small kingdom for me, one of which I seemed to be the only explorer. One edge looked down on Reservoir Road, another world where cars and buses passed. Another edge was populated with straight, slender ailanthus trees, which I later found were good for making hideouts and lightweight spears.

Beyond Hoban Road lay Glover-Archbold Park, a natural, stream-valley park one-quarter-mile wide and three miles long. I crossed into that larger kingdom, two blocks from our house, when I was five. I was awed and excited by the tall trees overhead that covered the slopes leading down to Foundry Branch. It was all mystery and enchantment, perhaps slightly tinged with fear of the unknown. There seemed to be an infinity of possibilities for exploration.

The park became an irresistible attraction. One day I was in our back yard with my mother. When she went into the house she said, "Now you stay here." If she hadn't said that, I probably would have stayed, but her words raised an opposite idea—run off. As fast as my little legs would carry me, I ran down Hadfield Lane and into Glover-Archbold Park. I walked on and on up the path along Foundry Branch, past the improvised shacks said to be occupied by hobos, and finally came out on Foxhall Road, a mile from home. I had never wandered that far from home, and felt somewhat scared as I followed Foxhall Road in what I hoped was the right direction. With considerable relief I reached Hoban Road. There I found a posse of children and parents organized to hunt for me. David Mast, older brother of my friend Joe, was decked out in his Indian costume, with feathered headdress, bow and arrows, apparently thinking there might be danger in searching for me. My mother, of course, was even more relieved than I was, and felt no need for punishment.

Glover-Archbold Park became for me a sanctuary as well as an attraction. I loved to throw things—rocks, spears, snowballs—preferably at some target. So, walking along Hoban Road, I was moved to throw a rock at a passing car. It hit the door, the car stopped, and the driver jumped out. I started running as fast as I could toward the park. I was only a hundred yards from this supposed safety when the man caught me. He walked me to our house and told my father what I'd done. I got a stern lecture from him and thereafter was more careful where and when I threw things, though some of my targets were still inappropriate.

Glover-Archbold is one of the National Capital Parks under jurisdiction of the National Park Service. In such parks one is not supposed to disturb plants, animals, and other natural features. I didn't know about this and thus practiced a bit of commercial exploitation. Joe Mast said, "Why don't we pick some violets and sell them?" So we did. I decided to charge one cent per violet. At Fontaine Bradley's house we found a willing buyer. I told him I'd sell him a violet for one cent. He said, "I'll give you ten cents for the whole bunch." I wasn't prepared for this possibility and said no. Joe sold his bunch for the ten cents. My take for the day was well under ten cents. Joe became a businessman, I didn't. I wasn't yet a naturalist, either, but certain events would soon change that.

Thus far, what *was* the character of my relationship with nature, with other living things? Glover-Archbold was a seemingly vast other world, a wilderness beyond the lawns and gardens of Colony Hill, pure adventure. But I do not remember having curiosity or feelings about any of the plants or animals in the park. That was reserved for pets at home, especially our Irish terrier that I named Teedo, for no apparent reason; it just came to me. I was crushed when a car on Reservoir Road killed him. My feelings about the natural world seemed to be directed mostly at the whole landscape around me.

Sometime after my sixth birthday, a new era began.

Napier, Mother, and Teedo

2

Six to Eight

When I opened that first box of sea shells, I was unwittingly opening a Pandora's box that led to fascination with the whole panoply of nature. My friend Paul Fundenberg, who lived in Fort Lauderdale, had collected those shells and sent them to me. I was struck with their beauty and variety and wondered what their names were. Some answers came when my father, always eager to encourage his only child's interests, bought me a sea shell book replete with illustrations of the more common species.

More boxes of shells arrived and occupied me for days on end. Lying on my bedroom floor, I leafed through the book looking for matches with what I had in hand. When I found one I carefully wrote a label and attached it next to the shell: angel wing, sunrise shell, fighting conch, and many others. My treasures got names— common names—but not yet the scientific Latin names, and thus a bond with me; I knew them in some new way.

Was this a dawning attachment to nature, or just the urge to collect, which seems almost instinctive in children and many adults? In time I collected bugs, minerals, bird nests, whatever objects intrigued me, but also postage stamps and toy soldiers. I think it *was* more than a desire to collect; I was interested in the things I collected (well, maybe not the toy soldiers). And my interests extended to things I couldn't collect, such as astronomy. I was becoming aware of a wider world, full of things beyond myself.

My father was the central person in my life. He was ecstatic when I was born. In his journal he wrote: "He was EVERYTHING I had prayed for. Fair – normal – blue eyes – handsomely shaped head – near well formed ears. Such a joyful moment. How I love him and the girl who produced him." Since my mother bore me at 38, considered a perilously advanced age in those days, my parents, and probably my mother's doctor, decided I should be the last child. So I got a lot of attention, general nurturing from my mother and character guidance and encouragement of my budding interests from my father. I tried, in spite of occasional impulses in the opposite direction, to be the good person he wanted, and found freedom to explore physically and mentally the world around me.

Our half-acre yard was a major part of that world. I developed, especially, a fondness for its trees. One black cherry was good for climbing, and I sometimes ascended it 30 or 40 feet, occasionally swaying in the wind like John Muir—the naturalist and geologist who later became a father of the American conservation movement-- in his Sierra Nevada pine. In a larger black cherry my father built me a treehouse platform, an eyrie good for dreaming and feeling superior to pedestrian life on the ground. My father, who loved to garden, planted roses on the yard's lower level, and I worked with him while a curious catbird sometimes followed us around, inspecting the diggings. Later, birds of many kinds visiting our yard captured my attention.

I became an author at age six when my father self-published a little book called *Gyp the Squirrel and Other Stories and Jingles*, by Napier Shelton and His Father. This consisted of my retelling of the Gyp bedtime stories my father had told me, and his poems and drawings about me and other, fanciful things. It also included some of my information about ghosts. I don't know how I got drawn to that subject, but I did. In my imagination I formed a "ghost army," whose job was to kill ghosts, and in letters to Paul Fundenberg, who had sent me the sea shells, I described various species of ghosts. My father put my drawing and description of the Virginia sharp-billed ghost in the book, along with my descriptions of the crazy hook-pants ghost, the loud snooter ghost, the chattle-doo ghost, and the hug-rug ghost. (Was this the work of a primitive taxonomist?)

I also described how to make ghost poison, from water, flour, sugar, and ginger ale. This concoction was perhaps reserved for nice ghosts, a much milder concoction than what I usually put together—from the most disgusting ingredients I could find in the house. When Willard Kiplinger, my father's associate on the *Kiplinger Letter*, found out about my ghost poison, he told me he had ghosts in his attic and bought a bottle of my poison for ten cents. Later he said, "Well, I got rid of the ghosts in my attic, but now I've got them in the basement. Please sell me another bottle." Kiplinger, quite the joker, seemed intrigued with this ghost business and on another occasion when we visited him dressed his son Austin in a white sheet and sent him into the woods next to his house. I caught glimpses of this apparition but did not, I think, believe it was a real ghost. It had no similarity to any of the species I'd described.

My imagination was further aroused by objects from an expedition to Ecuador. My father, ever open to ideas for investment, had helped to finance a friend's gold-hunting trip. Problems at home forced him to cut the trip short, so he found little gold. My father's dividends consisted of various artifacts—blowguns, spears, an Indian flute, an anaconda skin, and a pre-Inca burial urn that eventually ended up in a Smithsonian exhibit, plus a very small bottle of gold dust and nuggets. The blowguns and spears I practiced with in our yard. The anaconda skin, which stretched the length of our upstairs hallway, inspired in me great wonder and awe for its live self. All these things, along with stories about the men being shot at with arrows as they made their way down into the Amazon basin, conjured up exciting images of that distant tropical world. It would be 26 years before I saw a real tropical forest.

In the first grade I met someone who led me to a lifelong association with the National Park Service and to another of my favorite habitats—the Chesapeake and Ohio Canal. Bruce McHenry's father, Donald, was the first Chief Naturalist of the National Capital Parks, a unit of the National Park System. The McHenrys first lived in Brookmont, Maryland, a small settlement overlooking the canal and the Potomac River, but after a year or two moved into the lockhouse at Lock 7 on the canal. This small, whitewashed house, with thick stone walls and dark blue window boxes containing red geraniums, had downstairs a living room with a fireplace and a kitchen. Upstairs, Donald and Bona May McHenry occupied one bedroom and my friend Bruce and his younger brother Keith shared the other.

Outside, a weeping willow and a large sycamore hung over the lock. After the 1942 flood broke canal banks the McHenrys planted a vegetable garden in the dry canal bed upstream. Downstream from the house they built a chicken and rabbit house. During the day Bruce tethered their milk goats at the top of the jungly hill rising up to the Glen Echo amusement park, and in the evening he brought them down to a shed beside the house for milking. All this became my headquarters for exploring the canal lands and Potomac River shores with Bruce, while his parents opened my eyes to the plants and animals all around. It was a place I often visited, until the McHenrys moved to Yosemite National Park in 1946. Over the subsequent years I often passed by along the towpath that remained my favorite trail through nature and history.

Lockhouse at Lock 7

By age seven my personal geography included our yard, the twenty or so houses and yards of Colony Hill, the woods across Hadfield Lane from our house, down into Glover-Archbold Park, across Reservoir Road into Foxhall Village and to my school on Foxhall Road, and now to Lock 7 and the C&O Canal. I was allowed to reach the latter on the marvelous Cabin John streetcar, which rocked along a hillside overlooking the Potomac River.

Family trips in summer to visit relatives in Missouri introduced me to Webster Groves near St. Louis, Marshfield, my father's small town in southwest Missouri, and Mount Vernon, my mother's home town not far to the west, but at first I knew little of the natural surroundings of these places. My chief memory of Uncle George's farm near Marshfield was of firing his shotgun, propped in a tree fork, and nearly falling over backward at the recoil. One of those summers my father took me on a fox hunt led by a relative riding a horse followed by a pack of eager hounds. In Missouri a fox hunt consists of sitting around a hilltop campfire listening to each other's hounds as they chase a fox they'll never catch. (This ensures a live fox for the next hunt.) Later times in Missouri took me deeper into the nature of the Ozarks.

The summers I was seven and eight, my parents sent me to Camp LeConte in the Great Smokies, a place now within Great Smoky Mountains National Park. Nature was luxuriant there, and I was aware of its exuberance. I remember a huge black snake up in a tree, large insects fluttering around lights at night, a bobcat that made a brief appearance at the rifle range, and an unfortunate bat, one of many that came out at night, that got hit by a fly ball during a baseball game. We swam in a cold mountain stream, climbed eight miles up Blanket Mountain and camped overnight there. For some reason, this budding naturalist found a nature walk I went on with a counselor rather boring. Much more fun was trying to catch footballs punted by members of the University of Tennessee football team, who were also counselors.

Throughout this book I relate Stephen Kellert's typology of human valuations of nature to my own development as a naturalist. He describes nine fundamental aspects:

> an *aesthetic* attraction for animals and nature, a *dominionistic* interest in exercising mastery and control over wildlife, an *ecologistic and scientific* inclination to understand the biological functioning of organisms and their habitat, a *humanistic* affection and emotional bonding with animals, a *moralistic* concern for ethical relations with the natural world, a *naturalistic* interest in experiencing direct contact with wildlife and the outdoors, a *symbolic* use of animals and nature for communication and thought, a *utilitarian* interest in pragmatically exploiting wildlife and nature, and a *negativistic* avoidance of animals and the natural environment for reasons of fear, dislike, or indifference.

I would eventually come to share, in varying degrees, all of these valuations, but at seven or eight I fell mostly in the naturalistic and humanistic camps, with, inevitably, some of the negativistic. I just plain liked plants and animals, liked finding and observing them, liked learning their names. My negativistic reactions were primarily dislike of such things as poison-ivy and mosquitoes. I hadn't yet learned much fear of nature, since the environments I explored and the animals I met were generally non-threatening. Only in my dreams had I met a lion that ran around our house, trying to get inside to attack me.

Why did I get hooked on nature? Was there anything hereditary in it? When I climbed trees and asked my father to build me a treehouse, was my primate ancestry part of the reason? Did my father's love of farming and gardening have anything to do with genes he passed on to me? I like to think they did.

Once the hook was imbedded, that love was nurtured by my father, by books he gave me, by people like Donald McHenry, by the easy access to green spaces, and by natural history groups and institutions that I became involved with. All this launched me on a life of love and understanding of the natural world and a desire to communicate those things.

3

Hooked on Birds

By age eight I had become addicted to birdwatching. Nothing else in nature stirred and attracted me as much as birds. Why? I often wonder. Was it their beauty, diversity, their power of flight, which allowed them to come and go in seemingly mysterious ways, to travel great distances to (for me) unknown lands, their simple visibility, which brought a succession of these various sprites into my consciousness, making me wonder what is their name, where did they come from?

I once heard the famous ornithologist Roger Tory Peterson try to answer this question. He thought perhaps it was the *freedom* of birds, which gave him a personal sense of freedom. And in recent years I have come to a similar conclusion: Birds give flight to my spirit. But at age eight I had no such answer. I just loved birds. It was as unexplainable as falling in love with a person.

Some people get hooked on birds by seeing one they never knew existed, like the diminutive Ruby-crowned Kinglet, and beginning to wonder what else was out there to be discovered. Some people catch the excitement from others who show them what is out there. Roger Peterson attributed his partly to a schoolteacher when he was eleven. But I recall no one bird that got me started, and no one person who introduced me to the bird world. The addiction just happened, like my fascination with the sea shells from Florida. Then, others supported and expanded my involvement with birds.

Certain bird experiences in our yard remain sharply alive in memory. There was a black locust tree in our backyard, at the top of the slope down to the rose garden. One winter day, as I was glancing out the window, a Cooper's Hawk landed in the top of it. This was exciting enough, but then I noticed a Downy Woodpecker frozen to the trunk barely a dozen feet below the bird-hunting hawk. Would the hawk spot it and end its life? I was torn between concern for the little woodpecker and anticipation of predatory drama. After what seemed a long time in which nothing happened, the hawk flew off. And after a cautionary pause, the woodpecker flew in a different direction, to live another day.

I was then putting out bird food under the hemlock tree by our kitchen door and watching to see what came. It was either late fall or early spring when among the usual juncos and Song Sparrows appeared a Fox Sparrow, my first. This is a bird that still gives me great pleasure because I see it infrequently and because it is beautiful. That day my heart jumped at sight of the big, robust sparrow with the rich reddish-brown plumage and bold black spots and streaks on its breast. It vigorously kicked up seeds under the hemlock, looking in charge of the area among its smaller relatives. I was more than pleased to add it to my small but growing life list.

For two years a pair of Northern Parulas (a warbler), which I assumed was the same pair, built their nest in the bottom of a tent caterpillar's web in one of our black cherry trees, easily visible from our house. This small bird with a rainbow on its yellow breast usually nests in Usnea moss in the northern part of its range and in Spanish moss in the South. Around Washington, which is between the ranges of these plants, it chooses similarly thick concealment of other types. I concluded that this smart pair had put its nest in such a place, and right next to food for the young. I proudly reported my observations of this, I thought, unusual behavior to birdwatching adults.

Northern Parula
(photo by Kent Minichiello)

By this time I was used to seeing Barred Owls in Glover-Archbold Park, where one frequently roosted by day in a particular pine tree. But the night I heard one hooting in our yard or in the small woods across Hadfield Lane came as a surprise. It was as if Glover-Archbold Park had moved next to our house or the owl was being extremely adventurous. Never again did I hear that wild "who-cooks-for-you, who- cooks-for-you-all" so close to home.

To see birds close up, I asked my father if he would build a bird feeder on the outside sill of my bedroom window. He not only did that but also bought me a copy of Ada Govan's book, *Wings at My Window*, about watching birds at her window feeder. Ada Govan was an amateur ornithologist, bander of hundreds of birds, and a close friend of Rachel Carson. All of this came out of personal tragedy early in her married life.

> Ada Govan was a housewife with a young family when in 1930 she lost three infant children in succession and her ten-year-old son barely survived a prolonged illness. To regain her physical and mental health, she and her husband built a house in the Massachusetts woods. Shortly thereafter Govan suffered a terrible fall that reduced her to a housebound invalid. In great physical pain and deeply depressed, she looked out of her window during one terrible December blizzard to find a small chickadee clinging to her windowsill. She fed it, and the other birds that came, and soon found in their visits a reason to live.[1]

That led to writing, long-term communication with Rachel Carson, and bird-banding.

For days nothing came to my feeder—my window was on the second floor, rather far from any trees. Finally they did. I was enthralled with the procession of chickadees, titmice, nuthatches, and cardinals, just a few feet from my riveted eyes. So stirred was I that I wrote a letter to Mrs. Govan, describing in breathless detail what I was seeing. And she wrote back, thanking me and knitting me more firmly into the fraternity of bird enthusiasts.

Down on Hoban Road, next to Glover-Archbold Park, lived Charles Woodbury, a chemist and early member of the Wilderness Society. He learned that I was interested in birds and invited me to come any time to watch birds that came to his feeders out back. I lay on the floor looking through the glass doors that opened to the fringe of lawn between the house and his wildflower garden, beyond which rose the tall trees of the park. His feeders, next to such habitat, attracted even more kinds of birds than mine did, and I was blissfully lost for hours watching them. I was finding that adults love to share their knowledge and interests with like-minded youngsters. (A decade or more later, at Woodbury's house, I met Sigurd Olson, a chronicler of North Country wilderness, here for a Wilderness Society meeting. He shared with me some thoughts about effective writing about nature that stay with me today.)

One by one, I saw new birds and added them to my list. Each discovery, whether something common or uncommon, was wonderful to me. I had seen a male Brown-headed Cowbird, glistening black with a dark brown head, and said to another boy who was a birdwatcher, "Guess what? I saw a cowbird!" "That's nothing," he replied, "I saw a Red-eyed Vireo." Both, I learned later, are among the most common birds in North America.

I got some other boys in the neighborhood interested in birds and formed the Colony Hill Bird Club. I established ranks, rather like those the Boy Scouts had, based on tests I devised. Those ranks ranged from Beginner, whose requirements included such things as, "show a list of at least twenty birds seen that year," and being able to answer several questions, including "What near relative of the Mourning Dove is extinct? Why?," through Advanced Beginner, Second Class, First Class, Assistant Chief, and Chief. A Chief had to, among other things, "Be able to identify any bird seen reasonably well," "Show a list of at least 100 birds seen that year and have ready information on any one of them," "Know the songs of 75 birds." I don't know how I would have tested all those ranks, but the need never came up. None of my few members ever got beyond Advanced Beginner.

Each month I wrote stuff for a club magazine, about our activities and bird notes, produced a cover with my hand-colored drawing of a bird on it, and stapled the few small pages together. Mrs. McHenry, mother of my friend Bruce, saw one of these and asked me to bring it to a picnic of the District of Columbia Audubon Society. Behind us sat Roger Tory Peterson, already famous for his revolutionary bird guides and as an accomplished bird artist. Mrs. McHenry handed him my magazine, with a black and orange redstart on the cover—not too bad for a nine- or ten-year-old, as I recall. He looked at it and handed it back without a word. No encouragement for the budding ornithologist! I guess his standards were too high, even for children. This of course belied the influence he was having and would have on creating widespread interest in the natural world, among children as well as adults.

In my tenth year I was still watching birds without the benefit of binoculars, a major handicap, and was saving money to buy a pair. Meanwhile, I remedied this problem by going on walks with people who had binoculars—for instance, George Petrides, who led National Park Service bird walks around Washington. I would hop on a bus to attend these, whether near my home or across town in Fort DuPont Park. I always followed right behind Mr. Petrides so as not to miss anything, sometimes running into him when he stopped. (George Petrides later taught in the wildlife department at Michigan State University and wrote a popular field guide on trees and shrubs for the Peterson Field Guide Series.)

By the age of ten, I was adding Kellert's aesthetic and ecologistic and scientific valuations of nature to my earlier approaches, now drawing birds and learning their habits. I thought I was going to be an ornithologist.

4

Ten to Thirteen

During the summer I was ten I spent a month with my friend Jerry Seward on his parents' farm on the Choptank River near Cambridge, Maryland. There on the hot, humid Eastern Shore of Chesapeake Bay I had new encounters with nature. We avoided the honey bees that swirled around the house from their hives on the lawn. We raised a baby robin that had become separated from its parents. From a skiff we scooped up soft-shell crabs on the river bottom with long-handled nets and, with more difficulty, the more elusive crabs in their hard-shell phase. And, many days, we picked tomatoes.

The farm had a large field devoted to tomatoes, now ripening and being picked by migrant workers, plus us. I learned something about the working part of a migrant's life: the ache and sweat of stoop labor and the low pay: then 5 cents a bushel basketfull. By the end of the month I wanted never again to see another tomato. Only occasionally were those days in the field relieved by vignettes of nature: a box turtle munching on a fallen tomato, a Bald Eagle forcing an Osprey to drop its fish, down by the river. All those experiences on the farm, though, the hard as well as the enjoyable, expanded my mental and geographic horizons.

I had much to report to my friends. I told Joe Mast (he of the violet-selling incident) I'd made eight dollars that summer. He countered with $100 he'd made mowing lawns. Up on the canal, Bruce McHenry was more impressed. He knew something about farm-like work, tending and sometimes milking the family's goats.

Bruce's father had become a mentor for me, encouraging my interests as well as those of his two sons. He was president of the Audubon Society of the D.C., along with his many park service duties, and created a Junior Audubon Society for younger folks. At a meeting of this group he called for nominations for president, got me nominated, and very shortly thereafter closed the nominations. I may have been the only nominee and was duly elected. My principal duty was to attend meetings of the senior Audubon Society, held at the home of elderly Mrs. Edith Miner. Sitting on her stuffed chairs in her dark Victorian living room, I said not a word but perhaps later reported what had happened at the meetings to the Juniors. Mr. McHenry also tapped me to lead a bird walk for my group. In later years the Audubon Society of the D.C. would introduce me to many natural wonders of the Central Atlantic States and to many people involved in conservation.

The Christmas I was nine my parents gave me a red bicycle. This allowed me to go farther from home, faster, and before long Joe Mast and I were pedaling over a mile on Saturdays to the Calvert Theater on Wisconsin Avenue to see the adventures of the Green Hornet and other film stars. Automobile traffic in those days, fortunately, was light.

More significantly for my naturalist endeavors, in a few years my bicycle was taking me down the Virginia side of the Potomac to Theodore Roosevelt Island, with its woods and marshes, past the haunts of a pair of Red-shouldered Hawks (near the present sculpture of flying gulls honoring Lady Bird Johnson), to Roaches Run Wildfowl Sanctuary, a lake connected to the Potomac beside National Airport, where ducks congregated in winter, partly or mainly because they were fed. This to me was an adventure far exceeding those of the Green Hornet. One never knew what birds might show up at Roaches Run.

Not long after I began making these downriver trips, unbeknownst to me, Louis Halle, a State Department official and Audubon Society of the D.C. member, was making similar bicycle trips, chronicling a spring in Washington. His book by that name, published in 1947, became a local nature classic.[1] Halle put into words many experiences I probably had had but didn't try to describe so lyrically. I was focused on the bird facts.

January 28: "On the other side of Memorial Bridge you could smell spring in the air, never so intoxicatingly as in this first whiff.... I began unbuttoning my soul or inner man for the first time in an age of months."

February 5: "On the uplands of Wellington, halfway between Alexandria and Mount Vernon, we came on the first flock of grackles, sauntering in black-and-purple elegance along the grass borders, perched on spires of cedar, or dragging their tails in labored flight."

March 1, at sunrise: "The trees at Roaches Run and the marsh grasses stand in relief, flooded by radiance from the horizon. All the birds are sparkling and ebullient in the sharp dawn....This is life beginning all over again, emerging from the darkness and damp into the new day."

Shelton, August 8, 1944: "Charlie and I went to Roaches Run Wildlife Sanctuary where we saw 32 species of birds. Four new for the year. Watched Long-billed Marsh Wren and nest from position in marsh. Got excellent look at the bird. Were able to see the tiny lines of white on its back (upper). Other new birds for the year, Osprey, Common Tern, Laughing Gull."

Halle, March 11, Dyke Marsh: "For two hours I struggled through the marsh, filling the sky with ducks....They circled away...exploring the whole marsh with its myriad veins, before they decided it was safe to put down and, on suddenly set wings, scudded all together over the grass tops and disappeared into some inlet hidden from view."

Pushing through the Dyke marshes, May 21: "We heard the [marsh] wrens before there was light to see them. All over the marshes we heard them, singing in a steady chorus, each song a gurgling chatter, brief but repeated with hardly time for breath."

Shelton, May 14, 1945: "Went to Dyke, Va., with Mrs. Simpson [Bird Division, Smithsonian Institution], Robert Gibbs, Tom Bradley, Tommy Woodward, Clyde___, and Randolph___. Saw Double-crested Cormorant, Philadelphia Vireo, Bald Eagle, Horned Grebe, Prothonotary Warbler, Canada Warbler, Yellow-throated Warbler, Laughing Gull, and Long-billed Marsh Wren. Year list at 128." (I was very much into listing.)

Frequently, Halle's observations awoke philosophical thoughts, on many subjects. Central to many of them was that the majority of urban people live in a "hive" of work, oblivious to the seasonal wonders around them. He concluded that "Our civilization, apparently, has become divorced from the universe and is feeding on itself." Such thoughts have stayed with me ever since reading his book in 1947.

I have a small notebook I kept in 1943-44 titled "Woodcraft and Birds." The first part has hand-colored bird pictures; my drawings of how to set up a tepee, storm caps above the tepee, implements and instructions for fire-making with bow, drill, and wood block; and drawings and descriptions of six kinds of arrows. I find these drawings surprisingly good. The second part records bird counts I made between January 5, 1943 and October 7, 1944, in Colony Hill (where I lived), nearby residential areas, Glover-Archbold Park,

Thistlewood (my father's farm), and Roaches Run (near National Airport). Besides numbers of birds, I usually noted time of day, and sometimes temperature, observers, distance traveled, and weather. In 1943 the birds are probably listed in the order in which I saw them; in 1944 (when I was twelve), they are listed in roughly taxonomic order. The June 17, 1944 count, conducted at Thistlewood Farm, was a "record census"—51 species. The farm sometimes yielded "Migrant" Shrike, Henslow's Sparrow, Bewick's Wren, and Bobwhite, species now virtually extirpated from the area. In winter I often saw Tree Sparrows at the farm; now they're scarce in this region, perhaps because of the warming climate. These are, I think, my first bird counts, and I have ever since counted birds on many field trips, with others or alone.

The following is what memory tells me. I had visited the exhibits at the Smithsonian's natural history museum, but none of this compared with something my father arranged: meeting the man who became the Smithsonian's next secretary, the ornithologist Alexander Wetmore. Together we ascended to the office of this tall, august-looking but friendly man, who talked with me about our mutual interest, and pulled out a tray of colorful trogons from Panama, whose bird life he was describing in several large, authoritative volumes.

My journal reports meeting Wetmore differently. September 16, 1944: "Took Hudson Moore with me to see Dr. Wetmore at the National Museum of Natural History. I thought he would have a mustache and Hudson didn't. Hudson was right. Dr. Wetmore showed us how they keep and study their birds and later took us to the taxidermy shop. It was a swell afternoon."

I was to have more association with Roxie Collie Simpson (Laybourne, after her second marriage), a member of the museum's Bird Division who was an expert on identifying bird feathers. She taught me how to prepare a bird specimen and later mounted for me a Clapper Rail that I picked up dead on a street in Cape May, New Jersey. (That rail still peers out at me from a bookcase in our study.) Roxie, who had a car, took me birding with her to Greenbelt, Maryland, where I saw my first Bufflehead duck on a small lake, and later to the C&O Canal and to Dyke Marsh down the Potomac from Washington, a birding spot even richer than Roaches Run.

Carla Dove, who worked with Roxie for years in the feather lab at the Division of Birds, describes her as a "unique and wonderful person...a very friendly woman." She fondly remembers her

The Clapper Rail stares out at me from a bookcase

strong North Carolina accent, her loud laughs echoing down the hallways, and her help as a mentor. An obituary by Dove and other associates describes her many accomplishments and professional skills, especially feather identification:

> Known as the 'Feather Lady,' Roxie pioneered the field of forensic ornithology at the Smithsonian Institution by study-ing the detailed microscopic structures of plumulaceous (downy) feather barbules and creating a technique of iden-tifying species of birds from fragmentary feather samples. Her methods are now used throughout the world to iden-tify birds involved in collisions with aircraft (bird-strikes) and are routinely applied to studies of prey remains, evi-dence from criminal cases, and anthropological artifacts. She

worked long hours, weekends and holidays, and never took a vacation—believing that if you love what you do, there is no need for time off.[2]

Roxie helped other kids besides me. "She took a special interest in young people. From organizing birding trips for Boy Scouts to her evening bird-skinning classes at the museum, Roxie viewed her efforts to teach 'her' students with happiness and pride." [3]

The Smithsonian thus became an institutional home for me, where serious scientists were happy to take time from their work to share their knowledge and encouragement with, maybe, a budding ornithologist.

We now move into a few years when I killed certain birds or mammals. It seems incongruous in someone whose life was immersed in a love of nature. Why did I do it? Was it something in my genes that often crops out at a certain age? I had conscious reasons for why I killed things then, and a few times in later life. But I don't know if I had unconscious reasons. Now we will explore this subject.

By age eleven I was hoping for a .22 rifle, but my father opted for a bee-bee gun. This probably made sense in a place like Colony Hill, where firing a rifle was no doubt illegal. As it was, I made illegal use of my bee-bee gun, by shooting at a little round attic window in a house being built next door. I interpreted the police car parked in front of our house next day as something related to my activity, and so kept out of sight.

I knew the window shooting was wrong but developed a sliding moral scale for the shooting of certain birds that lasted several years. I viewed starlings and house sparrows as legitimate targets because they were nonnatives and aggressively competed with native birds like the Red-headed Woodpecker and bluebird for nesting sites. I thought they were bad, even evil. (And I threw rocks at cats because they catch birds.) Some of my journal entries show how I felt about targeted birds.

December 30, 1942: "Today a starling and a Red-bellied Woodpecker came to my feeding station. I shot the starling who is a terrible pest."

January 31, 1946: "At the farm [described later], I attempted to shoot some sparrows last trip, but only succeeded in killing one. Also grazed two others and two starlings. My next scheme for liquidating sparrows is to beat their roosting places at night in the barn with a flat board." (Not a very reliable method, I suspect.)

August 20, 1947: "My friend Lloyd Hinton and I were at the farm, helping with the haying. "I came down with a sore throat friday morning, the day we were to come home. I contented myself shooting english sparrows, killing six and seriously wounding several more. Lloyd only fired at two and dropped dead the first one."

I recoil now at this bloodthirstiness, but that was the way I thought then.

The grackle was a less clearcut case. On the negative side, it ate other birds' eggs and small young, but on the positive side it was a native species. I shot one grackle but then no more. Crows, in my estimation, for the same reasons, occupied a moral position similar to the grackle's. Another time at my father's farm I took an unsuccessful shot with a twenty-two at a crow flying overhead, then couldn't get close enough to crows pestering some raptor in the woods for another shot. Their sentinel kept them informed about my location. End of crow hunting.

The hunting instinct must be fairly strong in most of the young of our species. When visiting relatives in Rogers, Arkansas during my early teens, I saw a robin feeding on the lawn and on an impulse shot it with a bee-bee gun. The poor bird lay flopping on the grass as I approached it, then, when I nudged it with my foot, flew off. I was sorry I had shot it and hoped it might survive. Robins were way off my moral scale. No shooting whatsoever allowed. I don't know why I did it, other than for some primal, subconscious reason.

I recall killing things only six other times. At thirteen I shot a red squirrel at camp in the Adirondacks for its tail, the award in a bottle-shooting contest. (You had to go get your own red squirrel tail.) At the same camp that summer I clubbed a porcupine to death, because the camp gave a prize for killing the most porcupines, which chewed canoe paddles for the salt. At fourteen, in Colorado, I killed a marmot by throwing a rock 60 yards at it and hitting it in the head. I was as surprised as the marmot must have been. I just wanted to see how close I could come. Twice I killed a snake. The first was a prairie rattlesnake at Chaco Canyon in New Mexico that I nearly stepped on. I was fourteen. The other was a copperhead in Glover-Archbold Park, when I was probably fifteen. I guess I killed them because they were a threat, or near-threat, to human life—mine and, in the case of the copperhead, of people who walked in Glover-Archbold Park. Finally, when in my forties, I shot an impala on a large farm in South Africa, just to experience, if possible, the mystique of big-game hunting. With an Afrikaner friend guiding me we got downwind from a group. I fired at a brown spot among the acacia trees and the impala fell. When we approached, it jumped up and ran away, no doubt to die later. We couldn't follow the blood spots because a sudden rain was washing them away. Jack said it was a lung shot. This made me feel better about my accuracy, but I had no more desire to go big-game hunting.

Thus, I feebly demonstrated Kellert's dominionistic valuation of wildlife, a desire to exercise mastery of living things. But I didn't progress into a hunter, committed to the sport. And though I have no serious objection to others hunting for sport or meat, I came to the point where I didn't want to kill anything myself, except if necessary in self-defense. The question about the morality of killing animals that began with frogs in our backyard was settled for me with the impala in South Africa.

But why did I go through a killing period into my early teens? And why do so many people who frequently hunt in their youth give it up later?

Perhaps hunting is an instinct engraved in our genes from the 99 percent of human existence when we were hunter-gatherers. In his introduction to Ortega y Gasset's *Meditations on Hunting*, Paul Shepard says, "Ortega has grasped that essential human nature is inseparable from the hunting and killing of animals and that from this comes the most advanced aspects of human behavior."[4] Ortega writes: "...if we attend to the facts, we discover...that the most appreciated, enjoyable occupation for the normal man has always been hunting."[5] He describes it as "a vigorous discipline and an opportunity to show courage, endurance, and skill." But, at the same time, "every good hunter is uneasy in the depths of his conscience when faced with the death he is about to inflict on the enchanting animal." He comes closest to describing hunting as a human instinct when he writes, "Hunting was...the first form of life that man adopted, and this means—it should be fundamentally understood—that man's being consisted first in being a hunter."[6] But now, after so many years with an "ancestral proximity to animals, vegetables, and minerals—in sum, to Nature—[he] takes pleasure in the artificial return to it, the only occupation that permits him something like a vacation from his human condition." [7] (Another school of thought disputes the possibility that hunting "is an instinct engraved in our genes, " because of cultural mediation during the time we have not been hunter-gatherers.)

My killing of House Sparrows and starlings was only to a small degree "hunting" as Ortega used the term. I was primarily at war with these birds, ridding the world of invasive pests. That was my conscious justification. My other few killings caused "unease in the depths of [my] conscience."

Some of Ortega's thoughts on hunting resemble those of Henry David Thoreau in the mid-19th century:

> Once or twice…while I lived at [Walden Pond], I found myself ranging the woods, like a half-starved hound, with a strange abandonment, seeking some kind of venison which I might devour, and no morsel could have been too savage for me. The wildest scenes had become unaccountably familiar. I found in myself, and still find, an instinct toward a higher, or, as it is named, spiritual life, as do most men, and toward a primitive rank and savage one, and I reverence them both.[8]

> I like sometimes to take rank hold on life and spend my day more as the animals do. Perhaps I have owed to this employment and to hunting, when quite young, my closest acquaintance with Nature. They early introduce us to and detain us in scenery with which otherwise, at that age, we should have little acquaintance.[9]

> …when some of my friends have asked me anxiously about their boys, whether they should let them hunt, I have answered yes—remembering that it was one of the best parts of my education—*make* them hunters….[10]

Here Thoreau departs from Ortega:

> There is a period in the history of the individual, as of the race, when the hunters are the 'best men,' as the Algonquins called them. We cannot but pity the boy who has never fired a gun; he is no more humane, while his education has been sadly neglected. This was my answer with respect to those youths who were bent on this pursuit, trusting that they would soon outgrow it. *No human being, past the thoughtless age of boyhood, will wantonly murder any creature which holds its life by the same tenure that he does.*[11] [italics mine]

To a much lesser extent, after the Walden period, Thoreau has a similar feeling about fishing:

I have found repeatedly, of late years, that I cannot fish without falling a little in self-respect. I have tried it again and again…but always when I have done I feel that it would have been better if I had not fished.[12]

My father bought the farm referred to above in the early 1940s, 30 miles west of Washington between Manassas, Virginia and the future site of Dulles airport. Having lived part of his childhood on a farm in Missouri, he had nursed the idea of owning one for years, and finally he had enough money. "Thistlewood," he called it, a name that had some relation to the land granted by King Charles II to Lord Fairfax and other "Lords Proprietary" in 1669. My father hired a man named O'Meara to manage the farm and occasionally hired a wiry little man with a beard that he called Lord Fairfax. A house whose main part had been built with foot-thick logs and an older part built with stones that was pre-revolutionary, sat in the middle of the 300 acres. Oak woods covered the northeast section, fields the middle, and woods the southern part, beside Long Branch, a tributary of Bull Run.

My father and some of his Herefords

My father's main intention was to raise Hereford cattle, which he preferred over black Angus because you could recognize individual Herefords by their varying brown and white patterns; secondarily, he raised pigs. He tried turkeys for a while, but they kept getting colds and dying, so he switched to chickens. Most of the fields were devoted to lespedeza and orchard grass for the cattle; some went periodically into corn. A few walnut trees stood in the fields, surrounded by patches of blue grass. The cattle herd eventually numbered 100, presided over by Prince Mischief, a bull from Montana. (In the course of doing his duty he broke a cow's back, giving us a welcome supply of steaks during World War II. We got ham when one night my father butchered a pig in our garage in Washington, but we never quite knew what part we were eating.)

Some knowledge of farming filtered through to me, but my main interest was the birds and other wildlife the farm harbored. Some of the birds I saw on a regular basis are now gone from the area or very rare: Bewick's Wrens hung around the house. Henslow's Sparrows and Loggerhead Shrikes inhabited the fields; along a fence row I found a bush where shrikes had impaled grasshoppers and other prey on thorns. One day in August a Bachman's Sparrow—the only one I've ever seen—was singing beside a garden patch. That same August I found my first Sedge Wren, no doubt on migration, in a bushy spot out in a field.

On every visit to the farm, I circumnavigated it, checking out the various habitats. The front woods usually yielded Summer Tanagers, and one day I scared a whippoorwill off its nest in leaves on the ground. The stream at the southern edge was a special attraction—aren't streams always? I happened upon two large snapping turtles out of the water, mating. When Bruce McHenry and I started a snake collection, I hunted for snakes at the farm. One day I spotted a queen snake on the stream's steep bank. Hanging over the edge, I made a quick grab and caught it, nearly falling in. The stream was also home to water snakes, one of which I captured and carried home to Washington in a burlap bag. My mother was not happy when I opened it to reveal the snake and all the small fish it had regurgitated. Alongside the stream I established my "bird sanctuary." Management here consisted of building a brushpile and planting some trees.

I was witness to some unpleasant events: O'Meara pulling out a calf that was caught in a breech birth and needed help; O'Meara shooting a rabid dog that was walking across our farm, its mouth foaming. You see a lot of death on a farm, as well as life. The dog's carcass remains in memory along with the Grasshopper Sparrows, Henslow's Sparrows, and Horned Larks I also saw in that field.

Several years after he bought the farm, my father sold it. He had kept meticulous financial records and told me he had broken even on it. It had given him great pleasure and me a sample of farm life. I had not attempted, or even thought of, judging my father's management of his land, but I recall no degradation. The last time I visited, in the 1980s, the place was still a farm, where the owner was raising bison and hydroponic lettuce. Aside from a couple of houses along the north edge, it had not yet succumbed to the development eating up Loudoun County farmland elsewhere. I fear that development has eaten up the farm now.

Is there something about teenage boys that gives them a fascination with snakes? I don't know. But when I was around thirteen Bruce McHenry and I decided to start a collection, keeping them in the McHenrys's chicken house—in cages of course. We decided early on to collect no poisonous snakes, which along that part of the Potomac River meant just copperheads. Gradually we acquired 27 snakes of 9 species, from the very small ring-necked snake to a sizeable black rat snake.

I bought some white mice to propagate and feed our snakes. Unfortunately, they got loose in my house, occasionally made an appearance but evaded capture, and never served their original purpose. We got more mice, and one day demonstrated to a visiting Girl Scout troop how a black rat snake eats a mouse. We put them both in a trash barrel. The snake contemplated the mouse for a while, then struck and swallowed it, slowly. No constriction needed. No squealing of Girl Scouts. Apparently they were mesmerized. Somehow we kept our snakes going for perhaps a year. Then we let them all go.

The spring of 1944, when I was twelve, was a traumatic time for me. The trauma began around the end of April, just as the spring bird migration was picking up steam. I contracted measles. Bedridden, I invented a game to pass the time: our maid, Barbara, would read me the description of a bird from the Peterson field guide and I would identify it. As I remember it, I got them all right. Unfortunately, the measles led to infection of the mastoid bone behind my right ear. No drugs available at the time could cure it, and the doctor said I had a really "hot ear." Must go to the hospital.

Thus ensued two weeks at Doctors Hospital, which began with two hours of chiseling out infected bone. Besides the painful changes of bandages in the hole, I was dismayed to be missing the bird migration, with all its warblers and other small birds, many of which I had not yet seen. And all I could see out the window was the wall of another building. I was entirely cut off from the world of nature. As some sort of connection with it, I wrote a short treatise on the migration of birds, which impressed the nurses no end.

Shortly before I was due to be released from the hospital my father came in with a present—a $100 second-hand pair of Zeiss binoculars, which he had bought by adding his contribution to my 36 saved-up dollars. The day I left the hospital, binoculars in hand, my mother drove me to Rock Creek Park. The world seemed luminous, miraculous. I felt transformed. Now I think of it as a resurrection, one of the few peak experiences in my life. The image that sticks with me from that day is the male Hooded Warbler I spotted with my new binoculars, in a laurel thicket up on a hillside, bright yellow with a black hood, singing away.

The spring migration was essentially over, but I consoled myself sitting in a chair in our backyard, my head still swaddled in bandages, training my binoculars on everything that flew. A few weeks later, still wearing some bandages, much of my birding was still in our yard, where I kept close watch, especially on a nest of catbirds. June 22, 1944: "Our family of catbirds has left the nest (where I found a dead baby remaining). I am sure one is still alive for it was being fed by our back porch this morning. That leaves one which is still unaccounted for. The parents are very tame and seem to like me being near them. To illustrate this: Today I saw one of them on the clothes-line. I came nearer to hang some clothes up and what should he do but start singing softly when I had approached to a distance of about five feet. It makes me feel good."

I am grateful to my parents for sending me to summer camps, first in the Great Smokies, then on Chesapeake Bay, next in the Adirondacks, and finally, to be described in a later chapter, in the Rocky Mountains. These experiences acquainted me with some of the most cherished natural environments in America as I also learned skills and grew socially.

Closest to my heart are four summers at La Jeunesse in the Adirondacks. My first summer, at age thirteen, gave me an abiding love for the North Woods. Whenever I smell balsam fir or hear a loon calling, it takes me back to that experience.

La Jeunesse was run by Harry (Hank) Blagden, a gravel-voiced Teddy Roosevelt sort of guy who had gone out west for his health. For a while he operated an iron foundry but then decided he wanted to run, as it were, a foundry producing exemplary young men, and started his camp. At evening campfires he entertained us kids with stories from his western days, such as one about fighting a wolverine, but also tried to inculcate manly virtues, which might be described as shooting straight and honoring the king.

We began each day by running from our cabin and jumping, naked, into the cold water of Square Pond, which probably was supposed to build character. Most days saw us at the rifle range, where we learned the essentials of accurate shooting at targets. The most fun part of this was the bottle shoot, where we fired at a swinging bottle on a string. There were prizes for number of consecutive hits. One was a hawk's tail feather, which Hank acquired by shooting hawks that unluckily soared overhead. A higher prize was a red squirrel tail, which was infrequently won and required the winner to go off in the woods and shoot a red squirrel (thus my killing of one, in which, during the hunt, I saw my first Three-toed Woodpecker, a bird restricted to boreal forests.) I did even better, once making sixteen consecutive hits and winning a deer's feet rack for hanging a rifle, which I never owned. Once in a great while someone reached 25 hits, giving him a deer-hunting trip with Hank in the fall. We learned canoemanship, including "egg-shell landings," in which you ease gently up to the dock, and packing a canoe so it will ride evenly. We also learned how to row Adirondack guide boats, adapted for traveling on that region's lakes. A high point was going lake trout fishing in Saranac Lake with the father of one of the campers. On my trip I hooked one at the bottom but lost it near the boat when it broke the copper snelling above the hook. What excitement and then disappointment!

As the years at La Jeunesse had gone by, the area, near Saranac Lake, had acquired more visitors and Square Pond, once entered only by canoes and guide boats, began to experience the noise of motor boats coming from Saranac Lake. "Damn tin-canners!" Hank would grumble.

There were no tin-canners on Fish Pond, where Hank leased a campsite from the New York State Conservation Department. It was a serene place, visited only by people from La Jeunesse. To reach it, we traveled on foot and by canoe eight miles, portaging our food and equipment between Hoel Pond and Clamshell Pond, where canoes were kept, and then from Clamshell to Fish Pond, where we hollered across the half-mile-wide lake for someone from the camp to come get us.

The campsite consisted of a large wooden lean-to that Hank had constructed, with a stone fireplace at one end, and two tents whose cots were covered with aromatic fir boughs, upon which we placed our sleeping bags. A spring nearby provided water. Behind the camp rose the steep slope of Fish Pond Mountain, which paralleled Fish Pond and continued on to the east. A sign read: "This is a part of God's country. Do not set it on fire and make it look like hell."

A counselor, known as the Fish Pond monitor, was in charge. He and his assistant counselor took us on hikes, up to the top of Fish Pond Mountain behind us, off to other ponds, canoeing quietly around the shores of mile-long Fish Pond, watching for wildlife. Deer came in the evening to drink; loons called and raised their young; goldeneye ducks and mergansers nested; and one day at the top of Fish Pond Mountain we encountered a black bear eating berries. From the top one could see nothing but more forest, lakes, and mountains.

I guess I showed my love of this place, because I was allowed to make several week-long trips to Fish Pond that first summer. This was real North Woods, with spruce and fir, sugar maple and white pine, beavers and most of the other animal complements of this kind of environment. And no human sounds other than our own, which we tried to keep to a minimum. Lying on my fir boughs at night, I sometimes heard overhead the beating of a loon's wings, like a distant outboard, and its wild cry.

The author, second from left in the front row, at camp La Jeunesse.
Four summers later, he served at Fish Pond as a counselor with
J.D. MacDonald, third from right, front row

At the end of the camp season I was awarded the Best Woodsman cup, no doubt because of how I acted out there. If I have a most sacred place in the world, it is Fish Pond.

If I didn't think of Fish Pond in quite those terms when I was thirteen, my feelings were, I think, nevertheless akin to the religious. There was something about the peace, the beauty, the remoteness from human activities, and the seemingly pure nature of the place that lifted me to a higher realm of consciousness—perhaps "a peace which passeth all understanding."

5

Fourteen to Eighteen:
At School and Afar

St. Albans School

In the 6th grade I transferred from a public school to St. Albans, an Episcopal school for boys on the National Cathedral Close. My father thought I would get the best education there, and the school had male teachers—better for character building in his opinion. I guess I had scored well on the entrance exam, and perhaps they were impressed with my essay on the migration of salmon.

St. Albans did give me an excellent education, and probably helped a bit with my character, but gave no mentoring in my chief interest—natural history, especially birds. There were school companions in these pursuits, however. Tom Bradley went to the farm with me and on birding trips, but dropped out when he discovered that girls were more interesting than birds. Tom Donnelly, however, decided both were interesting, as did I, and kept on birding. In the Olmsted Woods (part of the landscape architect Frederick Law Olmsted, Jr.'s design for the cathedral Close), which lay between St. Albans and the athletic fields, he caught a young crow and reportedly taught it to say a few words. (Tom became a geologist and taught at SUNY Binghamton for many years, at the same time becoming an expert on the world's dragonflies.)

I remember seeing certain birds at St. Albans: A Black and White Warbler in a tree outside the A Form (sixth grade) classroom, a Bald Eagle flying over the athletic fields, and kestrels flying around the towers of the cathedral. But I know I saw many more, because the editor of *Cathedral Age* magazine had learned of my interest and asked me to write an article about birds on the Close. The result was my first published article, at age fifteen, one that impressed my now famous (to St. Albans graduates) English teacher, Ferdinand

Black and White Warbler
(photo by Kent Minichiello)

Ruge. It was a high point of my time at St. Albans when he walked into class one morning and said, "You all should read Napier Shelton's article about birds on the Close."

Missouri and Arkansas

My mother and father came from small towns in southwest Missouri, she from Mount Vernon, west of Springfield, and he from Marshfield, east of Springfield. We had relatives in those towns, St. Louis, Kansas City, and Rogers, Arkansas. So a visit out there was a part of several summers as I was growing up. When I was a little kid I rolled car tires in the streets of Marshfield with Artie Thomas, who lived next door to my father's parents. In later years we went fishing in a farm pond near Artie's house, rode inner tubes down the James River, cooked out in the woods along Turnbow Creek. A spring gushing from the limestone by the creek had the best water I ever tasted.

When birds became my greatest passion I kept detailed notes on those I saw on these trips to the Midwest.   The summer I was twelve my mother and I took the train out to St. Louis.   On the way I kept track of all birds I saw out the window: Maryland, 15 species; Ohio, "only 9 species because we traveled through most of the state at night;" Indiana, 18; Illinois, 15, "including Bobolink." That summer I added a few birds to my growing life list, among them Dickcissel, "calling out his name with a stutter," and Lark Sparrow—though I heard it often, its "song is a blank to me now." Bewick's Wrens and Loggerhead Shrikes—birds I'd seen on my father's farm—were more common in Missouri, and Red-headed Woodpeckers were everywhere.   Visiting my great aunt and uncle in Rogers, Arkansas, I recorded that "Arkansas has about the same birds as Wash. D.C.   One difference is the apparent scarcity of starlings, having many Purple Grackles instead.   Another bird scarcity is the Song Sparrow."   (If I had stayed until winter I would have seen Song Sparrows that had migrated southward.)   Another year I added Bell's Vireo to my life list, singing loudly from a thicket, and Blue Grosbeak.

Best of all was the family of King Rails.   On one of our trips to Rogers, I was introduced to a man named Frank Dean Crooks. I visited him at his large old frame house in the country outside Rogers.   Crooks sexed chickens for a living, but his heart was in natural history.   His house was full of things he had collected from the woods and fields around him.   The second floor was full of such things too, but he cautioned me not to go up there, the stairs were not dependable.   We went for a walk to see something he'd recently discovered, and found it—a King Rail with young in a grassy ditch, threading their way toward us.   This was another new and exciting bird for me, one I have seldom seen since.

At St. Albans I wrote an English class composition about Crooks. Most of it covers the facts above, with sixteen-year-old storytelling imagination.   It ends with the following three paragraphs:

> The physical appearance of Dean Crooks is slightly suggestive of a well-fed chipmunk.   He has a creased and suntanned face, bright eyes, a small mouth, and rather loose jowls, which look as if they could hold three baseball-sized walnuts.   His unceasing flow of conversation strengthens the comparison. [Thinking of a chipmunk's chatter, I guess.]
>
> Now the big question is, 'How does he earn money to live on?' This is the only problem which bothers Mr. Crooks.

When he has run out of food, he is faced with the nuisance of having to earn some money. His real profession is culling [actually sexing] poultry, and that is how he lives.

Frank Dean Crooks is a special kind of tramp. He does what he wants to do, goes where he wants to go, and is healthy and content. He is everybody's friend and nobody's enemy. There will never be one like him again.

In June 1949, when I was seventeen, I "collected some dragonflies" at the pond near my grandfather's house, and "was amazed to see a least tern [far from its breeding grounds] come bounding over the pond." I sent the dragonflies to my friend Tom Donnelly in Washington and later learned that one was a rarity. Further notes from that trip include a list of 65 species of birds I saw at Lake Taneycomo. Some comments: "kingbird—one nest found in dead fork over water (low); Purple Martin—very numerous; Prothonotary Warbler—about one dozen seen; two pairs feeding young out of nest; Blue Grosbeak—one female atop bluff in scrub oak and cedar." Climbing a bluff here I "found some interesting ferns, two species of which I have pressed in this book." [no longer extant] These notes show I was interested in many facets of nature, as I had been for some years.

My trips to the Midwest fixed in me a fondness for my ancestral homelands, from Kansas City south through former prairie to the Ozarks of southern Missouri and northwestern Arkansas. There were other trips over the succeeding years, eventually resulting in a book: *Natural Missouri: Working with the Land*, published in 2005. In it I described the work of people in such places as Prairie State Park, with its bison and prairie flowers; Mingo National Wildlife Refuge, in the wetlands of southeast Missouri; Mark Twain National Forest, with its great chunks of Ozark forest; and a farm in northeast Missouri, where Dave Mackey raised cattle on wildlife-friendly land. I'm sorry my father and mother didn't live to see this written appreciation of their native state. (See Chapter 10).

Colorado

The train had been rolling through mile after mile of sagebrush. Then I saw what looked like a line of clouds on the horizon. But as we approached I realized that was snow on the Rocky Mountains— my first sight of them and an exciting one. At fourteen I'd never been west of Missouri. This was the true West.

My father had found out about a summer camp in the Rockies for high-school-age boys, run by Ansel Hall, the first Chief Naturalist and first Chief Forester of the National Park Service. At the Explorers Camp, headquartered in the La Plata Mountains of southwest Colorado, you spent three weeks camping in the mountains, three weeks on an archeological dig, and three weeks exploring the Four Corners Country, looking for cliff dwellings and artifacts on the many flat-topped mesas. My father thought this would be a wonderful experience for someone like me, but at first I was reluctant to travel off alone into this unknown. I finally agreed and became glad I did.

My first stop en route to the camp was Denver, to which Hudson Moore, one of my Colony Hill Bird Club buddies, had moved. When I arrived he told me an Ovenbird, an eastern warbler that had strayed west, had been spotted in the Denver area. Robert Niedrach, ornithologist at the Denver Natural History Museum, welcomed youngsters and knew Hudson. He took us out hunting for the Ovenbird. We were unsuccessful, but our acceptance by the prominent naturalist made us feel like members of the scientific big leagues. It was like my experience at the Smithsonian in Washington.

The last leg of my journey was by narrow-gauge railroad from Pueblo, in the foothills, to Durango, across a succession of mountain ridges. This was slow and spectacular. At one point we were allowed to get out and walk a bit beside the laboring train. To heighten our sense of adventure, I suppose, the conductor pointed out an engine that had departed the track and ended up in a canyon far below.

Headquarters of the Explorers Camp, 20 miles north of Durango, reached along a winding gravel road, was at buildings of an abandoned gold mining operation, elevation 9500 feet. The air was cool and pure. At first, walking took my breath away, but after a few days it didn't, and I never felt so good in my life. Around the camp, some of us wandered into abandoned mine shafts, admiring or collecting beautiful minerals. One day I watched, entranced, as a pine marten pursued a chipmunk, back and forth, until capturing it.

We were divided into three tribes—I think I was a Choctaw—and each tribe went off on a different expedition for three weeks. On the mountain camping trip, we saddled up, each of us leading a pack animal with supplies. Eighteen miles later we arrived at our site, at the edge of a large meadow beside which ran a lively stream. From here we simply enjoyed the land, climbing 13,000-foot Mt. Hesperus one day, fishing another. The fishing was to acquire breakfast—small, delicious rainbow trout. I fashioned a fishing pole from a willow stem, baited the hook with a grasshopper, and let the bait drift downstream. Usually a trout struck—this stream was seldom fished. In a short time we had 60 trout, and a great breakfast. I may have thought about the lack of a fishing license and possible limits on number of fish caught, but the law seemed far away. It was here that I killed the marmot with a long, miraculous rock throw. I skinned it and inexpertly cleaned the pelt, which ended up in the Shelton Museum back home, smelling rather unpleasantly. I gloried in the mountains—the conifer forests, the snowy peaks, the clear, rushing streams, the wildlife.

The other expeditions took us out of the high mountains, into pinyon pine mesa land and sagebrush desert. This was Southwest Indian country, past and present. Those who had lived in the cliff dwellings now preserved at Mesa Verde National Park had left around 1300 C.E., those in the lowlands at Chaco Canyon (now in Chaco Culture National Historical Park) had abandoned their large sites during the 12th century, after 500 prosperous years, both groups primarily for environmental reasons.

Chaco Canyon sticks in my memory because of rattlesnakes. I was walking up a track with another camper when he grabbed me. I was about to step on a prairie rattlesnake coiled in weeds. Milky eyes indicated it was in a shedding stage, sluggish but certainly capable of striking me. I killed it and kept the skin. Another rattlesnake had spent the night on the stone floor of an open dwelling, a few feet from where we had slept. Somebody killed it and we ate it for breakfast. Tasted like chicken, as they say. So our group had killed two rattlesnakes in a national park, an offense we apparently were not aware of.

Elsewhere we climbed a mesa looking for traces of long-lost tribes. High up we came upon a small, disintegrating cliff dwelling. On top of the mesa potsherds were scattered all about. We imagined many other mesas held such treasures.

The archeological dig on top of a mesa, in southwestern Colorado, introduced me to that science. A former Marine (though Marines say, 'once a Marine, always a Marine') who was working on a Master's degree was in charge. We slept in cavities below the mesa rim with the woodrats, who built little stick nests there and occasionally ran over our sleeping bags. To wake us up the boss walked to the edge of the mesa and fired his pistol. My assignment was to sift any artifacts out of soil in a trench dug through a trash mound. In three weeks I found a bone needle and a dog's skull—not very exciting but teaching me something about archeological techniques. I believe the site was abandoned in the 14th century, which suggests that the people here met the same problems as those at Mesa Verde.

Hugh Kingery, a camper from Denver who was interested in birds, joined me in searching the pinyon pines along a stream channel at the foot of the mesa. There we found Pinyon Jays and Black-throated Gray Warblers. Later in life Hugh became a lawyer and continued his birding, directing the first Colorado Breeding Bird Atlas project.

We occasionally encountered present-day Natives—a lone man riding a horse through an empty, immense landscape; tending gardens beside their adobe hogans; at trading posts selling Navajo turquoise and silver jewelry (and a fiery liquid "that tastes like peppermint" and burned my throat long afterward).

Most memorable was the Indian rodeo near the Lukachukai Mountains of northeastern Arizona. The camp had two trucks to carry us. The newer one went over the mountains, the older, less powerful one with dubious brakes, driven by my 16-year-old friend Lloyd Hinton, went around. The only whites there, we arrived at the rodeo site to find a fenced area surrounded by Indian wagons. The women were decked out in all their finery, turquoise, and silver. Some families had brought sheep, perhaps for feasting. All through the rodeo, with horse racing and other events, a drummer drummed and chanted. We campers had been invited to put on a show, which was a comedy routine with guys wearing red underwear. The audience loved it.

The summer did what my father had hoped—tremendously expanded my geographic and mental horizons. I learned how different the West was—in general dry, but becoming wetter and more vegetated with elevation, each zone bearing different ecological communities. By summer's end, I relished my experiences but longed for the deciduous forests of my wetter East. I had learned something about how people—Native and others—lived in dry country (we saw few people who lived in the mountains). And when I returned home I felt triumphant.

Yosemite

In late June 1948, 16 years old, I boarded a bus in Kansas City, bound for Yosemite National Park. I was going there to be with the McHenrys and work in the park. When we crossed the Rockies I was in new territory: first, the Wasatch Mountains, Salt Lake City, and the Great Salt Lake flats, then the isolated mountain ranges and sagebrush desert of Nevada, and finally across the Sierra Nevada into San Francisco. My first view of Yosemite Valley is forever seared in my brain. It was unbelievable, magical, and inexpressibly beautiful, as if some divine hand had sculpted into the landscape the most majestic scene its divine head could imagine. Those soaring granite walls, gracefully leaping waterfalls, and the swift Merced River winding through the valley would be my home environment for two inspiring months.

The McHenrys' house stood in a forest of tall sugar pines and other conifers whose aroma I can almost smell now. A short walk brought us to Yosemite Falls, whose thunder gently shook the house day and night. Mr. McHenry arranged for me a bus-boy job with the Curry Company, the park concessioner, and borrowed a white shirt and black bow-tie from a friend. I lasted three days as a bus-boy, losing the job when I dropped a tray of food, and perhaps for other shortcomings. The substitute job—picking up trash around the cabins with a pointed stick—was much more to my liking. It kept me outdoors. I wandered among the cabins and past several trash cans on my beat. Often a mother black bear and her two cubs visited these trash cans, upsetting them and devouring anything edible. One day I challenged her by sitting on her food source and looking menacing. She just kept walking toward me. I got off. In my opinion, however, Bruce was less fortunate in his employment—cleaning restrooms. The job itself was made worse by his boss, a woman whose morning red-wine hangovers gave her a bad temper.

We dated two girls who were working as maids for the Curry Company and took them on an overnight hike to a High Country camp at Merced Lake. It started poorly. "After work Bruce and I rounded up the pack and Georgia and Pauline. We were on the trail to Merced Lake at 5:45 p.m. They brought everything but a kitchen stove, so the pack weighed fifty pounds. I started out cheerful, but reached Merced Lake, 13 miles away, feeling like a tired old bear. I was ready to toss Georgia in the lake." The next day "we fished in Merced River just below Washburn Lake. Bruce caught three and

I caught two. A ranger asked about our licenses. He let me buy one, and Bruce said he was fifteen [not true]....I saw a Yosemite Fox Sparrow near Washburn Lake." (Bird people paid more attention to subspecies in those days.) We started home at 5:15, walking 22 miles—"the farthest I have ever walked in a day"—and arrived at 2:00 a.m.

Bruce and I hiked all around Yosemite Valley. We climbed to the top of Yosemite Falls, watching the water plummet down 2,000 feet. We climbed to Glacier Point, from which we got an astounding view of the valley and blue mountains beyond it. And we pulled hand over hand on the rope up the back side of Half Dome. We walked over the flat top of the Dome to its lip, a rock projection into which we crawled and looked straight down 3,000 feet to the valley floor. (I wouldn't do that today.) While we were up there a Peregrine Falcon was performing powerful dives, presumably to impress a female. It was a perfect drama for all the space and magnificence around us.

Our hike down the John Muir Trail in August was the summer's highlight, and my journal was full of comments on nature. From Tuolumne Meadows Bruce, his younger brother Keith, and I started off at 7:30 a.m. up the Lyell Fork of the Tuolumne River and over Donahue Pass. I noted a female Williamson's Sapsucker among other birds. "We found a flock of sheep in the upper basin of Rush

The author, left, and Keith McHenry enjoy a view
from the John Muir Trail
(photo by Bruce McHenry)

Creek, much to our disgust." (I must have heard about John Muir's description of sheep—"hoofed locusts.") The next morning I "cut a willow pole for fishing and fished until nine. Not even a strike. Bruce came back with one." (Trout were supposed to be a major item in our diet.)

At Reds Meadows, site of the Devil's Postpile, a formation of basaltic columns, we eschewed the campground and ended up illegally on a hillside trail for privacy. Then we discovered we were only a hundred yards from the ranger station. In the morning our cooking fire was putting out thick smoke and we worried we'd be found. "Pretty soon Bruce said he heard someone coming so I jumped on the fire and buried it. Then I heard women's voices, and I got my pants on pretty quick, because I was running around in long underwear. Then we saw them come up through the brush with their two dogs and a shovel to put out the fire. The first words were, 'Wait till I catch my breath and I'll deal with you.' Then they bawled us out, and called us 'babes in the woods.' "

When we reported to the ranger's cabin he wrote up all the regulations we had broken, including insulting his wife, and told us to hike to Mammoth, 13 miles away, to see the District Ranger. Fortunately, before doing so, we learned we had been pardoned. The Veretts—the ranger and his wife-- helped us get more supplies, and even fed us breakfast next day. The Veretts and the McHenrys exchanged Christmas cards for several years. The experience was for me an early lesson in fire management.

I had experienced the Rockies two summers before, and now was getting a good look at the Sierra Nevada . "This country here is dry—the ground is soft pumice—and dusty. There are numerous little streams coming down the hills, but in between them the ground is not moist, and there is almost no undergrowth. On one side we have a volcanic ridge, along which are several hot springs, and on the other is the main Sierra Crest of granite and metamorphics. This is much different than the Rockies, which I feel I prefer to the Sierra. The Rockies are greener, and the ground is more moist, although there are not the great number of lakes." (I did not attempt to explain the difference, which might have to do with climatic and geologic factors. I just reported mainly what I saw.)

Nine days into our hike, having lost two or three days to illness, we decided to leave the Muir Trail and walk eastward to a highway where Bruce's parents could pick us up. "Our first task was to find the McGee Creek Trail. After a couple of false starts, and frequent reference to the book (Guide to the John Muir Trail and High

Sierra) we found its feeble origin in a meadow. We followed the trail up Fish Creek, found a Cooper's hawk, Cassin's Purple Finch, White-crowned Sparrow, and large bear tracks in the dusty trail.

> Scenery more magnificent the higher we climbed. At 10,000 the peaks surrounding the Fish Creek Basin came into view. At 11,000 we found an exotic alpine valley and meadows. There was a superabundance of Clark's Nutcrackers here. Also a pair of Sparrow hawks, a red-tailed hawk, white-crowned sparrows, and toads which had reddish-brown spots behind their ears. There was also a superabundance of grasshoppers, which undoubtedly support the sparrow hawks, and possibly the Clark's Crows. The red-tails up there probably live on the gophers which burrow in the meadows.
>
> The scene was beautiful, and weird. The peaks were highly-colored—red, white, black, silver. And magnificent peaks, all over 12,000 feet. We struggled over McGee Creek Pass at 12,000 feet, where the wind was blowing 30 miles an hour, and it was cold....we started down the precipitous trail over red slate and granite rocks...down past small lakes covered with butterfly-wing-blue ice. Rounding a turn, we startled five deer. There was a huge buck in the lead, and three small bucks and a doe trailing him. What a sight!

That evening, "we are keeping warm by a white-bark pine fire, which is not nearly so hot as lodgepole, but is hot enough to warm up by."

Next day, walking down McGee Creek, in a small, brushy meadow, I "found fresh beaver cuttings and slides and tunnels. Just above this point I saw a pine marten run across the road in front of us. Many mourning cloak butterflies along the road. Saw clark's crows at 7000 or 8,000 feet. Seems low for them."

In the Owens Valley there was a "lake teeming with waterfowl," "forty-four sage hens off in the grass and sagebrush," numerous other birds, and "green farmland and shade trees which contrasted sharply with the barren pinkish mountains and desert surrounding the valley." After meeting Bruce's parents we stopped at Mono Lake, where there were "hundreds of eared grebes and northern phalaropes, the latter feeding along the shore, dabbling and spinning and carrying on." Bruce and I each ate "three and ½ hamburger sandwiches and two milkshakes. Very Delicious." (My journal noted almost as much food eaten as nature observed.) Thus, "the happy end of a long, exciting trail through the High Sierra."

At sixteen, I was showing Kellert's aesthetic, ecologistic and scientific, humanistic, and naturalistic valuations of nature.

My journal that summer shows a fascination with a new environment, the Sierra Nevada. It is that of a naturalist rather than a conservationist, though I'm sure I was sympathetic to conservationist attitudes. I was living in John Muir's Range of Light, but didn't read any of his works, then or soon after. (However, in May 1949, one year later, I entered a conservation essay contest, affirming my concern about our relationships with nature.)

In 1950, two summers after the first visit, I worked as a museum assistant in Yosemite. One afternoon Bruce and I drove back to Mono Lake. My reaction that time, near sundown: "Complete stillness, loneliness, and peace. At my back the towering wall of the Sierra turning black; before me the quiet water going far away and soft with the last light of day. Nearby to the south rose three humps—the Mono Craters—and dark except for the top of each old volcanic cone, which the sun made red.

> Little things made lonely noises along the grassy beach. What is more reminiscent of desolation than a gull's crying? A few meadowlarks and killdeers inhabited the grass, as northern phalaropes in small sociable flocks spun about in the water just offshore. These few little things coming and going—otherwise only the stillness, and the quiet power of Nature sleeping.

It is interesting to note the difference between the sixteen-year-old's and the eighteen-year-old's reactions to Mono Lake. The sixteen-year-old says what he observes. The eighteen-year-old adds his feelings about what he sees. There is also an artistic element. (I had been painting all through high school.)

Return to Camp La Jeunesse

In 1949, at age 17, I went back to La Jeunesse as assistant Fish Pond Monitor, working with J.D.MacDonald. J. D. was well-liked and genial, worshipped by the kids. All summer he sang a song from *Guys and Dolls*—"I have the horse right here, his name is Paul Revere..." In addition to trips to and from Fish Pond, leading perhaps six boys and lugging heavy loads of supplies, I took boys on many hikes from Fish Pond, up nearby mountains and to other ponds, as well as doing some of the cooking and other chores around camp. My journal notes at age 13 described mostly what we did. My notes now more frequently describe the surroundings and what I felt about the place. Here are a few.

July 11: Fish Pond is the same quiet, wild place I visited four years ago. The unseen creatures in the woods at night do not excite me as they used to do when I was thirteen, but I find new beauty in the muted evening colors on the opposing hills, and in the rich, fresh sunset clouds, and in the glassy, tree-reflecting water at dusk.

The loons and gulls are still here. In fact, the herring gulls have a nest on one of the rocks in Fish Pond in which they raised two youngsters. Those two are not yet able to fly, so when we appear on shore or in canoes, the ever-watchful parents cry a warning, and the young swim across the pond. When they swim, they lower their heads like a hiding rabbit.

The woods about our camp are rich. I think of birch—silver, white—peeling off in great curls. Dark soil supporting luxuriant ferns, small, ground-hugging flowers and vines, such as shinleaf and partridgeberry. On the mountain slopes behind camp, fallen and bent trees of every size lie at all angles. Great gray boulders jut up unexpectedly back up the hill.

This evening I was out on the pond alone to watch the sunset—a burnished coral fire with duller offshoots streaking out and up from behind the trees at the west end of the pond. Above the north side, Fish Pond Mountain and its adjoining brothers hump up in black profile all along the ridge up to the top of St. Regis.

Often in the evening a solitary loon will leave the water in a long, splattering run, circle the pond with its stiff wings sounding like an outboard, and disappear into the sunset. The bird's weird laughter comes back as parting cry. After dusk the whip-poor-will's throbbing calls come out of the hills—one here and one off there.

July 14: In the morning [George Williams] and I and Marshall Swartz [a camper] sawed [a] twenty-foot stump into fireplace lengths, and in so doing we opened a cross-section through a woodpecker's hole. Shreds of our bumwad [toilet paper] were being used for padding along with sawdust, birch bark finely shredded, and fragments of maple leaves. The hole measured sixteen inches in depth.

July 17: I know that I can do the best job in the field of nature, and to the furthering of interest and love in the great outdoors. I must give my life. I hope, through writing, painting, and perhaps speaking, to spread my own love to others.

July 21: Randy [Harris, a counselor] and I took the boys up Fish Pond Mountain in the afternoon. I found fresh bear droppings in a raspberry patch on top. Scared up a grouse on the way down. Jerry Jones found a beautiful ring-necked snake under a rock. It was about 18 inches long, was gray on the back, and had a yellow ring on the neck, and salmon pink on the belly.

July 24: Now as I write [in the lean-to], moths and crane flies are flitting about my face and over my paper, attracted by the candle. In fifteen minutes a great swarm has arrived. Many are matted in the molten tallow.

August 2: Today's big event occurred tonight. Everybody was in bed except for J.D. and I. We were in the lean-to, talking, writing, and soaking J.D.'s foot by candle light. Suddenly a loud scampering noise among the pots and pans and food supplies brought us both to our feet. That was the opening of an amazing, ruthless, and gripping drama of Nature. By the candle light we caught several glimpses of a slender animal moving swiftly about. The thing disappeared and appeared several times in just that half-minute. We made a quick search with flashlights, but heard or saw nothing. We went back to writing and soaking. J. D., in preparation for the return of the supposed rat, walked over to the fireplace to pick up some rocks. As he was doing so, two green eyes appeared a foot away from his hand. He let out a surprised yell, and we grabbed sticks and flashlights. Several voices from the tents asked what was going on.

Then we saw the weasel's head poke out from the rocks. The creature came out, alert, intent on something—utterly oblivious of our presence. We sat and listened....Within seconds a shrill little shrieking noise came from the fireplace, and out of the rocks scrambled a small gray rat [woodrat], closely pursued by the weasel. The chase led under the table and all about the fireplace. The shrieking rose suddenly to a terrified intensity. We swung our beams to the ground, and there, right at our feet, the weasel and the rat squirmed about. The fight was no match. Quickly the weasel seized the rat's neck, and wrapped all four legs around its prey. The weasel dragged the rat slowly across the floor and behind some cans, and then into a hole.

All this was observed by a cluster of boys, all excited, and a couple afraid. They went back to their tents in great anxiety.

I had never experienced the ferocity of predation at such close range, then or since.

August 10: I thought again today as we climbed Long Pond Mountain that I love the mountains better than shore, plain, lake, or desert. That smoky blue high horizon holds a tremendous fascination for me. Give me the Great Smokies, the Rockies, the High Sierra, the Adirondacks.

August 14: The heat of day is really summer heat now; but the nights are growing cooler—45 degrees last night. But midday is really August. Dry bracken on the hillsides; grasshoppers galore flying everywhere; cicadas now droning monotonously. The winds have been shifting continuously lately. The prevailing southwest wind occurs seldom now. East and north winds are common.

August 15: At seven o'clock this morning I woke up to find everyone dressed and running around. Then I heard a whoop across the lake. It was Hank's whoop [the camp director]. When Hank shows up out here everybody moves. Hank must have left Hoel Pond at five o'clock.

Shortly after breakfast we were sitting around gabbing, when Remus [Hank's dog] got excited about something in the ground twenty yards down the trail. We thought it was

a chipmunk. But somebody went to see. Remus had discovered a cache! We started removing bottles from a badly
rusted old bread box in the ground. The bottles were full!
Hank came over and discovered that it was his father's!
There was Hawthorne Water, ink, Listerine, Apollinaris,
and other unidentified contents. All together we unearthed
about twenty bottles. Hank figured it was cached around
1904.

Turning cold tonight—northeast winds...

I see here my interest in and love of nature, expressed more lyrically than at earlier ages, and a life mission, but not yet any sign of
the philosophical advocacy for nature that developed later. I was
too focused on myself for that.

Maine

Early one morning in 1949, after La Jeunesse, I arrived at the west
shore of Muscongus Bay in Maine. From there I rowed a small boat
across to Hog Island, where the Binghams welcomed me to their
summer home.

Millicent Todd Bingham was a remarkable woman. She had
traveled widely with her astronomer father, including by elephant
in Thailand to see an eclipse of the sun; was the first woman to
receive a Ph.D. in geography at Radcliffe; researched in Peru for a
dissertation, and then had dropped that career to edit and publish
a large number of the poems of Emily Dickinson. Acquiring a pas-
sionate love of nature from her mother, like Rachel Carson, she had
encouraged that love and concern in countless others.

I had met her in the mid-1940s, when she joined the Audubon
Society of the District of Columbia (later renamed the Audubon
Naturalist Society of the Central Atlantic States). Her dedication
to conservation and her value as a wise counselor were soon recog-
nized. She became a Director in 1947 and was elected an Honorary
Vice President in 1954.

Most of Hog Island was purchased by her mother, Mabel Loom-
is Todd, soon after a visit in 1909, to save its age-old forest from
imminent logging. A friend, James M. Todd, later purchased the
rest, a 30-acre peninsula at the northern end of the island, as a gift
to the National Audubon Society, for use as the first Audubon Nature Camp. Here, teachers of natural history and other interested

participants could extend their knowledge and skills in this inspiring natural setting. Roger Peterson taught here in 1936, the first summer of the camp.

Millicent Bingham took an interest in youthful naturalists like me, and thus the invitation to Hog Island. I spent my days wandering around the 1 1/2-mile-long island, with its forest of spruce, pine, and birch, and my evenings with Millicent and her psychologist husband, Walter Van Dyke Bingham, in their rustic cottage. I saw my first White-winged Crossbills, denizens of northern conifer forests, and observed some of the camp activities.

Allan Cruikshank, who had been an instructor there since the camp's first summer, took groups out on a boat to see birds nesting on small islands in the Gulf of Maine. One day, as the boat returned, I saw Cruikshank on the deck, standing on his head. I learned later that this was how jokester Cruikshank announced that they had seen a "good" bird.

Allan Cruikshank with an immature Great Black-backed Gull
at the Hog Island Auduban Camp

My journal shows my admiration for this man:

On the first day I met Allan Cruikshank, an incomparable fellow, filled with the zest of life. He is a tall, rugged and ruddy Scotchman, of what percentage I know not. He is known as the Dean of Women at the Audubon Camp. What a joker he is! At the banquet he kept everybody laughing. He is kind and extremely energetic....I will try to follow his example as a real outdoors man.

The next Christmas Mrs. Bingham sent me a book of Cruik-shank's photographs: *Wings in the Wilderness*. Excerpts from a memorial article in *American Birds* sketch the many contributions of this man known so widely in America among people who love birds and nature:

...Allan was a many-faceted and complex person. As a teacher for the Bird Club of Long Island and for National Audubon, he estimated that he had lectured to 2,900,000 people (live), in some 5,860 talks with motion pictures, and thousands more in the early days of colored slides. He was an instructor at the Audubon Camp in Maine from 1936 to 1958 (with two years out for war service); teaching and inspiring teachers in the ways of birds....

He photographed more than 550 species of North American birds and was author or co-author of twelve books. When this "picture of rugged good health, boundless energy, and ageless enthusiasm" died—in October 1974—his "tens of thousands of friends and admirers" could hardly believe it. I was among them.[1]

I thank Millicent Todd Bingham for introducing me to another part of the Great North Woods I loved so well, and for pulling me further into the fraternity of conservationists.

I was to enter college that fall, and after the Cruikshank thoughts wrote in my journal: "I have suddenly realized that I am coming to the crossroads of my life. I am thinking that a decision must be made, and soon. Artist or writer; which shall it be? Naturalist I already am, but which kind shall I expand into?"

We now back up a few years to describe an organization and my involvement in it that greatly influenced my relationship with the natural world. (During my later years I served as Vice President for Publications and on the Board.)

6

Teenage Years with the
Audubon Society of the D.C.

During the 1940s, my experience of Washington's natural places and those of the Central Atlantic States was deepened and broadened by membership in the Audubon Society of the District of Columbia. My views of nature were similarly expanded by an amazing assortment of distinguished members.

The Society was founded in 1897 and is the second oldest still existing independent Audubon Society, after the Massachusetts Audubon Society (1896). The late 19th century had witnessed a slaughter of wildlife, for the market and for sport. The Audubon Societies that sprang up in many states were a response particularly to the slaughter of birds, many of which were killed to adorn women's hats. This inflamed the consciences of many other women, who formed a large part of those societies.

This was the case with the Audubon Society of the D.C. The founder was Mrs. John Dewhurst Patten. Women held many offices and chaired many committees. Photographs of the Society's outings show a preponderance of women, in formal attire wearing (featherless) hats. (The men wear suits and ties.) Many men, however, were also committed to the protection of and education about birds. Major General George M. Sternberg, Surgeon-General of the U.S. Army, was the Society's president for its first 18 years. Theodore Roosevelt, first as Assistant Secretary of the Navy and later as President of the United States, was an "interested and supportive" member. In 1908 he invited Society members, among others, to the White House for the first U.S. showing of motion pictures of birds. Mrs. Lucy Warner Maynard, one of those present, asked Roosevelt if he could provide a list of the birds he had seen on the White House grounds. Two days later she received lists of 56 he had recorded at the White House and 93 around the city. "Doubtless this list is incomplete," he wrote. "I have seen others that I have forgotten." Society members conducted classes on birds for school teachers, wrote and distributed publications about birds, worked for passage of legislation protecting birds, and led field trips to nearby spots in the D.C., Maryland, and Virginia. Their efforts, along with those of many other organizations and individuals, led to substantial protection of birds by 1918, when the Migratory Bird Treaty Act gave the federal government power to regulate the taking of migratory birds.

With protection of birds under better control, the Society was less active during the 1920s and 1930s. The bird classes for teachers and students were discontinued in 1935. Some conservation work was undertaken in 1926, when the Society appointed a committee, including Dr. Theodore Palmer, assistant chief of the U.S. Department of Agriculture's Biological Survey, and Dr. Paul Bartsch, curator of mollusks in the Smithsonian's National Museum of Natural History, to work with the District Fine Arts Commission and the City Planning Commission in an effort to protect parks and green spaces in Washington from highway and commercial development. After the federal government bought the C&O Canal in 1938, the Society, with other groups, pressed for preservation of natural conditions along the canal. The majority of Society members, however, were content in those years simply to enjoy nature on "bird picnics," with binoculars and luncheon.

Things picked up during the World War II years. In 1941, John Aldrich, who had just begun a long career with the U.S. Fish and Wildlife Service, became president of the Society. He organized the Society's first Christmas Bird Count, conducted in the metropolitan area in 1943, encouraged research projects, and enlarged the field trip program. He enlisted Donald McHenry, Chief Naturalist of the park service's National Capital Parks, as program chairman to increase Society activities. McHenry succeeded Aldrich as president in 1944 and started or expanded an array of programs in education, publications, field trips, and inclusion of children. He brought in some of the best scientific and natural history talent in Washington, such as Alexander Wetmore, Secretary of the Smithsonian, Roger Tory Peterson, and Irston Barnes, an economist with a deep interest in nature and conservation. When McHenry was transferred to Yosemite in 1946, Barnes became president and, with his energy, ideas, and commitment, greatly accelerated the Society's growth in numbers and activities. During the 1940s and 1950s, I thus found myself in the midst of nature and conservation stars.

The lives and accomplishments of the people presented below

have been critical for the successes of the Society, but in several cases have also greatly benefited the city, the nation, and even the world. They all enhanced my knowledge of natural history and deepened my devotion to conservation, through personal association and their writings.

John Aldrich (1906-1995) I became acquainted with John Aldrich when, as a Fish and Wildlife Service ornithologist, he was curator of the Service's collection of bird specimens at the Smithsonian's National Museum of Natural History. He also conducted regional bird surveys in the United States and its territories, and identified feathers and bones for the FWS and other agencies, often serving as an expert witness. (Roxie Collie Simpson followed him in the latter work.) In 1947, John was appointed chief of the FWS Section of Distribution and Migration of Birds, which included the national bird banding program, and in 1951 the mammal investigations were joined with the bird studies, all under Aldrich's supervision. He retired from the Fish and Wildlife Service in 1972 but continued working for many years as a retired annuitant.

I appreciated his enthusiasm for Christmas Bird Counts, one of my favorite activities. In this he was like his fellow Fish and Wildlife Service ornithologist Chandler Robbins.

Donald McHenry (1895-1969) We've already met him as the father of my friend Bruce. Bruce had been born at Stillwater, Oklahoma, where his father taught biology at Oklahoma State University. Botany was Donald's chief interest among the many segments of nature, but in his talks he brought them all in. Under his presidency of the Audubon Society of the D.C. he initiated or helped to carry out a great range of activities: the (National) Audubon Lectures; monthly Society meetings, with speakers; the Society's first breeding bird census, at Glen Echo along the Potomac River; study seminars on birds, led by John Aldrich; *The Wood Thrush*, a publication about nature and the Society's activities; field trips broadened to include more than birds, and to farther destinations; expansion of Audubon Junior Clubs throughout the public school system. Donald McHenry carried out such a busy presidency at the same time he was initiating park service programs, some of which, such as bird walks, he arranged as joint activities with the Society. I remember with fondness the smiling bespectacled face, the balding pate, and rapid rides through Rock Creek Park in his little green Mercury as he pointed out features with one hand and negotiated curves with the other. More than anyone else, he was a mentor for me.

Donald McHenry

Alexander Wetmore (1886-1978) While he was Secretary of the Smithsonian, Alexander Wetmore was also a guiding presence in the Society, particularly in sharing his scientific expertise as an ornithologist. In 1948 he was elected an Honorary Vice President, and in 1964 was given the Society's highest honor, the Paul Bartsch Award. Prominent in scientific circles, he was a member of the National Geographic Society's board of trustees for almost 40 years and was a member and in some cases president of many other organizations. One Smithsonian colleague said, "his stupendous work in ornithology is staggering." In addition to hundreds of scientific publications and description of 189 species and subspecies of birds previously unknown, he contributed 26,058 mammal and bird skins to the national collections. Wetmore's *magnum opus* was on the birds of Panama, which he studied for 20 years. The results were published by the Smithsonian in four volumes.

Wetmore took delight in the information and fun gained from Christmas Bird Counts; he was one of the three who inaugurated the Washington count. On the 1947 count he joined John Aldrich's

Alexander Wetmore

team to scour Arlington, and helped them spot one of the Barn Owls that occupied the Smithsonian Tower. He had spent hours up in the tower studying these owls and their food supply (mainly rats as I recall). A later Smithsonian administration decided to close the tower to owls, but Secretary Dillon Ripley, an ornithologist, reopened it. Adversities, natural and/or human, finally ended the reign of the Smithsonian Barn Owls.

Alexander Wetmore was always friendly and encouraging to youngsters. My contact with him began when I was eleven or so, with his showing me in his office a brightly colored trogon specimen, probably collected in Panama. We both had a close association with the Potomac River, he because of membership in the Washington Biologists' Field Club, whose clubhouse was on Plummer's Island, and I joined him at least once as we paddled our canoes up to the foot of Stubblefield Falls. One day in the early 1960s, as I was researching a term paper on bird taxonomy in the Smithsonian's Bird Division, he came into the room and excitedly announced that a Snowy Owl had been seen on top of one of the Department of

Agriculture buildings. Years later I was asked to propose several subjects related to the Smithsonian for possible publication by the Smithsonian Press. One was chosen, but not the biography of Wetmore that I would have preferred to write. After he died in 1978, a plaque was installed on his beloved Plummer's Island honoring this popular and admired ornithologist.

Paul Bartsch (1871-1960) Employed for much of his professional career as curator of mollusks at the Smithsonian—and known as a foremost authority in this field—Paul Bartsch was also interested in all other disciplines of biology, especially botany and ornithology, as well as conservation of natural resources and biological foundations of medical training. He taught botany and biology at George Washington University, and then started the school's graduate program in the natural sciences. For thirty-seven years he also taught histology at Howard University, later serving as director of its Histological and Physiological Laboratory. On Smithsonian expeditions to the Philippines, West Indies, South America, and elsewhere he collected thousands of marine invertebrates but also observed with keen interest all other forms of life, including the human. In reading about this, one is instantly reminded of the voyage, nearly a century earlier, of another man with broad curiosity in natural sciences—Charles Darwin on the *Beagle*.

An early member of the Society, Paul Bartsch was for many years deeply involved in its activities, serving as chairman of the Conservation and Legislative Committee and on the board of directors. He was elected an Honorary Vice President along with such luminaries as Gilbert Grosvenor and Roger Tory Peterson. He was so well loved and respected that after his death in 1960, the Society named its highest award, given only for long and outstanding service, the Paul Bartsch Award.

I knew him first as one of the Smithsonian scientists happy to show collections to interested youngsters. An example from my journal, March 17, 1945: "Counsel Meeting at National museum. Dr. Bartsch was speaker. Showed him Charles' [duck] wings that we could not identify. He took them to Dr. Friedman and together they figured them out. As I can remember right now there were several ring-necked, canvasback, redhead (?), Gadwall, Pintail, Black Duck, and Baldpate. He also gave me some of his [bird] checklists."

Later he was our host at his sanctuary on Mason's Neck, Virginia, called Lebanon. He and his wife Elizabeth bought these 458 acres in 1942 and began restoring its 18th-century home. When Paul became curator emeritus at the National Museum of Natural History in 1945, they moved to Lebanon, where Paul "could indulge his unquenchable appetite for natural history in a natural setting," and Elizabeth "her affection for flowers." [1] They welcomed all groups interested in nature, including of course our Society. We wandered down through wooded hills and a deep ravine, where the Bartsches had planted wildflowers and ferns from all over the East, to a bottomland swamp and a 48-acre marsh on Pohick Bay. We passed a slide otters had made into a pond. Birds abounded. Over 200 species were eventually recorded at Lebanon, including a male Bachman's Warbler, a species now thought to be extinct that sang in the swamp along Pohick Creek for three weeks in May 1954, and then disappeared.

My journal entry for May 1, 1949, contained the following:

ASDC trip to Lebanon. I drove Tom Donnelly, George DuBois down. We got about 90 [bird] species. Dr. Bartsch had a special treat for us. A young man from the Linnaean Society had discovered the first nest of the yellow-throated warbler at Lebanon Sanctuary. Of the twelve or fourteen breeding warblers at Lebanon, Dr. Bartsch had found all the nests except the pine and yellow-throated. Today George DuBois and I found the nest of a pine warbler. It was being built by the female on the limb of a white oak about fifty feet above the ground. Dr. Bartsch was overjoyed.

Another highlight of the day was seeing Dr. Bartsch's wildflower garden....It was a fabulous garden. He, at 86 or so [more like 78], is amazingly robust.

Roger Tory Peterson (1908-1996) In 1943, Private Roger Tory Peterson arrived at Fort Belvoir, Virginia, a short distance down the Potomac from Washington. There he would spend the last two years of World War II preparing and illustrating manuals on defusing land mines, building roads and bridges, and camouflage. *Life* magazine used his field guide principles for a plane-identification manual, and later the Air Corps did the same.

Always with birds on his mind and in his concern, he persuaded his commanding officer to reroute the line of march away from the area on the parade grounds where Peterson had found a Horned Lark's nest. (Some years later, Jackson Abbott, a birder who worked at Fort Belvoir, showed me a Horned Lark's nest on what was probably the same parade ground.)

By 1943 Peterson had gained considerable fame for his eastern and western field guides, for his bird paintings, many of which had appeared in *Life* magazine, and for his photography, lectures, and writing. At night, in the bathroom of the tiny apartment he and his second wife, Barbara, had rented in Alexandria, he continued painting. The Army would not totally interrupt his burgeoning career.

Peterson soon learned of all the kindred souls in the Audubon Society of the D.C. and joined. He was elected to the board of directors, served as chairman of the Policy Committee, gave lectures, and led bird walks along the C&O Canal, to Dyke Marsh, and elsewhere. One May morning I was witness to Peterson's legendary ability to hear and identify bird songs, as we gathered for one of his walks in Rock Creek Park. Before we started he rattled off the names of some twenty birds he could hear singing.

After the War, in 1947, Nettie Mae Burgess, a member of the Society, rented to the Petersons what she described as "the remodeled slave quarters of the old Wm Reading Farm," in Glen Echo, Maryland, near the C&O Canal. Later, Barbara recalled hiking the canal towpath, "which was in bad shape from floods, non upkeep, ignored...." [2] More enthusiastically, Roger wrote to his boyhood friend Clarence Beal, "We are right on the edge of the woods, and I can see Pileated Woodpeckers from my window; Barred Owls hoot at night; both Scarlet and Summer Tanagers live in the huge oaks over the roof; Louisiana Water-thrushes, Kentucky [Warblers], etc. nest in the back of the house, and even Bald Eagles fly over—saw two yesterday. Also Osprey..." [3] He also described chipmunks that reached their living-room garden through a drainage hole, a five-foot black snake searching out the chipmunks, and flying squirrels entering their bedroom through open windows at night—all things that seemed to delight Roger but perhaps not Barbara.

In 1955 the Petersons moved to Old Lyme, Connecticut, but Roger would keep in touch with many of his Washington friends and associates.

William Vogt (1902-1963) The lives of William Vogt and Roger Peterson intersected fortuitously in the late 1920s. Vogt was a drama critic and nature columnist for five Westchester, New York newspapers, Peterson was going to art school and decorating furniture at a factory in New York. They met in the men's room at the American Museum of Natural History when Peterson was washing paint off his hands. They learned of their mutual interest in natural history and became friends and field companions.

Vogt gets the credit for pushing Peterson toward the event that launched him on his famous career: publication of *A Field Guide to the Birds* at age 25. One morning they were taking part in the 1930 census of birds along the Hudson River. "Roger possessed a prodigious keenness of sight and hearing, and on this particular December morning I was again impressed by his expertness...." 'Roger,' I said to him, 'you know more about identifying the birds of this region than almost anyone else, and you can paint. Why don't you pass on your knowledge to other people in a book?'....I guaranteed the book's sale, with no justification whatever, that if he would do the book I would get it published." [4] Peterson did, and Vogt took the field guide to several publishers before Peterson himself had success at Houghton Mifflin.

The two subsequently both worked for the National Audubon Society, Vogt editing its magazine, *Bird Lore*, and Peterson acting as art director, along with other duties. During Peterson's Army years, his wife Barbara worked as secretary for Vogt when he was head of the Department of Conservation at the Pan-American Union in Washington. He had landed there after research on conservation issues in Peru, including the production of guano by seabirds, an important economic resource for the country.

During the 1940s he was another of the notable conservationists in the Audubon Society of the D.C., serving on the board, giving lectures, and advising on Society stance regarding conservation issues. He had by then considerable experience in man-land relationships and put this knowledge into a book, *Road to Survival*, published in 1948. It was acclaimed by fellow Society members (and still takes an honored place on my bookshelf). In it he lays forth the damage expanding populations were doing to the earth and the remedy: bringing human "behavior into conformity with natural limitations," through research, education, action on the land, and "outwitting the libido" [population stabilization].

It's too bad his views were not taken to heart more widely at the time, because we're still struggling with these problems, now magnified. David Cameron Duffy, in an article about Vogt, described him as "a prophet before his time." His life seems bittersweet. A teenage bout with polio left Vogt with a bad limp, which may have made him feel different from his fellows. His message to the world did not receive the attention it deserved. In the late 1960s, having retired as Secretary at the Conservation Foundation, he "planned a series of visits to see friends in Latin America, but a stroke prevented this and, despondent and with greatly reduced mobility, he took his own life in 1969." [5]

Louis Halle (1910-1998) By vocation a diplomat and expert on international relations, Louis Halle was also an eloquent writer on nature and humanity's place in it. One of the leading literary lights in our Society, he won the John Burroughs Medal in 1938 for *Birds Against Men*. In 1945 he monitored spring along the Potomac from January to June. Reviewing the resulting book in the Society's publication, *The Wood Thrush*, Roger Peterson wrote:

> *Spring in Washington*...is much more than a fine recording of the ever-changing phenomenon of spring. It is a deeply felt and philosophical inquiry into man's capacity or incapacity to live in the universe. It is a declaration of independence against the somnambulism of the hive that dominates our daily existence and a plea for a larger and richer life based on a true perception of man's relation to nature.[6]

Halle joined the Society in the late 1940s, served on the board of directors and Conservation Committee, and was subsequently elected an Honorary Vice President. After moving to Switzerland, he continued sending articles about birds to the Society's publication *The Atlantic Naturalist*, and in 1960 gave the Society the rights to *Spring in Washington*. This book is one that local outdoor people return to again and again, to relive Halle's experience and reabsorb his wise philosophy. For all his contributions, he was given the Paul Bartsch Award in 1979.

Chandler Robbins (1918-2017) Few in America have given as much as Chandler Robbins to the study and monitoring of bird populations, and to people concerned with the losses recorded. From his base at the U.S. Fish and Wildlife Service (FWS) Patuxent Research Center, he, with Robert Stewart, produced *Birds of Maryland and the District of Columbia* in 1957, an examination of the abundance, habitats, and seasons of occurrence of this region's birds. He and his associates developed the FWS Breeding Bird Survey in 1966, in which volunteers each year record numbers of birds, by species, along randomly selected routes throughout the United States and Canada; this is the best source of information on population trends of our breeding birds. In 1966, with Bertel Bruun and Herbert S. Zim, he published a very popular field guide, the Golden Press *Birds of North America*, and used his royalties to buy land for sanctuaries of the Maryland Ornithological Society. Well after retirement age, he traveled to Central America to study North American migrant birds in their winter home, a serious concern because of the cutting of tropical forests.

After Robbins joined the Society, he took a special interest in seasonal observations of birds—his and others'—and recording them in *The Wood Thrush* and its successor, *The Atlantic Naturalist*. One of the most endearing traits of Chan Robbins was his welcoming of amateurs in the study of birds, something not found in all professional ornithologists. Even into his 90s, he still had enthusiasm for going afield on Christmas Bird Counts. Long ago, he established six counts in Maryland, from Garrett County in the mountains east to Ocean City on the coast, and for many years he participated in all of them. I remember with great fondness joining his Blackwater Refuge and Ocean City counts and his delight in hearing the experiences of his fellow counters. He had perhaps been on more Christmas Bird Counts in North America than anyone else—412.

For his long dedication and service to the Society, Chandler Robbins was honored with the Paul Bartsch Award in 1979.

Rachel Carson (1907-1964) In 1945, Rachel Carson met Shirley Briggs, who became a close birding companion and brought Carson into the Society. They soon found they had similar interests, in both nature and the arts, and began taking trips together, to the shore, Hawk Mountain, Rock Creek Park, and elsewhere. In the Society, Briggs became editor of *The Wood Thrush* and its successor, *The Atlantic Naturalist*. Carson lent her deep editorial experience and contributed, among other things, a review of Roger Peterson's *Birds Over America* [7] and two articles: "Design for Nature Writing," remarks made at her acceptance of the John Burroughs Medal, awarded for *The Sea Around Us*; [8] and "Lost Worlds: The Challenge of the Islands," material "drawn from a chapter in a new book which Rachel Carson is now writing"[*The Sea Around Us*]. [9]

During her association with the Society, Carson became deeply concerned about local and national conservation issues. The latter included wilderness areas, the proposed Echo Park Dam on the Green River in Dinosaur National Monument, and of course pesticides. After *Silent Spring* and Carson's death, Shirley Briggs continued the campaign against harmful pesticides with The Rachel Carson Trust for the Living Environment. For Carson's service to the Society, including work on the board in the late 1940s and late 1950s, and major contributions to conservation and the appreciation of nature, the Society gave her the Paul Bartsch Award in 1963, a few months before her death.

Rachel Carson's books became part of my thinking and feeling about nature and conservation, as of the thinking and feeling of so many others, but her public speaking was not suited to her personality and had much less effect. I heard her give (read) a talk at one of the Society's annual dinner meetings, but it was so quiet and unemotional I have no recollection of what she said.

Louis Halle described Carson as "quiet, diffident, neat, proper and without any affectations....She had dignity; she was serious; and as with Lear's Cordelia, her voice was ever soft, gentle and low." [10] The portrait is enlarged by Shirley Briggs, a closer friend, who enjoyed Carson's sly humor.

Quiet voice or no, what matters is that Rachel Carson's writing spoke like the most beautiful ocean sunrise and, when necessary, like a stiletto.

Shirley Briggs (1918-2004) In the late 1940s, the arrival of Shirley Briggs, who became editor of publications, and Irston Barnes, who became president in 1946, propelled the Society to a new era of growth and action.

An artist and writer, Shirley came to the Society after jobs at North Dakota State University, the Glenn L. Martin Corporation, and the Bureau of Commercial Fisheries, part of the U.S. Fish and Wildlife Service. She soon began helping with production of *The Wood Thrush*, and in 1948 became its editor, turning a mimeographed newsletter into an attractive small magazine, which was renamed *The Atlantic Naturalist* in 1951.

In the 1940s, birds dominated the interests of the Society and filled most of *The Wood Thrush*'s pages with reports of bird sightings and good places to see birds, Christmas and regional bird counts, and so on. I faithfully sent in my bird observations for the section Birds of the Month and contributed a few paragraphs about Birding at Seneca in March, a camping trip I took up the C&O Canal with Tom Donnelly. I find this interesting to read now because of changes in some species's abundance. "By far the most common [duck] was the Black Duck, of which we saw hundreds [and only "about 10" mallards; the reverse is true now]. "Red-headed Woodpeckers were as common as Downies, and we had no trouble in finding 13 or 14 near Seneca." Today the red-headed is quite scarce around Washington.

The Society began conducting Christmas Bird Counts in 1943. I first participated in 1946, joining the group along the C&O Canal. As reported in *The Wood Thrush*, "Twenty courageous members of the Society in seven teams left their comfortable beds and sallied forth on the miserably wet dawn of the 21st of December with the temperature hovering around 32 degrees." On a later Christmas count I rode around with John Aldrich, the former Society president, in the Arlington sector. Spotting a kestrel (then called sparrow hawk), he tried to get a better look and accidentally bumped over the curb and up a grassy bank. *Life* magazine sent two men to cover the 1947 count. *The Wood Thrush* for January 1948 included a wonderful photo, taken by *Life*'s Arthur Shay, of the group at Dyke Marsh, silhouetted at dawn on a small bridge. Roger Peterson, in the lead, points out some bird ahead.

Shirley ran a series of articles on the best birding places around Washington. For instance, Irston Barnes did one on the C&O Canal, John Taylor (my youthful contemporary) on the Kenilworth Aquatic Gardens and Soldiers Home, Paul Bartsch on his Masons Neck sanctuary, Lebanon, and Louis Halle on Dyke Marsh. Because I had spent so much time in Glover-Archbold Park, Shirley tapped me to write about that place. After a lengthy and, I thought, rather literary description of the seasonal progression of birds, I (and Shirley) ended with paragraphs about the threat to the park of a planned four-lane highway.

Shirley Briggs was a fierce conservationist, and as the 1940s moved into the 1950s, she put more and more articles on conservation issues, both local and national, into *The Wood Thrush* and then *The Atlantic Naturalist*. Locally, there were threats to the C&O Canal, Dyke Marsh, Theodore Roosevelt Island, Rock Creek Park, Glover-Archbold Park, and the Potomac River (dams) to be fought. Nationally, hawk-shooting at Hawk Mountain and Cape May, threats to national parks, pesticides, private and state ownership of federal land, and wilderness were among the many topics addressed. I and the other Society members were being sensitized to the conditions of our land and life.

During Briggs's 23 years as editor, the Society also published seven scholarly but popular booklets on topics such as the Potomac Valley, bird habitats in the Middle Atlantic States, and *Washington: City in the Woods*. Conservation was an ever-present theme.

The Society, up until 1960, was entirely run by volunteers like Shirley Briggs. Before 1960, when Dr. and Mrs. Walter W. Boyd underwrote the rental of a small headquarters in Georgetown, "We met principally at the Smithsonian," Briggs wrote. "We conducted the work of the Society in our homes, stored material in our attics, and relied on a Post Office box as our address, taking turns getting the mail and distributing it."[11] One can only be amazed at this freely given dedication. (The first paid staff were hired to run the bookstore at the headquarters.)

For her complete and long-term dedication to the affairs of the Society and to the cause of conservation, Shirley received the Paul Bartsch Award in 1972.

Irston Barnes (1904-1988) The chief propellant of the Society's growth during his presidency (1946-1961) was Irston Barnes. He came to Washington from Yale University to take important posts as an economist with the Justice Department, the Civil Aeronautics Board, and last, the Federal Trade Commission. Somehow he found the time to institute a great range of Society activities and write a column for *The Washington Post*, "The Naturalist."

His presence was everywhere. He promoted the Society's publication program and filled many pages of *The Wood Thrush* and *The Atlantic Naturalist* with commentary and learned information on conservation and natural history. As Edward Rivinus and Shirley Briggs wrote, "His ability to generate new activities and goals quickly led to new programs and far wider participation by members in the growing number of committees that directed these new enterprises—seminars in many aspects of ornithology and other aspects of natural history, a lecture-movie series begun in 1945, monthly meetings for timely speakers and informal discussions, field identification courses, providing speakers for schools and other organizations, and in time the Natural History Field Studies program....it is abundantly clear that many of the exceptional achievements during those years are traceable to the strong and imaginative leadership of Irston Barnes, and his ability to enlist the most capable people and to encourage their many ideas for Society programs. To complain of a lack, or to suggest something new, was a sure way to be appointed to the job of taking care of the matter." [12]

Barnes's thinking was never small. In 1959 he persuaded the board of directors to change the Society's name to Audubon Naturalist Society of the Central Atlantic States, reflecting its broadening interests and distribution of members and activities. He pushed for acquisition of a headquarters and got one, first the small rented building on Wisconsin Avenue in Georgetown. Then, in 1967, after he'd moved to Columbia University but remained Chairman of the Board, Mrs. Chester Wells bequeathed Woodend, her Chevy Chase estate, to the Society after numerous discussions, primarily with Irston Barnes. In 1969, after the death of Mrs. Wells, the Society made its headquarters at Woodend.

As with anything else he did, a field trip with Irston Barnes was not casual. He pursued birds with energy and total concentration. When we were birding with a string of cars, Barnes in the lead, drivers had to be alert. When he spotted something of interest he suddenly swerved to the side of the road and the rest of us just as suddenly had to follow. A trip along marshes near Cape May, for instance, would be a succession of such pull-offs, rewarded by good birds but with a certain amount of tension.

Looking through the dozens of articles Barnes wrote for the Society's publications, one notes, from 1946 to 1951, almost exclusive attention to birds, but beginning in 1952 an increasing focus on conservation issues, both local and national. It seems appropriate that in 1972 Irston Barnes was given the Paul Bartsch Award at a meeting devoted to "The Pressing Need for an Environmental Ethic."

Irston Barnes, Shirley Briggs, Rear Admiral Neill Phillips, and other members of the Society had a great deal to do with preserving the best natural areas around Washington. They are an important part of the story, now to be told, about the green Washington that I grew up in. Here we switch from a chronological account of my life to a largely topical one--a bit of history.

7

How Washington Remained Green

I was lucky to live in a city with so much natural parkland, where I could immerse myself in forests growing back toward maturity and even in a good-sized marsh. These landscapes were preserved because some people thought they were valuable. But not without a fight with people who thought they stood in the way of progress.

The land chosen by George Washington and approved by Congress in 1791 to become the site of our national capital consisted of farms, forests, marshes, and probably swamps (forested wetlands). Tiber Creek, whose estuary flowed through what became the Mall and entered the Potomac near the present Lincoln Memorial, overflowed at high tide. Siltation during the 19th century provided new shallows conducive to marsh growth. In 1900 marshes extended on the Potomac's western shore from Analostan Island (now renamed Theodore Roosevelt Island) almost uninterruptedly to Four Mile Run, at the site of the present Reagan National Airport, and south of Alexandria to Dyke Marsh and beyond. On the eastern shore of the Potomac marshes occupied the area of present East Potomac Park and part of West Potomac Park. Wild rice marshes grew along both shores of the Eastern Branch of the Potomac (Anacostia River) from present Hyattsville to Anacostia. [1]

Rock Creek and its wooded hills were from early times a sanctuary from politics and other stresses of Washington life. John Quincy Adams called it "this romantic glen," where he could listen "to the singing of a thousand birds." His grandson, the historian Henry Adams, thought "Rock Creek was as wild as the Rocky Mountains." The naturalist John Burroughs found parts of Rock Creek "as wild and savage...as anything one meets with in the mountain sources of the Hudson or the Delaware." Perhaps the most famous and enthusiastic visitor was Theodore Roosevelt, who frequently rode his big horse Bleistein there, climbed its cliffs, and even skinny-dipped in Rock Creek.

A key figure in the establishment of Rock Creek Park was Charles C. Glover. As described by John Rhodes, who had many conversations with him, Glover was "tall, well-built, and impressive....His physical stature was consonant with his leadership in local society and financial circles. He [was the first president of Riggs Bank, in 1896] and was the close friend of Presidents and other high government officials from the time of the Cleveland administration until his death in 1936." [2]

When Glover was a boy, he and friends walked "all over the Rock Creek Country....I became attached to almost every foot of it." Later he went horseback riding "all over this country," sometimes with the historian George Bancroft, Senator Randall Lee Gibson from Louisiana, and a brother-in-law of Justice White, who was later Chief Justice of the Supreme Court. Sometimes they saw a new subdivision taking the old oaks, hickories, and chestnuts. "We would bewail the fact that all of this country would not be taken in as a national park." (If not covered by subdivisions, the Rock Creek valley could have been drowned by a reservoir proposed by the Engineer Department of the District of Columbia in 1880.)

One day in 1888, while riding with different friends, Glover said, "Boys, this is Thanksgiving Day. Let us...enter a solemn resolve that we will never cease working until the Rock Creek Park is a reality." After learning that some of the landowners wanted "tremendous prices for their property," he decided to ask Congress for an appropriation, and condemnation of the ground. With friends he put together a bill and presented it to Senator John Sherman, who "was immensely helpful afterwards in the passage of the bill."

The first attempt had failed, however, because Congressmen feared their constituents would not like paying for a park in the District of Columbia. The second attempt, in which the cost would "be equally divided between the National Government and the District," passed, "against the vigorous objections of many Senators." Rhodes concluded that "The final fortunate result was very largely due to the groundwork laid by Mr. Glover," with the help of many friends, among them Senator John J. Hemphill of South Carolina.

The first part of the Rock Creek valley to become a public park was the 175-acre National Zoological Park, created by an Act of Congress in March 1889. Frederick Law Olmsted, designer of many urban parks in America, carried out the recommendations of Samuel P. Langley, the man who had conceived the zoo idea.

The next year, 1890, Congress authorized acquisition of 1,606 acres for Rock Creek Park, for its "pleasant valleys and deep ravines, primeval forests and open fields, its running waters, its rocks clothed with rich ferns and mosses, its repose and tranquility, its light and shade, its ever-varying shrubbery, its beautiful and extensive views." [3] Subsequent additions expanded the park to 1,800 acres, and later to 2,700 additional acres in Maryland.

Sedimentation from farms upstream after the early 1800s had led to creation of extensive marshes along the Potomac and Anacostia rivers. Most of the marshes didn't last much past 1900, particularly along the Anacostia. In a 1910 government report, Hugh Taggart stated that "The Washington yard was accessible for many years to the largest vessels in the navy." Since then, "The utility of the upper portion of the river, for purposes of navigation, has been destroyed by [the marshes], and below that point it has been seriously impaired. The betterment of the present objectionable conditions on the river by the elimination of the pestilential and unsightly flats, and the making of other needed improvements, has long been imperatively demanded by considerations of public health and utility." [4] Marshes in the lower part of the river soon gave way to those requirements of "public health and utility."

For the same reasons, marshes on the eastern shore of the Potomac were destroyed. Following a proposal in the 1902 Senate Park Commission Plan, West Potomac Park (1907) and East Potomac Park (1913) were created, largely on land dredged from the Potomac, where marshes had been. These marshes, it was said, had "become so malarial as to affect seriously the health of residents of the city." [5] The parks that replaced the marshes were lovely but landscaped, not natural.

Marshes along the Virginia shore lasted a little longer. Until around 1920, Moorhens, Virginia Rails, and American Bitterns nested in some of this marshland. By the 1940s most of it was gone, supplanted by developments such as the George Washington Memorial Parkway, the Pentagon, and National Airport (now Reagan National Airport). The marshes at the mouth of Four Mile Run had been a popular hunting area. Building the airport had taken most of this marsh, but a fringe along the southern edge of the airport remained, and was a favorite birdwatching site, for me as well as many others. Concern about planes hitting birds led to a study by Jackson Abbott, a well-known local bird expert, who concluded that this strip of marsh, too, a roosting place for large flocks of birds, should be cleared. And it was.

Today, small marshes on Theodore Roosevelt Island and at Roaches Run, a lake across the George Washington Parkway from the airport, and the larger Dyke Marsh, south of Alexandria, are about all that remain on the Virginia side of the Potomac near Washington.

From the beginning of Washington's development, however, there were those who bemoaned the loss of natural landscapes. Though he approved of L'Enfant's plan for the city, Thomas Jefferson was sad to see forest destroyed to make way for L'Enfant's avenues. Momentarily he wished "that, in the possession of absolute power, I might enforce the preservation of these valuable groves." By the beginning of the 20th century, enough pressure for preservation had built up to create the Senate Park Commission, which was established in 1901. The following year it produced its proposed park system plan. Rock Creek Park had already been established. East and West Potomac parks, as described above, replaced marshes. Battery Kemble Park, the southern part of Glover-Archbold Park, lands along the C&O Canal, Analostan Island (Theodore Roosevelt Island), lands along both shores of the upper Anacostia River, and Fort DuPont Park all became parts of the system. Thin strips of parkland along certain roads were proposed, but most of these did not survive subsequent development. Most of the rest, with certain changes in acreage or quality, is natural parkland today. But not without some fierce fights to protect them.

In the 1920s, a boost for park planning and authorization had begun. Frederic A. Delano, Franklin Roosevelt's uncle, became chairman of the American Civic Association, and was "asked to undertake the revival of the recommendations of the 1901 [Senate Park Commission]." In 1924 his Committee of 100 on the Federal City recommended "a major extension of Washington's park and forest preserves under the guidance of an overall planning agency that would focus on park planning as one of its major responsibilities." Congress created such an agency—the National Capital Park Commission—in 1924, and renamed it the National Capital Park and Planning Commission in 1926. (This commission continues such planning today.)

Delano was chairman of the NCPPC during its early years and helped promote passage of the Capper-Crampton Act of 1930, "which authorized funds for parkland acquisition within the District and for the George Washington Memorial Parkway on both sides of the Potomac [now renamed the Clara Barton Parkway on the Maryland side], and acquisition of land for extension of the parks along Rock Creek and the Anacostia River into suburban Maryland." In 1924 Charles Glover and Mrs. Anne Archbold had given land to the District that completed the present Glover-Archbold Park.

In the late 1930s and 1940s, I was venturing to parks beyond Glover-Archbold, which adjoined my home community, and the C&O Canal, locus of my friend Bruce's lockhouse. I traveled to Rock Creek Park, Dyke Marsh, and even Fort DuPont Park, a crosstown bus ride away. At the same time, Washington was rapidly changing. As David Brinkley wrote in his book *Washington Goes to War*, "[World War II] transformed not just the government. It transformed Washington itself. A languid Southern town with a pace so slow that much of it simply closed down for the summer grew almost overnight into a crowded, harried, almost frantic metropolis struggling desperately to assume the mantle of global power, moving haltingly and haphazardly and only partially successfully to change itself into the capital of the free world." [6]

As the federal government expanded to deal with the Depression and the war, workers flocked into the city by the thousands. Car traffic increased enormously. After the war, the city continued to expand. In 1940, the metropolitan area population was 1,000,000 and the developed area 50 square miles. By 1970 the population had grown to 2,800,000, the developed area to 600 square miles.[7] Roadways proposed to handle the ever-increasing traffic threatened neighborhoods and parkland. Some of my favorite parks were targeted.

The highways-through-parks issue arose in 1951 and wasn't settled until 1976. It all began with a metropolitan area origin and destination survey sought by the National Capital Park and Planning Commission. This survey was undertaken by the District Highway Department, the highway authorities of Virginia and Maryland, and the U.S. Bureau of Public Roads. Their conclusions were published as a *Program of Highway Improvements for the Metropolitan Area*. The section concerned with the District was made public on January 31, 1951.

The report called for a system of freeways, two of which would run through Rock Creek Park and Glover-Archbold Park and connect with an Inner Loop and a Capital Beltway, as well as a connection from I-66 in Virginia to the Glover Park Freeway crossing the Potomac at Three Sisters Islands.

> The Inner Loop would have demolished the Georgetown waterfront, cut a swath through DuPont Circle, Shaw, and the northern edge of Capital [sic] Hill, slashed through the

center of Capital Hill at Lincoln Park and through the western edge of the Mall, and gone under K Street to a highway
interchange in the neighborhood of Farragut Square."[8]

Park defenders were joined by Washington residents who were
incensed by the prospect of bulldozed neighborhoods. The highway plan would have destroyed more than 200,000 housing units.
In opposition, the Emergency Committee on the Transportation
Crisis was formed, "a loosely knit but militant cross section of civic
organizations and ministers, as adamantly opposed to freeways as
the builders, planners, and businessmen [were] for them."[9] Among
the members were prominent civil-rights activists Marion Barry
and Julius Hobson, and the D.C. Federation of Civic Associations
and Neighborhoods.

Among parks, the highway plan threatened most directly Rock
Creek and Glover-Archbold.

Rock Creek Park

Outbursts from the Audubon Naturalist Society suggest the rage of
pro-park civic groups.

> …a four-lane divided freeway through Rock Creek Park…
> two to three hundred feet in width…would sever the Park
> as effectively as a canyon several thousand feet deep. It
> would also…destroy the forested and natural character of
> the Park for the greater part of its length. To the south…
> the hills would have to be cut back to make room for the
> freeway. The rare scenic gorge of Rock Creek would be
> mutilated to the point of destruction.[10] (The existing two-
> lane road through the park mostly paralleled Rock Creek
> without damaging natural contours; car noise was its main
> drawback.)

Glover-Archbold Park

> In the case of a narrow park like Glover-Archbold, the de-
> struction [by a four-lane freeway would be] almost com-
> plete….With the removal of the bottomland habitat, at least
> two-thirds of its wildlife would be obliterated….The spell
> of the quiet woodland sounds would be gone forever.[11]

Charles Glover, Jr., whose father had given land for the park, and Mrs. Anne Archbold, who had given to the District most of the rest, were of course outraged by the highway plan. It would be, Mrs. Archbold said, "a violation of the purpose for which so much land has been given, so that it might be kept in its natural state for a bird sanctuary and the enjoyment of people in this rapidly growing part of the city...." [12]

She instituted a suit to restrain the District Commissioners, Secretary Seaton of the Interior Department, and Director Wirth of the National Park Service from using the park for a four-lane highway, and Glover joined the suit. "The defendants sought to avoid the necessity for a trial on the merits by motions to dismiss the suit or for a summary judgment. Judge Burnita S. Matthews denied their motions and rejected their arguments." [13]

The freeway battle went on and on. Lawyer Peter Craig, when with the U.S. Department of Transportation, studied the Highway Department's origin-and-destination studies and data and determined that the statistics were "full of helium." The D.C. City Council in August 1969 voted to comply with the 1968 Highway Act approving the Three Sisters Bridge, a condition imposed by Congress before funds could be given to the city for Metrorail. In August 1970 Judge John Sirica issued an injunction stopping work on the Three Sisters Bridge. Congress continued to press for the freeway system. In 1976 new Mayor Walter Washington appeared to turn the tide, by proposing that $493 million in federal highway funds be made available for Metrorail, saying that "most of this money would come from elimination, once and for all, of plans to build the Three Sisters Bridge and the K Street Tunnel."

Now the only sign of the planned freeway through Glover-Archbold Park is a plant-covered pile of broken concrete slabs in the lower end of the park. Not much has changed since I was a kid roaming here, except that big, flashy Pileated Woodpeckers and deer have moved in, and nonnative plants, such as the ground-carpeting lesser celandine, have also. But it looks and feels the same.

C&O Canal

In 1948 the 80th Congress directed the Bureau of Public Roads of the Department of Commerce and the Interior Department's National Park Service to report on "the advisability and practicability of constructing a parkway along the route of the Chesapeake &

Ohio Canal between Great Falls and Cumberland, Md." The resulting report transmitted in August 1950 by the Assistant Secretary of
the Interior concluded that "it is entirely practicable to construct a
parkway along this canal and that it is advisable to do so provided
that the necessary additional right-of-way can be obtained." [14] Thus
began an 11-year battle to preserve the canal and adjacent lands for
their historic and natural values.

The park service was then enamored with parkways and supportive of a canal parkway. According to the Audubon Naturalist
Society, the highway scheme "was devised as a means of raising
the real estate value of the tract and clinching National Park Service control of it. Arguments for its usefulness as a highway were
contrived to fit that purpose...."[15] Maryland was prepared to buy
the necessary land ($325,000) if the Federal Government built the
highway ($8,000,000). Cumberland hoped for increased tourism.

C&O Canal at Lock 7

Considering the proposed destruction of the canal's historic and natural values, and the adequacy of existing highways in the region, it seems unlikely that the parkway idea ever had a chance. Many Washington residents were "shocked and aroused."[16] Maryland communities in Montgomery, Frederick, and Washington counties did not want to be by-passed by an express highway. The District of Columbia Daughters of the American Revolution called upon the Congress "to refrain from appropriating any funds whatever... [for] one or more motor highways" on the bed of the canal. At a meeting in Washington "on May 7, 1964, representatives of more than 20 organizations—local, state and national; naturalist, conservation, civic and historical—constituted themselves the Potomac Valley Conservation and Recreation Council to work for the preservation of the Canal and other threatened areas."[17] As recorded in the administrative history of the C&O Canal National Historical Park, the Council more specifically came about this way:

> The D.C. Audubon Society called a meeting at the home of Mrs. Gifford Pinchot on May 7 [1954] to mobilize the opposition. Some fifty people attended, including Irston Barnes, Shirley A. Briggs, and Constant Southworth of the society; Howard Zahniser, executive secretary of The Wilderness Society; and [Anthony Wayne] Smith, [a CIO attorney active in the National Parks Association]....The group voted to form the Potomac Valley Conservation and Recreation Council, with Barnes as chairman, to fight the parkway and promote conservation objectives for the valley.[18]

The Washington Post took both sides of the issue. A column on January 11, 1953 proposed a historical and natural recreational park from Washington to Cumberland. A later editorial supported the parkway idea. In 1954, Supreme Court Justice William O. Douglas organized a hike along the canal from Cumberland to Georgetown, taking along *Washington Post* editors who had supported the parkway, as well as conservationists. Seeing what would be destroyed, the *Post* editors reversed their earlier position, and publicity from the walk helped to further build public sentiment in favor of a park rather than a parkway. Over the next few years that sentiment swelled, and in 1956 Secretary of the Interior Douglas McKay, a parkway advocate, was succeeded by Fred A. Seaton, who "showed little interest in resurrecting the parkway issue.[19] In 1961 President Eisenhower established the Chesapeake and Ohio

Canal National Monument by proclamation, and in 1971 President Nixon signed the act of Congress changing the canal's status to the more firmly protected Chesapeake and Ohio Canal National Historical Park.

The canal, however, was not totally free from freeways. The George Washington Parkway on the Maryland side of the Potomac was planned to run from Great Falls to Chain Bridge. With many others from the Audubon Naturalist Society, I wrote a letter to Senator "Scoop" Jackson opposing this assault on the peacefulness along the canal. He replied that some of the parkway would be placed farther from the canal. And so it was, but much of the canal between Georgetown and Angler's Inn, near Great Falls, is now serenaded by automobile noise, first along Canal Road and then the parkway (completed in 1965, later renamed the Clara Barton Parkway). The quality of a walk along these noisy parts is diminished, but thankfully there are many more miles toward Cumberland where the sounds are nature's alone.

For a time, the canal was also threatened with being buried, not just under a highway but also by water. After World War II, the Army Corps of Engineers unveiled a plan for 14 dams on the Potomac and its tributaries, for flood control, hydroelectric power, and recreation, which would have flooded much of the canal. A scaled-down version of the Engineers' plan was still floating around as late as the Nixon Administration, when the national historical park was finally authorized. This effectively ruled out most of the dams, but one was built, creating the Randolph Jennings Reservoir, on the North Branch of the Potomac above Cumberland. This water is now a backup supply for Washington. The District of Columbia has an agreement with the reservoir authority to release water for the D.C. if the flow of the Potomac at Little Falls drops below 360 million gallons per day. Such a situation has not occurred since the 1960s.

The canal is still my favorite walking place, though I tend to start beyond earshot of cars. I still see virtually all the wildlife I saw as a boy: ducks of many kinds thronging the river in winter; migrating birds and wildflowers everywhere in spring (although the migrant "waves" are diminished); turtles on logs, herons stalking fish, the almost tropical luxuriance of forests in the somnolence of summer; and the return of migrants in the color and brisk air of autumn. There are as well new things: beavers that reclaimed their canal territory during the twentieth century, otters that repopulated the Upper Potomac late in that century, and even convincing reports of cougars in the mountainous region. I am happy these days to also see so many people—bikers, joggers, walkers, birdwatchers, anglers, and others enjoying the canal. It is fortunate that the public demanded keeping the canal as it was.

Theodore Roosevelt Island

In 1931 the Roosevelt Memorial Association bought Analostan Island, a forested island in the Potomac downstream from Georgetown. Renaming it Theodore Roosevelt Island, the association gave it to the Nation to honor our greatest conservationist president, and to preserve a place in the middle of the city where people could come for refreshment in a peaceful, unspoiled environment. Part of its purpose was to be "an island of solitude where men may find lost values and perspectives amid the tumult and confusion of national politics and international controversy."

At first these values were protected. The only access was by a National Park Service ferry from Georgetown, on which I, as a 10- or 12-year old, made my first visit to the island. Later, pedestrians could cross to the island on a causeway from the Virginia shore, and car traffic over it, with parking on the island, was considered. By 1960, a bridge carrying I-66 across the Potomac to E Street over the southern end of the island was under construction. And instead of a modest memorial to Roosevelt, in keeping with the island's quiet naturalness, a sphere 50 feet high surrounded by granite slabs 10 and 20 feet high was planned. A *Washington Post* editorial (7/8/60) panned this idea: "It would be difficult to contrive a more monstrous monument than the gargantuan Freedom Wall....The bulging excrescence [the sphere]...has been charitably dubbed a glorified gyroscope."

Such opinions had an effect. The resulting monument has a circular moat, lined with willow oaks, ringing a plaza, with a bowl-shaped fountain at the east and west sides. On the north side stands a 20-foot limestone slab with a statue of Theodore Roosevelt in front of it. Behind, under trees, four smaller slabs along the edge of the plaza bear Roosevelt quotations. Two of these read:

NATURE
There are no words that can tell the hidden spirit of the wilderness o that can reveal its mystery o its melancholy and its charm

THE STATE
A GREAT DEMOCRACY has got to be progressive or it will soon cease to be great or a democracy.

As you approach the plaza on a trail through the forest, the statue strikes you. This is probably appropriate. Theodore Roosevelt was not one to stand back in the shadows. The monument in general still seems a bit formal for this lover of wilderness.

A forest of oaks, ash, hickories, and beech, with sycamores and silver maples near the shores, shades the island. A perimeter loop trail and cross trails provide access to all parts. The perimeter trail goes on a boardwalk over wet areas on the south end, where a marsh lines a small stream flowing out to the river. On a June 2011 visit, I stood on the bridge over this stream, watching a great blue heron fishing. It was low tide, and schools of small fish flashed in the shallows. Farther along two male Pileated Woodpeckers, close together, whacked on an ash tree. In the distance a Red-shouldered Hawk called.

Walking on the island is a pleasant experience, but it is not the peaceful environment it was in the 1930s. Planes flying to and from Reagan National Airport pass over at short intervals, and occasionally helicopters. In summer, foliage at the south end makes a visual but not auditory screen for the I-66 Bridge.

It's another example of the fact that nature preservation often has to be a compromise.

Dyke Marsh

According to a 2011 U.S. Geological Survey study, Dyke Marsh began forming about 530 years ago. Early in the 19th century, Col. Augustine J. Smith, who owned the marsh, attempted to drain it to make grazing land by building an earthen dike around the perimeter. He wasn't successful, and during the 20th century Dyke (the British spelling of "dike") became a popular birdwatching area. I didn't get that far by bicycle, but in my early teens I went with birders who had cars. I especially remember one trip with Roxie

Dyke Marsh

Collie Simpson, an ornithologist at the Smithsonian who frequently took young birders places. That day in May 1945, we walked out along the dike, by then mostly vegetated with shrubs and trees, and crossed openings in the dike on wooden foot bridges. It was an exciting place, full of possibilities for birds of marsh, open water, and forest.

I was unaware then that the Smoot Sand and Gravel Company owned most of the marsh and planned to dredge it for sand and gravel. By the 1950s the Audubon Naturalist Society and other organizations were pressing for preservation of this eroding 2-mile-long marshland, where ducks, herons, rails, bitterns, Ospreys and many other birds lived among or near the wild rice, cattails, and other marsh plants. Swampy woods added another habitat for wildlife.

The preservation campaign, aided by conservationists in Congress led by Representatives John D. Dingell, Henry S. Reuss, and John Saylor, in 1959 succeeded in getting an Act of Congress (Public Law 86-41, H.R. 2228) that was an apparently workable compromise with Smoot Sand and Gravel. Under the agreement, 1) Smoot deeded to the U.S.A. 110 acres, and deeded another 150 acres with a right to dredge for 30 years (until 1989); 2) the U.S. agreed to permit Smoot to dredge in another 85 acres for 20 years (until 1979); another section owned by the government was not to be dredged. Thus, Smoot could dredge in the outer part of the area—235 acres.

Dredged areas were to be restored to within ½ foot to 3 feet below the mean water level—shallow enough for marsh plant growth. The Potomac Sand and Gravel Company—successor to Smoot—agreed to continue the agreement.

By 1970, 500,000 cubic feet—mostly fill from demolition and construction projects—had been placed in the 85-acre section. Seven and a half million cubic feet remained to be filled. However, by 1972 or 1973 dredge mining ended, and in 1974, pushed by individuals and groups concerned with the deteriorating condition of Dyke Marsh, Congress mandated its restoration. In 1976, Friends of Dyke Marsh was established and became the major private organization advocating for protection and restoration of the marsh. Among other activities, members carried out research on flora and fauna of the marsh and conducted walks to promote interest in the marsh and concern about it.

The mandated restoration has been slow in coming, but a major foundation for future work was created with publication in 2011 of the U.S. Geological Survey study, *Analysis of the Deconstruction of Dyke Marsh*. This study identified the major causes of erosion and the rates of erosion since 1937, before dredging began.

"[It was concluded that] storm waves driven northward up the Potomac River valley, from tropical storms and hurricanes in the summer and nor'easters in the winter, were the primary agents of marsh erosion." Actual marsh acreage calculated from photographs declined from about 184 acres in 1937 to about 60 acres in 2006, with losses accelerating over the years. From 2002 to 2006, 1.5 acres were being lost each year.

> Historically, the shallow western river bottom and a forested promontory south of the marsh...jointly buffered most storm activity directed toward the marsh...Dredge mining before 1959 removed those protections, destabilizing the marsh and exposing it to repeated storm erosion. Also, deep mining scar channels...now exist in the western river bottom adjacent to the present shoreline [and] cut into what originally was emergent marsh inside the park boundary. These mining channels have become active scour channels along this stretch of the Potomac, increasing the intensity of storm erosion at the shoreline, and adding to the marsh's instability.

Restoration could begin once the Environmental Impact Statement process is completed. It would consist primarily of recreating protection from storm waves at the southern end of the marsh, rendering the mining scour channels "nonfunctional" as scour channels, and protecting from further storm erosion the outflow of the last major tidal creek in the marsh (down which sediment flows that builds up the marsh substrate). Whether the marsh could be expanded to the 1937 boundary depends primarily on physical conditions.

Restoring Anacostia River Marshes

During the 19th and early 20th centuries, the Anacostia River marshes, and especially the Benning marsh, which spread upstream for three miles from the old Baltimore and Potomac Railroad Bridge to the D.C.-Maryland line, were a magnet for hunters in early fall. "All classes in society are represented," wrote Dr. Elliott Coues in 1882, "from the gentleman sportsman with his pusher and favorite breech-loader…to the ragged contraband with the cheap, old-fashioned, single-barreled muzzle-loader, or old-style army musket, 'wading' the marshes from knee to waist deep….It is a common thing on the first day of the season for one [market gunner] to secure from twelve to twenty dozen [rails] and as many [bobolinks]." [20] Red-winged Blackbirds also fell to the less sporting gunners.

In the 1920s and 1930s, filling of the "pestilential marshes" began. A seawall was constructed on the banks of the river, the bottom of the river was dredged and the sediment dumped behind the wall to fill the marshes. Today most of that new land is used for golf courses, other recreational activities, and various facilities. It is Anacostia Park, administered by the National Park Service. The most natural area of the park is that surrounding the Kenilworth Aquatic Gardens.

Marsh restoration has been underway in parts of the Benning marsh area since the 1990s. The most ambitious project is adjacent to the Kenilworth Aquatic Gardens. The Gardens were created by Walter B. Shaw, a clerk in the U.S. Treasury Department, who bought 30 acres from his mother-in-law in 1882 and developed a "pleasure garden" of lily-filled ponds. His daughter, Lucy Helen Fowler, managed the ponds after 1921 and opened the commercial operation to the public. In 1938 Congress bought the 8 acres of ponds and turned them over to the National Park Service. They now occupy 12 acres.

The area around the ponds contained some remnant marsh but was mostly swampy woodland. In 1992 and 1993, the National Park Service, the District of Columbia government, U.S. Army Corps of Engineers, Metropolitan Council of Governments, and others joined to build new marshland. Openings were dredged in the woodlands and various marsh plants were introduced. At high tide the water depths could range up to three feet, creating conditions for a variety of plants. Today one sees hibiscus and buttonbush in the High Marsh zone, cattails and wild rice among other species in the Mid-Marsh zone, and spatterdock in Low Marsh, where water is deepest. Marsh and woodland now occupy 77 acres, including 32 acres of newly created marsh.

In the last few decades beavers have moved in. In March 2012 I saw many cuttings, and along the River Trail a dam and ponded water with a mud-and-stick-packed lodge in it. Mallards and Canada geese were getting ready to nest. A pair of Hooded Mergansers, tree-cavity nesters, were perhaps checking out these wetlands as a potential breeding site. Later, Red-winged Blackbirds and Marsh Wrens would arrive and nest in the greening marshes.

Downriver, at Kingman Lake, some of the shores have been graded to make gradual slopes suitable for a variety of marsh plants. All this marsh work is part of a long-term effort to return the badly-polluted Anacostia River to a cleaner, more wildlife- and people-friendly condition.

Two popular natural areas in the 1930s and '40s have succumbed to overuse (Fort DuPont Park) and development (Soldiers Home).

In 2010, Washington, D.C., with 19 percent of its land area in parks, ranked second among high-density U.S. cities. Only New York City, with 19.5 percent, ranked higher, and natural Rock Creek Park is more than twice the size of Central Park, which is only part natural.[21] "Parks" include remote natural areas, playgrounds, flower gardens, paved plazas, sports fields, reflective retreats, bike trails, dog parks, river walks, cemeteries, and boulevards. Ninety-one percent of Washington's 7,464 acres of parks is managed by the National Park Service. Parkland contributes to a high urban tree canopy of 35 percent.[22] After a period of neglect of Washington's trees outside natural parks, Casey Trees was established by Betty Brown Casey in 2002 to "restore, enhance and protect the tree canopy of the nation's capital." Since then it has funded a great surge in tree care and tree planting in the District. Officials of Casey Trees and the D.C. government have a target of 40 percent tree canopy by 2035. From the air, Washington looks green indeed.

Next we pick up my own story, from my late teens to 36.

PART II
Speaking for Nature

8

Finding My Mission

While some of the battles over Washington-area parks were going on, my life was taking a turn for the worse. When I was twelve I had no doubt I was going to be an ornithologist. In my late teens, I wasn't so sure. My father, who had been so important to me in my childhood, and so supportive of my interests, had become alcoholic when I was ten. This bothered me more and more until, by the time I was a teenager, that difficult time of life under the best of circumstances, this was affecting me in a bad way, and by my late teens I had gone into an emotional shell, an attempted escape, I suppose, from my changed father, whose life was now ruled by alcohol. Although I maintained good grades at school, I felt inferior, outside the realm of the most popular boys.

During my freshman year at Amherst College, I sank further psychologically. I majored in English because I liked to read and write, but found that I wasn't good at literary criticism, the main content of these courses. I got low grades in English as well as everything else. In my sophomore year I nearly flunked out but was saved by a biology professor who got my studying organized. Then I decided it was time to decide on a career. I was still interested in birds and nature, but my psychological difficulties, no doubt, made me think I should go into psychiatry. I thought of it, rather fuzzily, as healing people's souls. This meant, first, an M.D., so I took some pre-med courses. My work in these was mediocre or worse; I flunked introductory chemistry twice. But I did better in philosophy, religion, and psychology, subjects that had more meaning for my mental state.

After college I still considered psychiatry, but didn't go to medical school. I then turned to religion and wrote the Princeton theological seminary about studying there for a Ph.D. in religion. They replied that I needed more philosophy. I didn't want to study more philosophy. (Guess I wasn't really serious about this degree, either.)

But I did need to get a job. I investigated two possibilities: working at a settlement house and working at the Corcoran Art Gallery (I had done a lot of painting in high school). The settlement house said I would need a Masters degree in social work. The Corcoran said maybe I could crate paintings for shipment. These lines of work, apparently, were not serious ideas—just fliers.

Then, fortunately, in 1957 I went to see an editor at *U.S. News & World Report* who was a family friend. He got me a job as copy boy, which then led into proofreading. I worked in the newsroom, the hub of magazine production, and loved it. By this time I wanted to be involved with conservation, a move back toward my earlier interests. If the magazine had been covering environment, I might have stayed there and tried to be an environment reporter, but it was 1960, before Rachel Carson's *Silent Spring* and the awakening environmentalism in America. Newspapers and magazines were not yet interested in this. I had to do something else.

If I were to do something involving conservation, I decided I needed more knowledge of the subjects basic to conservation, beginning with botany. After summer courses at the University of Virginia's Mountain Lake Biological Station, including plant ecology, I was accepted at Duke University for a Master's degree in this subject—the relation of plants to their environment.

For a long time I had had a fascination with the Arctic and decided to do the research for my Master's thesis in Mt. McKinley National Park, Alaska, which wasn't quite Arctic, but had elements of that region. I compared vegetation on north- and south-facing slopes, where spruce-fir forest gave way upslope to a shrub zone and finally to alpine tundra. In my free time I explored, following a river 10 miles to the Alaska Range, where the river issued from a glacier; camping out at Wonder Lake to see the sun rise on Mount McKinley (now called Denali—The Great One); canoeing down the Nenana River with a park ranger. And always birdwatching, caribou-watching, and grizzly-bear watching—this last sometimes with Adolph Murie, a park service biologist who was studying grizzly bears.

Blueberries were ripening that August and I had seen a grizzly bear eating them near my research area. I had thrown stones and chased it off. But one day I met a grizzly under more dangerous circumstances. I was taking a core from a foot-thick spruce tree at timberline when I heard a roar just down the mountainside, where my pack lay. Apparently the bear had been attracted by the squeaking of my increment borer, and perhaps was a female with cubs. I went up the tree. Grizzly bears aren't adapted to climbing trees and ten feet up I thought I was safe. But this tree was leaning, with ladder-like branches sticking out from the trunk, making climbing easier. I felt the bear's teeth slash through my left leg and fasten onto my boot. I couldn't hang on, the bear was pulling me down. Then I felt release, the bear had lost its grip in the tree and slid down.

I climbed to the top of this 20-foot spruce and found the bear had scrambled up behind me. Like a fighting dog, it was growling and its palomino hair was standing on end. I kicked its massive head, the bear lunged and bit me in the other leg, then slid to the bottom again.

I couldn't tell if the bear was in the thick shrubbery or was going off. Half an hour later, taking my chances, I came down, hobbled to my car at the bottom of the mountain, and drove away. I happened to meet Adolph Murie driving toward me and told him what had happened. (I was lucky. Just before coring the foot-thick spruce I'd been coring a 4-inch-thick spruce. If the bear had approached then, it would have caught me with nothing to climb.) At the Muries' cabin his wife Louise applied some first aid and they drove me to

Author at the bear tree, when he returned to pick up his pack.

the hotel at the park entrance, 30 miles away, where a nurse applied more first aid. She searched the hotel guest list and found an M.D., who inspected my wounds, said little, and walked off. He was a psychiatrist. A bush pilot in Fairbanks was called to come get me.

After five days in a hospital and two days on the front page of the *Fairbanks News-Miner*, with a photo of thin, red-bearded me, I returned to the park and completed my research.

If I didn't already, I now knew firsthand that nature could kill me. I loved nature, but nature didn't love me. I'd experienced a terrifying example of Kellert's negativistic valuation of nature. (See Chapter 2).

Pondering my next career move, I discussed it with Murie. He suggested that a Ph.D. in botany would provide a good background for work in conservation. But I didn't want to be a botanist. What to do? Not being sure, in 1963 I took a job in Washington with the National Park Service as a writer and editor, producing publications for park visitors. This was fun, and they actually paid me to do it.

During this time, two things happened that further focused my life. First, I took some courses in geography at George Washington University and found that I felt very much at home in this subject. Geography has two principal themes: study of the spatial arrangement of things, and the relations of humans to their environment, which can be considered human ecology. The latter kind of geography seemed a perfect foundation for understanding environmental issues.

Second, I met Elizabeth Worth, who was to become my wife. She entered the Foreign Service, and, after Junior Officer training, was posted to Thailand. While she was there, we decided to get married — in Thailand. This meant, however, that the current regulations — female diplomats couldn't be married — would require her to resign from the Foreign Service.

Meanwhile, I'd applied to the University of Michigan for graduate work in geography and was accepted. So, at the end of May 1964 I flew to Bangkok to get married. We spent two months wandering the Far East, and in September I began my studies in Ann Arbor.

(My dissertation topic was about vegetation patterns around certain Midwestern cities and their values for urban residents. But later I wished I had studied the bird species present in woodlots of different sizes and shapes, a subject I had casually wondered about and which was just beginning to be addressed. It turned out that individual species *require* different-sized forests.)

During the time I was pursuing a Ph.D. I was a teaching fellow for two years. And I discovered I was very uncomfortable doing this, in both large and small classes. After one lecture on ecology, in which I drew a diagram on the blackboard supposed to show how things were related in nature, with arrows going all over the place, I heard one student say to another, "That's the most confusing lecture I ever heard." I was both uncomfortable and hard to understand.

Then something happened that pointed my way more decisively. Both I and my wife had thought I was going to be a professor of geography, but my experience with teaching told me that was the wrong path. In 1968, my former boss in the park service asked me to go to Arizona to revise an NPS book about Saguaro National Monument. I went. On the train I realized that this sort of thing was what I was intended to do. I right then wrote a letter to Bruce McHenry's mother in California—she from the lockhouse on the C&O Canal—about this realization. I was, so to speak, at 36, finally on the right track. And that's where I've been ever since, back to my first loves of nature and writing. The Ph.D. helped to inform my writing, not lectures.

During good times and bad, birding has been a near-constant in my life. I'll pause here and single out a few experiences. I didn't do much birding at Amherst, but I do remember seeing my first redpoll, while walking down a nearby railroad track with a classmate; encountering a swarm of Pine Grosbeaks eating barberries at a classroom building entrance; and a screech owl perched on a branch in someone's back yard.

During graduate work in plant ecology at Duke, I persuaded three of my fellow students to canoe down the Waccamaw River, a slow dark-tannic stream through swamps in southeastern North Carolina. Before we shoved off, a county sheriff warned us: "Those cottonmouth rattlers will eat you alive." From my journal:

> We went down the river through Spanish-moss hung trees and snakes dropping into the water. One appeared definitely to be a water moccasin [but it didn't eat us]....Many thrashers and catbirds were in there. Heard and saw Pileated Woodpecker, and a number of egrets and herons. Saw one wood ibis [Wood Stork], the biggest bird treat of the day.

May 1964: Biggest adventure in recent weeks was my drive down to Florida. Stopped to see mother a couple of days in Delray Beach....Went to Okefenoke Swamp, Lake Okeechobee, Loxahatchee National Wildlife Refuge, Everglades National Park, and Key Largo. Saw a lot of birds, including seven life birds: Reddish Egret, Great White Heron, Roseate Spoonbill, Limpkin, Purple Gallinule, Mottled Duck, and Fulvous Tree Duck. Loxahatchee had the most birds—a truly wonderful concentration.

My contacts with Ann Arbor [during Ph.D. graduate work] and its people have come mostly through the Washtenaw County Audubon Society. Doug Fulton, its president this year, is a photographer and outdoor writer on the Ann Arbor News. Dr. Tordoff, ornithologist at the University [Natural History] Museum, joins some of their activities. May 7 weekend [1965] I camped at Point Pelee, along with Doug Fulton and some others. Saw some 125 species (113 on Saturday), including Harris's Sparrow, a life bird. May 15 I was in charge of the Washtenaw County 'Century Run,' in which 15 of us saw 122 species around Ann Arbor.

April 19-25, 1967: This can be considered the baby period! I throw in the 19th because that day before the birth [of our first child] we went out to Waterloo Recreation area—I to see the cranes, Elizabeth for the ride since she was feeling too heavy to walk much. We did a lot of bouncing around on dirt roads, and maybe it was more than coincidental that the baby was born the next day.

January 29, 1968: We are at By-the-Sea Cottages on Sanibel Island, Fla., in the midst of a six-week stay [while I studied for Ph.D. exams]. Mother is with us. Eleanor is crawling around happily.

One day on the beach Elizabeth said, "That bird looks different." It turned out to be a Glaucous Gull, far south of its usual wintering grounds. I learned that Whitney Eastman, one of America's most active birders, was on the island and I excitedly went to tell him about our Glaucous Gull. He concurred with my identification and told me a bit about his search for Ivory-billed Woodpeckers, back in the 1950s. "He says he camped all over Florida looking for them, and finally did find one or two along the Chipola (I believe) River in the north part of the state."

9

Writer/Editor for the
National Park Service

It's not surprising that I ended up working in one way or another for the National Park Service. My association with it began in first grade, when I met Bruce McHenry, whose father was the first Chief Naturalist of the National Capitol area. This friendship led me to spend many days with the McHenrys when they lived in the lockhouse at Lock 7 on the C&O Canal, and two summers when I worked in Yosemite National Park, where Donald McHenry was the Chief Naturalist after D.C.

I always thought of national parks as the most inspiring landscapes or places in America for their natural or historical values, and their preservation as a moral duty.

I worked for the National Park Service during three different periods totaling 14 years. During that time I wrote and edited publications, supervised the publication of books on research done in the parks, wrote speeches, got involved with the production of video programs, and was picked for several other interesting projects.

I spent 1963-64 mostly editing park folders, which describe the parks and things to do there, and are handed out to visitors. These folders were written in the parks and then sent to the Washington office for design, editing, creation of a park map, and finishing touches. When I arrived at the Office of Publications the folders were serviceable but undistinguished. When Vince Gleason became the new publications chief, everything changed. Vince had been an advertising executive at Alcoa and had advanced ideas about the quality of publications. He announced a three-stage improvement: first in design, then maps, and finally text. The other two editors and I were held to higher text standards, which sometimes required total rewriting of the manuscripts that came in.

Vince's greatest concern seemed to be design. I'll never forget the day the superintendent of Cape Cod National Seashore came in to complain about the cover of the new Cape Cod folder. Cape Cod had wanted something with sand dunes and terns. The expensive outside designer Gleason had hired came up with a lighthouse crowned by a Pilgrim hat. Vince asked me to be present at the meeting in his bare, Spartan office. It started as a discussion and ended with Gleason, a short man with a bristly crewcut, backing the tall superintendent into a corner of the room and shouting, "You don't know *anything* about design!" I believe the lighthouse stayed on the Cape Cod cover. It was my first awareness of the intensity of Vince's feelings about his work. We did end up with first-class folders. However, his attempt to replace the beloved arrowhead NPS logo with an extremely unpopular modern cannonball and triangle design was shot down.

My second period as a park service employee, 1978-81, made me the director of scientific publications. We published in book form the results of research on species and natural resource problems in the parks. This involved me in all stages of book production: deciding whether to publish, editing, and selection of and oversight of a company to design and print the book. To decide whether to publish I sent the manuscript to two experts on the subject for review. If both or neither said publish, the decision was obvious. If they split, I decided. I did much of the editing myself. Selecting the book-maker was interesting, as I compared bids and companies. This job gave me some insight into the world of publishing as I entered that world as a writer.

One day Vince Gleason asked me to revise a manuscript on elk in Yellowstone, to make it more readable, for a wider audience. To do this I took a train out there, bringing Elizabeth and our three girls with me. It was late September, and four inches of snow decorated the lodgepole pines. After consultation with the author I attempted the revision, but ended up with something that was neither good scientific writing nor adequate popular writing. It would have to be entirely rewritten, I decided, if intended for a general audience, and this approach was not wanted by the author. Well, it was a nice train ride, and we had a memorable moment in a picnic ground when a cow moose ran through, followed in full pursuit by an amorous bull.

During my third time in the park service, from 1986 to 1994, I was a writer and editor in the Natural Resource Management Division. This taught me a lot about natural resource problems in the parks and led me into a variety of interesting assignments. One was co-editing a hefty manual on natural resource management—

NPS 41. Chapters on various kinds of management were sent to the Division and Lissa Fox and I edited them. With so many authors there was a great range of writing organization, clarity, and so on, and a challenge to maintain a certain standard of presentation. One chapter I found particularly interesting dealt with "hazard trees." These procedures were developed after a tent camper in Yellowstone, I believe, was killed by a falling tree. The management instructions defined a hazard tree, which must be taken down or trimmed, in great detail, such as distance from a trail and condition of the tree. I hope no more park visitors have been killed by such trees. (And when I'm out walking in a high wind, I keep an eye out for falling limbs or trees.)

During these years, the Watchable Wildlife program was started. State by state, the best places for seeing wildlife were identified, a book describing them was privately published, and signs with binoculars on them were placed on approaching roads. The philosophy behind the program was that if more people could see wildlife there would be more inspiration to protect it and its habitats. Since many of the sites selected would be NPS areas, I was asked to represent the park service at planning sessions, along with others from the Fish and Wildlife Service, Forest Service, and other agencies and organizations. We met at some interesting places. One was the Rocky Mountain Arsenal near Denver, where chemical weapons were developed and stored during World War II and now were being cleaned up. (It later became a national wildlife refuge.) Burrowing Owls, Bald Eagles, and deer herds were easily seen within the fence that enclosed this large area. Groups were allowed in to see the wildlife. Another meeting place was the Marine base at Quantico, Virginia. Many military bases, with their extensive natural habitats and restricted entry, are managed partly for wildlife. By now, most states are sprinkled with the familiar binoculars signs.

Quite unexpected was the request to represent the park service in a group planning year-long educational trips for high-school-age students around the world on a sailboat leaving from Florida. We met in Palm Beach. My contribution was suggestions for stopping at several National Park Service areas in the Caribbean. Unfortunately, the leaders of the project failed to get adequate funding and the trips never happened.

One member of the group, Tania Aebi, had sailed solo around the world at age 18 and wrote a book about it, *Maiden Voyage*. She had been a bicycle messenger in New York when her father, worried about the direction of her life, offered to finance college or a sail around the world. It was an amazing story. She had done some ocean sailing with her father but didn't have GPS, just a compass, and didn't know celestial navigation. By luck she found Bermuda, but she entirely missed the Galapagos Islands. After capsizing in the Mediterranean during a violent storm she wanted to quit, but her father persuaded her to complete the voyage back to New York.

Over my years with the National Park Service, I studied or used various forms of communication. I went to Cumberland Island National Seashore in Georgia and Voyageurs National Park in Minnesota to learn how park staffs were explaining to neighbors NPS management activities that might be unpopular. At our Harpers Ferry center, with the help of an exhibit specialist who could design exhibits with a computer, I created one about how research led to informed management. The whole thing could be folded up and shipped around the country as needed. Selecting companies to make video programs, editing their film scripts, and sometimes helping in the field was interesting. With my boss, Anne Frondorf, we reviewed sample video programs and chose companies, balancing quality and cost. To increase my understanding of the process I took a course at American University on film script writing and then wrote one about research in Shenandoah National Park.

Speech writing was another new avenue of communication for me. I wrote one for our director, William P. Mott, Jr. about the devastating fires in Yellowstone—their causes and the regrowth that would eventually occur. Another was a Columbus Day speech for an assistant secretary of the Interior Department (and former governor of Kansas). I imagined Christopher Columbus coming back and marveling at all the changes (though he had never been in North America). My associates liked it but the assistant secretary didn't. Perhaps not politically useful. Instead, he stole the park service director's speech, about all the good things the park service was doing. In the course of writing several speeches I learned a surprising thing: it appeared that you could make policy if no reviewer objected.

10

Writing Books

Though I've published over 100 articles, I think of books as my principal offering to the world. The first four were written under contract to the National Park Service, which published them. The next five were published elsewhere. Now in my eighties I'm writing two more. I hope they won't be my last.

Saguaro National Monument (now a national park). Earlier I described the train ride to Arizona, when I realized that writing would be my work. The purpose then was to revise the existing NPS book by Natt Dodge. It was late September but the days were still hot. Early every morning I left my trailer home and drove around the loop road through desert scrub with tall saguaro cactuses rising all about. I would get out to watch peccaries feeding in a wash, or cactus wrens and other birds stirring in the coolness. One morning a coyote put on an amusing show as it tried to subdue a large centipede. By 9:00 a.m. it was 90 degrees and very quiet. Birds and other life had disappeared into shade.

The desert section was what most visitors saw, but trails led upward through zones of grassland, oak/pine woodland, and ponderosa pine forest to patches of Douglas fir at the highest elevations. To investigate these I rode a horse before dawn with others taking supplies to the Manning ranger station on Mica Mountain. As the sun came up I walked back down the Tanque Verde Ridge Trail toward the visitor center and my trailer. I had time to study the changes in plants and animals as I descended. Since most chapters of the book required only editing, I was able to write my seven new chapters and finish most of the revision before I left this wonderful piece of the Sonoran Desert.

The Nature of Shenandoah. The next book was entirely mine. I proposed doing a book about this national park to Vince Gleason because it was near my home in Washington and I was especially fond of it. I thought of it as my "home park." Not only that, my long-time friend Bruce McHenry was the assistant chief naturalist. Elizabeth and I had many opportunities to visit Bruce and his wife Martha. I even found a way to put Bruce into my book:

" 'If I were an Indian, I'd sit under this oak tree waiting for game.' Assistant Chief Naturalist Bruce McHenry got nods of agreement from the group of visitors he had led out along the quartzite backbone of Rocky Mountain. Along the way he had told them how Indians once used these ridges as sources of stone for weapon points and, no doubt, as lookouts. Now, having absorbed the view from a projecting outcrop and having tried to imagine themselves Indians, the hikers were filing back toward Skyline Drive. The naturalist had hardly made his comment about sitting under the oak tree when he suddenly stopped, bent down, and with a triumphant smile picked up a perfect quartz arrowhead. In one instant the yesteryear he had been trying to evoke became real."

Bruce McHenry

I wrote *The Nature of Shenandoah* the way I wrote all my national park books—I went there until I was overflowing with knowledge about the park, then started to write. There must have been a lot of love in this book, because a total stranger called me from his office in the National Press Building in Washington to say how much he enjoyed it; I was given an interim job as editor at the Wildlife Management Institute because Larry Jahn, its vice president, was so impressed by it; and the Association of Government Communicators gave it their Blue Pencil Award.

I still go to the park every December for the Christmas Bird Count that Bruce and I resurrected in 1968—Shenandoah National Park/Luray, VA. The count circle includes the highest parts of the Blue Ridge here and a wide swath of the Shenandoah Valley beside it. Standing in that valley on a frosty morning as the sun rises over the Blue Ridge brings back happy memories: researching my book up there, hiking the Appalachian Trail along the ridge, and many other days with friends on other park trails.

The Life of Isle Royale. Writing about this national park, in Lake Superior, put me in another part of the North Woods that I had learned to love so much at camp in the Adirondacks 25 years earlier. In the first chapter I describe arriving at the island:

> We see long outcroppings of gray rock. We see thick forest, pale green with birches and dark with the spires of spruce and fir. Across the water drifts the faint pungency of those firs, saying, as nothing else can, 'North Woods.'

I spent two periods on Isle Royale, one in the fall and one all the next summer. On the second trip I took my wife, our three daughters, Bruce McHenry's younger son Brucie, Elizabeth's sister's boy Chris, and a very large tent. We camped in a forest area designated for researchers for two weeks, walked nearby trails, and fished one day. When Elizabeth developed stomach trouble we moved to the cabin home so graciously offered by ranger Frank Deckert and his wife at the west end of the island. My entourage stayed awhile, then flew off toward home.

Then I began traveling in my aluminum canoe around the island's perimeter and portaging inland to investigate the interior. It was exciting and somewhat nerve-wracking paddling around the rocks and cliffs of the Lake Superior shore. I hoped I wouldn't capsize in the three-foot waves and lose my note-filled notebook. Another researcher, studying leeches, had done just that. Besides, the water was 50 degrees and landing would be hazardous. I decided to transport my canoe around the most dangerous waters on a boat that regularly circled the island.

My book was mostly to be, after introductory chapters about human history on the island and geology, a description of the natural communities. For each type I chose a bird or mammal representative of that environment, and spent time in the selected place watching what these particular creatures did. That way I could describe both the habitat and actual events I saw. A Herring Gull (Shorelines) chases another gull away from a dead sucker and tries to snatch a Red-breasted Merganser duckling, but the mother drives it off. A red squirrel (Spruce-Fir Forest) climbs out of an old woodpecker hole, angrily answers the call of another squirrel invading his territory, and wanders about, seeking food. A Black-throated Blue Warbler (Maple-Birch Forest) picks insects from tree leaves, hears the Black-throated Blue Warbler at the other end of the rise, which stays in its territory, watches the Broad-winged Hawk, a potential danger, on its nest, and feeds its own young. A loon (Inland Lakes) dives for fish to feed his young, which are guarded by the female as they swim about. A pair of beavers (Ponds and Streams) carries branches from an aspen they have cut down to their pond and eats tender parts. A young kestrel (Open Ridges), sitting on the tip of a spruce tree, cries for food, then flies to an aspen, where its mother has caught a grasshopper. The youngster lands awkwardly, pitching forward.

In each environment I fleshed out the scene with the activities of other animals and the vegetation they live with. Readers told me they liked this way of presenting ecological information.

After living all summer on Isle Royale, often alone, in close association with nature, I could say near the end of my book,

> [An] important part of the Isle Royale experience is the opportunity it gives us to be human. In this basic situation, we learn again the simple joys of eating after hunger, getting warm after being cold, drying out after being soaked or resting after a long day's hike. And we learn again the value of the individual. With pressures removed, fewer people around, and a dependence on those few in case of emergency, we recognize our need for each other and have the chance to know each other simply as unique human beings. The common experience of all these things creates a special fellowship.

Great Smoky Mountains. My association with the Great Smokies goes back to the summer I was seven. I went to Camp LeConte near the small settlement of Elkmont, in the park, a few years after the park's establishment in 1930. My mother stayed in Elkmont at the Wonderland Hotel. My father played golf in North Carolina at High Hampton. I did what is done at boys' summer camps, as described earlier (Chapter 2). My father, in pursuit of family genealogy, also visited Shelton Laurel in the mountains north of the park. Our line of Sheltons had gone from Virginia to North Carolina and Tennessee, then Alabama, and finally Missouri.

Aside from short family visits to the park area and a one-day botany research exercise from Duke around 1960, I didn't go to the park again until I co-authored *Great Smoky Mountains*, one of the NPS park handbooks. In research for the book I walked 30 miles on the Appalachian Trail; hiked many other trails; stayed overnight at the lodge atop Mt. LeConte; camped out in the southwestern part of the park, where a screech owl serenaded me at night and the rare Red-cockaded Woodpecker appeared, to my surprise; conducted the usual interviews and read numerous publications. I even took off my clothes and jumped into a high-mountain stream to see what the world looks like to a brook trout. It all gave me a greater wonder at the amazing richness and impressiveness of plant and animal life here—the huge cove hardwood trees, the many species of breeding birds, salamanders, lesser plants, insects, and microbes—a wonder that I tried to share in the book.

That made me known to park people, who asked me to give a lecture about the park as a biosphere reserve shortly before I retired from the park service, and later to write articles for a new magazine, *Smokies Life*.

Retirement from the park service in 1994 launched me into the present phase of my life. The first thing I did was to hop into my Isuzu Trooper and spend two months traveling through the West visiting friends and national parks, such as Grand Canyon, that I'd never seen before. Retirement also allowed me to spend more time overseas with Elizabeth (described in Part III), and to write more books.

Superior Wilderness: Isle Royale National Park. This was a revision of my first book about this park that the Isle Royale Natural History Association asked me to do. It was a great pleasure to revisit that alluring island, see what changes had occurred, and to add new material. Among that material were three new chapters, many new illustrations, and sidebars about various aspects of Isle Royale life.

In one of those new chapters, "The Lake Trout: Lake Superior," I presented this fish and its environment, then moved on to other aspects of the lake's ecology, such as food chains, the effects of introduced species such as the sea lamprey, air and water pollution. Shipwrecks bring in weather and the appeal of diving on these wrecks.

Sidebars are sprinkled through the chapters. One about the life of a fir tree I imagined, based on personal observation and literature about the balsam fir. It grows from a winged seed carried by wind to a small tree browsed back every year by moose until there's a moose decline, then at 50 reaches 30 feet, with beard moss dangling from its dead lower branches, and dies at 70, weakened by spruce budworm defoliation and heart rot. A northeaster breaks it in half, hairy woodpeckers nest in the still standing half for several years. "The rest of it lies rotting on the ground, returning its nutrients to thimbleberries, blue-bead lilies, and a few small fir trees."

Another side bar tells about the life of a loon, from birth to growing up in a sheltered nursing area with its parents, to migrations back and forth from the Atlantic until maturity and raising its own young. Specific human lives are also featured in these sidebars. I interviewed fisherman Milford Johnson at his log cabin at Crystal Cove on Amygdaloid Island and consulted stories and tapes recorded by others about him. I remember him as "a bear of a man with a gravelly voice and a lot of good stories, and a veteran fisherman with a deep respect for the power of Lake Superior." On one occasion he was traveling through the interior of the island with Dr. Frank Oastler when his companion offered him 50 dollars to ride a moose. On Lake Richie they paddled up to a moose that was swimming across, "and I hopped on….Lying on my stomach, I grabbed him by the antlers." When the moose touched bottom, Milford rolled off quick and swam for the canoe, which "should have been closer….He got his picture and I got my fifty bucks."

"A Researcher's Life" chronicles the long-term moose-wolf studies continued by Rolf Peterson after 1975.

> The research has winter and summer phases. Each year from early January to mid-March, weather permitting, Rolf and his graduate students, assisted by park staff members who come out for two-week shifts, headquarter in cabins at Windigo. Besides directing the research, Rolf sets the

bunkhouse rules and bakes the bread. Each good flying day, Rolf and pilot Don E. Glaser track wolf packs by air, flying in a small plane a few hundred feet above the tree-tops....Rolf's summer research focuses on further seeking and examining moose kills...trapping and radio-collaring wolves, and tracking collared wolves from the ground and air." Year after year, as new information is collected, new understanding of the wolf-moose relationship is gained — on the complex roles of vegetation changes, weather, snow depth, disease, and other factors that influence the numbers of wolves and moose.

Sometimes there are scares, such as being caught by a sudden snowstorm and finding their way back to Windigo by flying just above the treetops along the lake shore, and being chased away from a mother moose's dead calf on lake ice and barely beating her to a shoreline tree, which Rolf climbed. "She was only a few feet away, and we just stared at each other for what seemed like an eternity."

In "A Ranger's Life" I briefly described Elen Maurer's 13 years as an NPS ranger, much of it typical of park rangers' experience anywhere. She began as a seasonal, first operating the Feldtmann Fire Tower on Isle Royale, and then working as an interpreter at Rock Harbor and Windigo. During a summer at Apostle Islands National Lakeshore in Wisconsin she received training in law enforcement, boat- handling, and diving, which qualified her for a job as a "permanent" at Isle Royale. Her duties for the next nine years included leading a weekly interpretive walk, giving information to visitors, making sure they followed safety and resource protection regulations, and helping in emergencies. "People are pretty careful here," she said, but they do get in trouble. Sometimes hikers are injured or become ill. "I've had a few carryouts," and sometimes they have to rescue a boat in trouble. She loves her work and just living on Isle Royale. "I love watching the seasons here, the northern lights, paddling along the shore in my kayak, fishing or just enjoying...being close to moose."

Many people feel the same way about Isle Royale, myself included. It is indeed a special place.

Huron: The Seasons of a Great Lake. In 1967 my wife's parents bought a small blue cottage on the Lake Huron shore at Port Sanilac, Michigan. This was the beginning of a long family association with this lake and this town. It led to my next book.

Eleanor, our oldest, on the beach at Port Sanilac

Becoming familiar with a Great Lake is a large undertaking. I'd had years of casual acquaintance with Lake Huron before I decided to write a book about it. It was time now to deepen and broaden the relationship. Elizabeth was overseas and our children were on their own. I would live in the cottage for a year, observing the changing seasons and life, both natural and human, around the lake. Harry Greening, a local builder who had extended our first floor and added a bedroom above the living room, put up a styrofoam wall between the kitchen and living room, leaving just half of the first floor to heat with our Franklin stove in the front parlor. I would live and write in that half.

I arrived early in January 1995, seeing our yard and cottage under several inches of beautiful fresh snow. Every morning, because the Styrofoam wall blocked the view from inside, I went outside to see the changes of ice formations on the lake. I watched Buffleheads and other winter ducks diving in the patches of open water. Later that winter I drove around the lake, participating in Christmas bird counts on Manitoulin Island at the north end of the lake. In spring heart-stopping Vs of Tundra Swans flew over, on their way to the Arctic. Other waterfowl came through, followed by Bonaparte's Gulls, Double-crested Cormorants, and loons, and then warblers and other small birds in shoreline trees. In June I drove around the lake again, studying the shoreline plants, the colony of little massasauga rattlesnakes on the far Canadian side, and other things of interest, from geology to human activities. Fall saw me watching duck hunters from a platform at the Fish Point State Wildlife Area on Saginaw Bay, fishermen catching salmon from the breakwall at Port Sanilac harbor, maples turning brilliant red and orange, and other sights of that season. By winter I had most of a draft written (beside that Franklin stove in cold weather).

It was based partly on what I saw from the shore, but also on what I saw and learned from boats. I tried to travel on a freighter of the American Steamship Lines, but they turned me down, I suppose because of a concern for liability and for anything that might slow down loading, sailing, and unloading. The U.S. Coast Guard was more accommodating, possibly because of an opportunity for favorable publicity. They let me stay overnight on the *Neah Bay* as she helped a tug pushing a barge make its way through ice in the St. Clair River south of Port Huron. It was early March, a time when ice floes often pile up in the lower reaches of this river. The *Neah Bay* was breaking a path to Lake St. Clair for the tug *Mary E. Hannah* and her barge, which was followed by the *Samuel Risley*, a Canadian icebreaker. I stood on the bridge with the amazingly young people who were operating this vessel, moving it forward, then turning it around in the river and rebreaking the path back to the tug and barge. The bow would ride up on the ice, then break through it with a loud crunching sound. When we got to Lake St. Clair we just had a smooth sheet of ice to break through. As the ship moved forward a web of cracks radiated out before it and the ice flowed aside, leaving behind us a clear path. I was fascinated with the ice formations we passed. Besides this plate ice there was ball ice, round and cannon-ball-sized; and pancake ice, flat and round, with raised edges. Later I could identify these ice types in front of our cottage. In my book I made sure I described all the good work—rescues and so on—the *Neah Bay* had done in her lifetime.

One morning in early May I climbed aboard Mike Hanson's patrol boat. He had invited me to go along while he checked fishermen for violations of fishing regulations, one of his duties as the Sanilac County Conservation Officer. We donned orange coveralls against the chill and headed out. A mile offshore we passed a long string of Long-tailed Ducks (formerly called Oldsquaw) resting on the water. Before long they would be on their breeding grounds in the Arctic. With the sun behind us we headed north toward boats fishing. Mike explained that he traveled with the sun behind him so fishermen couldn't easily recognize his boat and stop doing anything illegal. When we reached the first boat he looked to see how many people were aboard and how many fishing lines were out. Two per person is the rule. Mike asked how the fishing was going and gave them advice about where fish were likely to be, then asked to see their licenses. He was this way with each fishing party—generally friendly and helpful, though he did have to hand out one citation. I admired his technique. I got to know Mike pretty well and relied on him for information about Lake Huron fish.

One of the Lake Huron fishes of concern was the lake trout. Lampreys had decimated their population and fish biologists were monitoring lake trout reproduction. As a volunteer assistant among other volunteers and scientists I was on board the 75-foot research boat *Grayling* one foggy May morning, headed out of Alpena toward Six Fathom Bank, four and a half hours away in the middle of Lake Huron. There had been some reproduction on this ledge and we were going to find out if reproduction continued.

Next morning we began dragging the bottom across the ledge with a small-beam trawl, then dumped the contents—pieces of limestone, algae, tiny snails, and other material—on the deck. We volunteers carried pans filled with this stuff inside and carefully sorted through it looking for tiny lake-trout fry. I and others found a few, happily confirming reproduction. A long gill net set along the ledge caught a good sample of the fish present, including lake trout and their prey.

Being out in the middle of Lake Huron was an interesting experience in other ways. Herring Gulls hung around because they knew we were "fishing." And a few small migrants had landed on our boat for rest. Occasionally a little Savannah Sparrow would fly off, circle around, and land back on the boat. On one flight a Herring Gull swooped down on it and swallowed it. Further predatory drama appeared likely when a Great Egret, headed north that spring beyond northern limits of the species' nesting in Michigan, passed by. Some of the gulls immediately attacked it, and as they did the egret stabbed upward at them. I watched this fearful action until the birds disappeared from sight. I held little hope for the egret.

I traveled on a few other boats used for fishing or other purposes. I went with Rob Taylor in his 16-foot aluminum Starcraft to check his long catfish lines in Saginaw Bay. He sells his catfish live to Bay Port Fish Company, who sells them live to fish farmers. This company runs trapnetting boats in Saginaw Bay, and I went out on

Forrest Williams, an owner of the Bay Port Fish Company,
lifts fish from trap net

one to see this operation. Long nets on the bottom arranged like an arrow lead fish to a "pot" at the end, in which the fish are trapped. At Manitoulin Island in the northern, Canadian, end of Lake Huron, George Purvis allowed me aboard his 78-foot gillnetter *Blue Fin*. I watched as long gill nets, which had been set on the bottom, were pulled in mechanically through an opening in the port side of the bow and the whitefish every few feet were removed by hand inside. From these and other fishermen I learned much about the methods, economics, and perils of commercial fishing.

On board Dick Schaffner's sailboat out of Port Sanilac I heard about his trips across the lake with other sailors to the Canadian side, the local races, and what it was like to encounter 12-foot waves. (Scary) I paddled my canoe near the northern shores of the lake and got an idea of the voyageurs' experience. And I rode the large ferry that runs from Manitoulin Island to Tobermory on the Bruce Peninsula.

Over the years many ships have sunk along the Michigan shore of Lake Huron, and divers love to explore them. I thought maybe I should learn to scuba dive, but when I found out that your ears filled with water doing this I decided not to. Instead, I went out on policeman Garry Biniecki's dive boat from Port Sanilac with two divers. They were going to the *Regina*, a 249-foot package freighter that sank during the huge storm in November 1913, three and one-half miles offshore in 77 feet of water. When they were down on the wreck the 806-foot *Charles M. Beeghly* churned by, only 200 feet away. They said it was like being in a washing machine.

By December it was time to go back to Washington. Before leaving, I took a last walk along the snow-covered beach to the Port Sanilac harbor. Christmas lights were shining in a couple of houses. Perched on the break wall, a Northern Shrike eyed a small flock of Snow Buntings on the beach but flew off as I approached. I had a happy sense of completion but also a sadness that this memorable year in my life was over.

Natural Missouri: Working with the Land. In 2004 I wrote this book "because Missouri is my ancestral home and I wanted to know it better, especially its natural side." All my most recent ancestors, back to the "great-greats," ended up in southwest Missouri; grandfather Samuel Azariah Shelton right after the Civil War; great-grandfather Cyrus Napier, with his half-Cherokee wife, about 1858; great-great grandfather James McCanse, with his six slaves, in 1840; and great-great grandfather James Hopper in 1853. They were all farmers. I dedicated this book "to all my Missouri relatives."

I had been going back to Missouri to see relatives ever since I was a baby, with my parents for many years, and then on my own. Whenever possible I roamed the woods and fields, birdwatching and soaking up the landscapes.

Missouri has many kinds of landscapes, from swamps and big river bottoms to extensive forests and low mountains in the south, and rich farmland and remnant bits of prairie in the north. I wanted to sample natural places in these landscapes and the range of management practices in them, from largely hands-off in state parks to largely hands-on in a northeast Missouri farm. I thought it would be interesting to look at these places mostly through the ways people work in them. I defined "working with the land" broadly. Usually it was direct manipulation of the land, such as burning or planting or removing certain kinds of vegetation, or timber cutting. But I stretched my definition as far as a writer, photographer, and Christmas bird counters, who need to know the land in order to find birds.

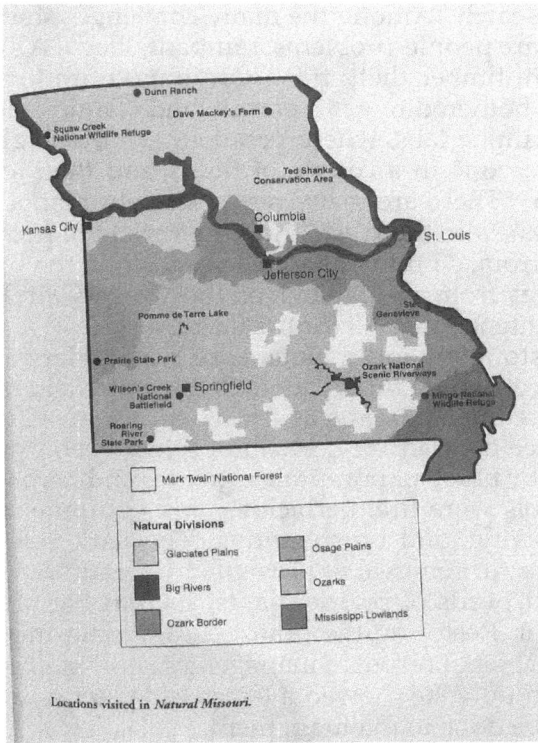

Map of natural places in Missouri covered in this book

Most varied in management and use was the Mark Twain National Forest, spread in nine large pieces across southern Missouri. Practicing the Forest Service multiple-use philosophy, the foresters here supervised selective cutting in some areas and total hands-off in others. Recreational use ranged from hiking, camping, bird-watching, fishing, and other low-impact activities to hunting, trapping, and dirt-bike riding on 125 miles of trails.

My lead character, among many people I talked to, was Jenny Farenbaugh, the District Ranger in charge of the national forest's middle three sections. She had been a fire-fighter in California, done recreational work on the Toiyabe National Forest in Nevada, reforestation on Cibola National Forest in New Mexico, timber sale administration at Lincoln National Forest in New Mexico, and use permitting at Arapaho National Forest in Colorado. One of her jobs on the Lincoln National Forest was cave management, which required her to rappel down to deep passageways to conduct inventories and research. Among the many challenges she meets on the Mark Twain are people-problems: rampant, illegal ATV travel; vandalism; arson; timber theft; trash dumping; outfitters and guides who haven't bothered to get a permit; and clandestine, temporary methamphetamine labs, where people make this highly addictive and cheap narcotic in a couple of hours and then leave. But she loves her job. "There are many new, different plants and animals from what I knew in the West." And the variety of people she's met and learned from. "I think I have the best job in the world."

I came away from my research on the Mark Twain National Forest with heightened respect for the forest service.

Prairie restoration and maintenance was underway at three of the areas I wrote about. At Wilson's Creek Battlefield they were trying to recreate the landscape as it was during the Civil War battle that took place there in 1861. Much of it had been prairie but now was covered by brush or non-prairie grasses and herbaceous plants. The main tools were fire, herbicides, and equipment for disking, plowing, mowing, and brush-cutting. The park was experimenting with goats for removal of unwanted vegetation. When the bed was prepared, seeds of prairie plants, such as big bluestem, were scattered on it. Restoring the prairie was a main mission of Gary Sullivan, the chief of resource management and maintenance at the battlefield. Proudly, he showed me restored patches, and explained what had to be done to maintain them.

Keith Kinne, the manager of Dunn Ranch, a 3,500-acre complex including Pawnee Prairie, in northern Missouri—owned by The Nature Conservancy—was also trying to restore prairie where it once had been. One thousand acres of the ranch had been "battered," he said, by decades of heavy grazing, haying, and planting of fescue, but never plowed. Other sections had been farmed. On much of the land, seeds and roots of prairie plants remained in the rich soil but were smothered, as it were, by the fescue and other non-natives, such as sericea lespedeza. Keith was using all the methods for restoring prairie—burning, early intensive grazing, which reduces fescue (by cows kept on the ranch for that purpose), mowing, brush removal, and spraying or plowing followed by seeding.

Keith pulled out maps of the 32 units and described the successes and failures.

> D1, when I got here in '99, really looked like a fescue field, with a little bit of scattered prairie grass in it. We've early intensely grazed it now for four years and we've got a lot of

big bluestem, little blue, and cordgrass. There's very little fescue left in that. That's mostly from grazing. We've never burned it. It's forb-poor, though [forbs are nongrass, herbaceous plants]. It's mainly a grass-dominant prairie.

And so on through the various units. Though prairie restoration was in an early stage at Dunn Ranch, it *was* a grassland, and all the grassland birds were there in abundance, unlike as in Missouri generally and most of the East, where they are seriously declining. "Bobolinks, Dickcissels, and meadowlarks were everywhere. Tiny Grasshopper Sparrows sat on many a fence post. After a few days I lost count of the Upland Sandpipers and Loggerhead Shrikes I'd seen." Dunn Ranch has one of the largest populations of prairie chickens in Missouri, and visitors such as I could enjoy their dancing from a blind at one of their leks during the breeding season.

The Nature Conservancy was sure the restoration of prairie at Dunn Ranch would be successful. Bison would soon be brought in to replace the cattle and do the necessary grazing.

I felt pretty optimistic about it as I walked around unit D7B, one of the best, shortly before leaving Dunn Ranch.

As I walked under a warm blue sky filled with puffy white clouds, a meadowlark and a Bobolink mellifluously serenaded me. Bumble bees attended big patches of tube beardtongue. Regal fritillaries festooned purple-flowered milkweeds. I found [other prairie plants] and native grasses, short and tall. The land seemed to be saying, 'this Dunn Ranch prairie *will* be fully restored.'

Prairie State Park, which preserves the state's largest remaining piece of public prairie, in southwest Missouri, *is* restored. It just needs maintenance by prescribed fire and grazing.

Standing amid its more than three thousand acres of waving grasses in summer, you can imagine the way the prairie once was, extending to the horizon and far beyond. Around you, wildflowers of all sorts and colors bloom. Dickcissels and meadowlarks sing. On a distant rise, the patient, humped shapes of bison graze, following the lead cow. It's an experience too few have known, one to be sought and treasured, one of space, freedom, and peace.

My several visits here allowed me to see the changing seasons. In March the first tiny green shoots of grasses and sedges were poking up through the dead mats of last year's grasses. I heard the "prrreep" of western chorus frogs and the quacks of southern leopard frogs in swales pooled with rain water. Male prairie chickens were booming on a lek, waiting for females to arrive and chasing other males off their piece of the lek. Snow Geese flew over. A Northern Harrier did roller-coaster courtship dives. A Short-eared Owl bounded low across the landscape. One day I watched a herd of bison beside the road. One at a time, three of them rubbed their massive heads and necks on a sign by a service track that said Authorized Vehicles Only.

In late May,

> Regal Prairie was producing an entrancing variety of wildflowers nestled among the foot-high grasses: prairie parsley, with its umbrellas of tiny yellow flowers; lavender prairie phlox; tube and foxglove beardtongue, with tall stems bearing white flowers; green milkweed; blue-flowered common spiderwort; ...deep yellow large-flowered coreopsis; bright red Indian paintbrush; white and pink shooting star; and others.

I was there in the late fall, when deer begin to mate, and "downy gentian, one of the last wildflowers to bloom in Missouri, hits its flowering peak." In early November I saw the round up of bison for their annual vaccinations. "Range cubes"—fifty-pound sacks with protein feed—enticed many of the bison into the corral. Men in trucks and on an ATV rounded up most of the rest, leaving outside a few, such as an obstinate calf and two bulls considered too difficult and dangerous—they might gore other bison in the chutes. Some twenty people, including the park staff, neighboring ranchers, and four men from Roaring River State Park, using long poles and cattle prods, worked the bison a few at a time into successive compartments. The last chamber had sides that could be pressed tight to hold an animal securely and a head-sized opening at the end, which was clamped when the bison, seeing daylight, thrust its head through. Then one veterinarian took a blood sample and another, working through a side panel, administered the vaccine. The front of the chamber was swung open and the desperate animal, wearing an identifying tag on its ear, lunged to freedom.

I talked to many of the park people and watched as they worked.

Kevin Badgley took part in many facets of resource management and interpretation; I joined the group he led to the prairie chicken lek. Park Naturalist Cyndi Evans described the seasons to me in great detail. Winter "can be beautiful with snow or ice," she said. "The bison may have light snow on their backs, like powdered sugar. Some plants have 'frost flowers' at their bases. I like to get here early on those days." Chris Crabtree, doing seasonal maintenance work, said he was one-sixteenth (6%) Cherokee. I think I'm also 6% Cherokee, but Chris looked a lot more Indian than I do, with his black hair tied in a queue hanging down his back. He had developed an extraordinarily close relationship with nature. He had camped in the park just to experience the prairie at night, and wandered so close to unseen bison that he could smell them. Chris collected cattail pollen for flour, and made a salad with wild mushrooms, day lilies, and yucca flowers. He wanted to do graduate work in mycology. "I'm always looking for mushrooms," he said, "even when I'm driving. I should have a bumper sticker that says, "I Brake for Mushrooms.'"

I also visited Prairie State Park in January for a Christmas Bird Count, which I'll describe later.

People I talked to for other chapters of *Natural Missouri* had other ways of "working with the land." In one case it was both "the land" and "the river." Ste. Genevieve, on the Mississippi River, is the oldest permanent settlement in Missouri. Settled in the 1790s, its oldest remaining houses, mostly French, date from that period into the early 1800s. Built at the inland edge of the floodplain, Ste. Genevieve has frequently been threatened by floods. The highest came in 1993, and severe flooding of the town was only prevented by a huge mobilization of volunteers and others hauling materials and piling sandbags on the existing levee. Authorization to build a new levee had been passed by Congress in 1986, but funding was not available until after 1993. Construction began in 1997. Jim Zerega from the U.S. Army Corps of Engineers office in St. Louis was assigned the planning of it.

The new levee was built on the floodplain halfway between the town and the river so as not to impinge visually on historic Ste. Genevieve. It is 3 ½ miles long, tying to the bluffs north and south of the town. Twenty-five feet high, it is designed to withstand a 53- to 54-foot flood as measured by a nearby gauge on the Mississippi—more than 3 feet above the record '93 flood level. Clay is preferred for the core of a levee because its fine particles pack closely together, but, Zerega said, "A relatively small clay deposit was the only clay we found in the floodplain," and clay shipped from long distances would be much more expensive. The clay at hand was just enough for a thin layer on the river side of the levee. Sand pumped from the river was used for the core.

On August 10, 2002, I was among seventy-five people gathered at a tent on the levee for the dedication of the Ste. Genevieve "urban design levee." Many of them had filled or stacked sandbags during the '93 flood. Others had worked for years to get the levee. Still others had constructed it. This was a time of celebration and deep emotion. Various speakers praised everyone involved with the new levee. One concluded that "Ste. Genevieve is now ready for another 250 years." A different speaker put it at 500 years.

The featured speaker, Representative Richard A. Gephardt of Missouri, who had pushed Congress for construction funding, was introduced as "a gentleman without whom we would not be standing here." He ended his speech with a dramatic flourish: "I promised the people they'd never be flooded again....The levee will be here forever for the people of Ste. Genevieve and the nation. From space will be seen the Great Wall of China and the levee of Ste. Genevieve."

Later I asked Vern Bauman, whose ancestry here went back a long way and who had known the river as intimately as anyone, for his opinion. He said, "The Mississippi River is amazing and mighty. It has power beyond belief. The levee may be good for a couple of hundred years, but I think you ultimately lose, no matter what. The river never quits working."

Joel Vance worked with the land and life of Missouri as a writer. For many years he was employed in that capacity by the Department of Conservation, chronicling the state's and people's relationships with its natural resources in the department's magazine, *Missouri Conservationist*. He had a free hand. He wrote, for instance, about bicycling through Squaw Creek National Wildlife and canoeing on the Current River, and about natural history, hunting and fishing, and environmental issues. "I wrote about air pollution, water pollution, habitat degradation. I got most of the industry in Missouri mad at me at one time or another."After retirement he continued writing for outdoor and other magazines from his home, Cedar Glade, nestled in a woodsy forty acres west of Jefferson City. He showed me around the place, whose wildlife and changing seasons he and his wife Marty deeply enjoyed. "It's never boring," he said. "Maybe it would be to an urbanite...but I haven't been an urbanite since I was thirteen years old, and don't intend ever to be again."

Joel told me about his friend Dave Mackey and his wildlife-friendly farm in northeastern Missouri, and I put him too in my Missouri book. I first met Joel at the Wildbranch outdoor and environmental writing workshop in Vermont, where he was one of the instructors. We have kept in touch, sharing notes on the writing life.

When I walked into "Glenn Chambers's home, in a pleasantly wooded section of Columbia, [I] knew at once what the man is all about: wildlife and the outdoors. A sculpted otter [stood] by the front door. Inside, paintings and photographs of wildlife [adorned] the walls. Duck decoys [sat] around, as if waiting for the next hunt."

The otter out front said what his number one interest was then. Before his retirement from the Missouri Department of Conservation he had taken many thousands of photographs and produced seven award-winning feature-length films on forests, furbearers, bald eagles, fishing, and other subjects. Now he was still photographing and filming, but he spent the majority of his time going around the state with his two otters—Splash and Slide—displaying them and giving talks about otters and the somewhat controversial otter restoration program then underway in Missouri. Many fishermen and aquaculturists objected to the program because of the otter's voracious appetite for fish—any kind of fish. Glenn was championing the otter, making friends for it.

I caught his popular show in Springfield. Glenn and his assistant wheeled a large fiberglass tank to the auditorium and up a ramp to the stage. They filled it with water and arranged a wire fence across the front of the stage. Beside the tank they placed the artificial log that Glenn kept in the otters' pen in his home and covered it with towels. When the audience had settled in—this time it was mostly members of the Missouri Ozark Mountain Paddlers—he began telling them, in his strong, country-boy accent, about the restoration program and his raising of otters. He didn't shrink from the problems. Describing otter predation at farm ponds, he said, "they leave you with only heads on the pond bank."

Having set the stage, Glenn and his assistant carried in Splash and Slide and released them behind the fence. Rapidly they ran all over, investigating, poking behind the curtains, diving in and out of the tank. They climbed onto the log and urinated and pooped on it, marking their territory. Glenn then dumped dozens of live minnows into the tank and the otters twisted and turned in pursuit, capturing them with ease. In no time there were no more minnows.

Winding down the show, Glenn fielded questions from the audience. It had all been fun, informative, professional. Everyone went away with a warm glow about Glenn and his otters.

In 2002, at sixty-seven, after three open-heart surgeries, removal of his cancerous prostate, arthroscopic surgery on his knees, and other medical problems, he was still combining fifty talks a year with filmmaking around the Midwest. He had slowed down little from the days when he filmed as far afield as the Yukon-Kuskokwim Delta in Alaska or worked at both research and photography, starting his days at 3:00 a.m. As Joel Vance, a former associate at the Department of Conservation, put it, "The hyperkinetic wildlife biologist crams more into life than a baker's dozen of ordinary folks."

One of my greatest joys in life is Christmas bird counts, so I couldn't help ending my Missouri book with a chapter called "Challenge of the Christmas Bird Count." A CBC is a count of birds within a 15-mile-diameter circle, on a day between December 14 and January 5. These counts began in 25 places in the United States and Canada in 1900 and now number well over 2,000 in North, Central, and South America, the Caribbean, and Pacific islands.

I love these counts for their tradition, the camaraderie, seeing friends year after year, and the friendly competition to see the largest number of species. The counts are also a valuable long-term record of the numbers and kinds of birds in early winter—their distribution and trends.

I can say that they involve "working with the land" because you have to know something about habitats and the species that inhabit them to come up with a good list. You look in weedy, seed-bearing patches for sparrows, mature woods for most woodpeckers, fallow fields for the voles that attract hawks by day and owls by night. Large water bodies are apt to have more waterbirds and a greater diversity of them than do small water bodies. And so on.

The people I joined on three Missouri Christmas bird counts in December 2003 and January 2004 certainly knew the land they searched in their assigned sectors of the count circles. At an experimental farm of the University of Missouri on the Columbia count I followed Brad Jacobs, an ornithologist with the Department of Conservation, into a wide strip of tall Indian grass. We were looking for LeConte's Sparrows, which are hard to identify unless, when they flush, they perch momentarily on a grass stem. We flushed three or four sparrows, but none perched for the ID. Brad had recorded as many as 30 on earlier counts here, he said in frustration. This year, no LeConte's Sparrow was found on the Columbia count, but plenty of other species were. After a potluck supper that evening in a church basement, the tally was 96 species, a number also recorded on an earlier Columbia count that had been the highest for Missouri that year.

As opposed to the 71 people on the Columbia count, there were only 13 of us on the Squaw Creek CBC in northwest Missouri. But we had expertise: Mark Robbins, the compiler, an ornithologist at the University of Kansas; Don Arney, compiler of the Kansas City count; Brad Jacobs and others from the Department of Conservation, and several more experienced birders. Most of the ponds in the Squaw Creek National Wildlife Refuge had frozen, but Snow Geese flew over, and 300 Bald Eagles were feeding on the carcasses of 1,000 sick or injured Snow Geese that were frozen in the ice. We considered our 80 species pretty good, in view of the frozen water and three years of drought that depleted the food supply.

I returned to Prairie State Park for the Liberal count, teaming with Cyndi Evans, the park naturalist, and Connie Laughlin from Joplin. Fifteen other participants covered other parts of the count circle. We enjoyed watching Red-tailed Hawks, Rough-legged Hawks, and Northern Harriers hunting over the prairie, now in various shades of brown, and found the only Lincoln's Sparrow on the count, as I recall, in a brushpile, but our main responsibility was prairie chickens; our sector was the only one likely to have them. After not seeing any in the western side of the park, we headed to the eastern side, where Cyndi had been seeing them lately. Since prairie chickens band together in winter, we could have covered most of the park without finding any. Luckily, after we'd walked a long way down a grassy track, forty burst from the edge of corn stubble and flew far into the distance. This may have been all the prairie chickens in the park. Later I learned the count's total: 83 species. "Very good," Larry Herbert, the compiler, said.

After doing these three counts, I called around to see how the normally top counts had done. In first place the Mingo count, centered on Mingo National Wildlife Refuge in southeastern Missouri, had come up with 101 species, including the first American Redstart found on Missouri Christmas counts. Mingo had had the top list for many years, but in the late 1990s Horton/Four Rivers, a new one, began challenging Mingo, recording 110 species in 1997. In 2003, the year I've described, six to eight inches of snow, restricting road access, and frozen water held Horton/Four Rivers down to 96 species.

Top list or small list, I'm sure all the participants on Missouri's 27 Christmas bird counts that year had a good time, and added a bit more to knowledge about Missouri's birds.

Potomac Pathway: A Nature Guide to the C&O Canal. None of my books, except possibly the one I'm now writing, had as long a gestation as *Potomac Pathway*. One could say it began when I was six, hanging around Lock 7 with my friend Bruce McHenry, who lived in the lockhouse there. I of course did not have a book in mind, but it wasn't long before I got interested in writing, and my attachment to the canal continued to the present. In the 1970s, having written three national park books, I persuaded the NPS Publications Division to let me write one about natural history of the C&O Canal National Historical Park for the NPS Handbook series. The first part of this was an account of my experiences and observations one spring backpacking the entire 184 miles to Cumberland, Maryland. The rest consisted of specific valley-wide topics, such as geology of the Potomac valley.

After I handed in the manuscript, Vince Gleason, head of the division, decided a book about the *human* history of the canal would be more appropriate, since it was a national *historical* park. So Handbook 142 was produced, in house. My manuscript languished in a drawer until the 1990s, when I received permission to get a revised version published privately. I turned most of it into a mile-

Elizabeth and the children meeting me as I neared Harper's Ferry

by-mile guide to natural things one could see along the canal, along with several side trips onto adjacent public land and a number of topical discussions, retained from the first version, such as Floodplain Trees.

Eventually, Schiffer Publishing accepted it. Just one unexpected thing was required: high-quality color photographs. Fortunately, Connie Durnan, wife of a high-school classmate of mine, had done much photography along the canal and agreed to help. With many of her photographs and a few of mine, the book got published. I was very pleased with Schiffer's product, after all the years of hoping for such a book of mine—the first detailed guide to nature along the canal.

While writing the mile-by-mile section of the book I revisited each mile of the canal. I drove to the end of the last stretch I'd walked, hiked upstream five miles and then back to the car. In that way I rewalked the entire canal twice. I noted such things as beaver dams, rock outcrops, good places for spring wildflowers, and so on. I had many unexpected wildlife encounters, such as a woodcock in the snow, an albino fox squirrel identified by an orange streak in its tail, a screech owl sunbathing at the base of a cliff one afternoon, regarding me calmly through half-closed eyes. Most memorable was a February day around Snyder's Landing, when American Pipits searched for food on an ice floe in the river, dozens of robins drank at the river's edge, and 14 species of waterfowl, from small ducks to Tundra Swans, rested on the river.

Nature is always changing. That's the main challenge for writers of guides to natural places. So today, in my 80s, I walk again many parts of the canal towpath, noting changes in case I revise my book a second time. Eagles sometimes abandon a nest and build a new one elsewhere. Great Blue Heron colonies wax and wane, and sometimes disappear entirely. Beavers move as water conditions in the canal change or their woody food supplies diminish. I've seen a movement up the Potomac of nesting cormorants and maybe Great Egrets, and new colonies of Cliff Swallows on a bridge and aqueducts. Nonnative plants continue to invade, and management tries to halt them. Having written about the thousands of cougar sightings reported in the Appalachians (many of which seem reliable, including two near Orleans on the canal), I wouldn't be surprised if more occur in the mountain sections of the canal. Some changes in the canal environments may be subtle, but those noted above aren't.

After two visits to Newfoundland, I wanted very much to write a book about that wonderful island of forests, mountains, lakes, ocean shores, and friendly, humorous people. That is now unlikely, but one of the accounts in the next chapter will give you a taste of it.

11

Six Memorable (Mostly Birding) Expeditions

Unlike Phoebe Snetsinger, the first person to see 8,000 of the earth's bird species, and slighting her family to do it, I am not obsessed about my life list but do enjoy adding to it. Here are six of my forays abroad that added to the list.

Africa

I'd always wanted to visit Africa, and in January 1978 Elizabeth persuaded me to do it, though it would take the last few thousand dollars of my dwindling investment account. It also took a bit of courage: at that time I had a fear of flying. While pondering what to do about that, I ran across *Kicking the Fear* Habit, a book that told me what to do: practice orienting. That is, while flying I should focus on other things, such as the clouds out the window and the other passengers. Relate myself to those things, connect with them. So I bought plane tickets for me and our two older children. The night before the flight I took a tranquilizer and fell right to sleep. That might help too.

On the plane I sketched passengers, then took a tranquilizer, and drank two Scotch and sodas. The latter two actions made me so groggy I hardly knew what was going on. No fear could creep in through that barrier! I managed the next flight to Johannesburg, where my friend Jack van Wyk met us with his small plane. I managed that too, to Potchefstroom, though Libby threw up on me.

Jack, a botany professor and hunting partner of the president of South Africa, had arranged for us a Volkswagen bus and meetings with superintendents in several national parks. Best of these was Kruger, with its large size and exciting large animals. It's one thing to see these animals in a zoo and another to see them in their native landscapes. I'll never forget that large, dark bull elephant that came walking toward us across the plain. As it neared, I remembered stories about elephants that sat on Volkswagens, and drove farther up the road. My first sight of a giraffe was unbelievable! That long neck and head appeared close in front of us rising up through foliage as it ate leaves on the top of a tree. It was so *real*!

Of course I was watching birds all along and Kruger had lots of beautiful new ones for me. Libby and Eleanor became annoyed at my many stops to look at birds out the window, so I let them steer the car in between stops. The scops owl in the dining room that night, perched on a high beam, delighted even the girls.

In Kenya, though some viral illness dampened my enthusiasm, thousands of flamingos at Lake Nakuru and a long line of elephants in Masai-Mara National Park, spread out before us as if for inspection, made me forget the illness. I can't remember where we saw circling vultures that our guide said meant a kill. We drove toward them and came upon cheetahs eating an impala, encircled by tourists in vehicles. The cheetahs seemed used to that sort of thing.

Mexico

Ro Wauer, a Texan and one of the founders of the American Birding Association, had made many birding trips to Mexico. Shortly before Christmas, when Ro was Chief of the Natural Resources Management Division in the park service, and I was working with him, he invited me to go on a trip to Mexico, a country I'd never been to. I was on jury duty at the time, but fortunately was not selected as a juror, so was free to go.

Ro and I and three other people met in Mexico City, rented a decrepit old car, and set off eastward toward the coast south of Vera Cruz. Ro Wauer is not a casual birder. Every morning we rose before dawn and drove through the dark while Ro shone a spotlight into trees to catch the shining eyes of perched owls. Around nine o'clock we stopped, pulled out a briefcase full of Granola bars, and had "breakfast." For one whose favorite meal is breakfast, with *coffee*, this didn't quite do. And it happened for nine days.

It was , however, a good nine days for birds. In the rain forests, when it cleared up after a long period of rain, we saw fifteen species of raptors. One of our last quests was the Slender-billed Wren, one of Ro's "most wanted birds." After a long drive on a rough road, frequently scraping the bottom of our weighted-down car, we arrived in the wren's habitat—forested limestone hills where wild *Impatiens* covered every rock. After many minutes sitting still in the underbrush, everyone but me saw the bird. I wasn't too disappointed though. The Emerald Toucans were a much more fetching sight than the wren would have been.

On the last day we drove to timberline on Popocatepetl volcano near Mexico City, watched Red Crossbills in the conifers and distant climbers on the snow above, then entered a lodge. Here we had *breakfast—huevo rancheros* and hot *coffee*. Oh happy morning!

At the beginning of our trip, Ro had predicted we'd see 325 species of birds. Our final list was 328. Probably half or more were life birds for me.

Ecuador

When the Audubon Naturalist Society announced a modestly priced trip to Ecuador I signed up, and then arranged my own trip to the Galapogos Islands beforehand. The first few days in the Islands I was on board the *Angelique*. There were sixteen passengers, mostly young European couples, a congenial group. At each island our guide led us along well-marked trails past nesting boobies, frigatebirds, and other famously unafraid birds. Because there are so many visitors, the guides have to keep their groups moving to avoid jams. I had little time to chase down unidentified birds. That might account for my identifying only six of Darwin's thirteen finches.

Swimming and sunbathing with sea lions was a first for me. Especially endearing was a small group of Galapagos Penguins that swam beside our panga as we headed back to our boat. During the long cruises between islands I spotted the White-vented Storm-petrel, Wedge-rumped Petrel, and Dark-rumped Petrel, which flies like a shearwater and is much bigger than Audubon's Shearwater, which I often also saw. Most exciting was the large manta ray that repeatedly leapt out of the water; some think they do that to dislodge parasites.

Exhibits at the Darwin Research Center described some of the management conducted to maintain the native plants and animals. For instance, tortoise eggs are brought from various islands for hatching and raising, to restore populations that are declining. The baby turtles are kept in separate areas according to their subspecies and marked with a number, as well as a chip implanted under their skin, to keep track of them when released. When three or four years old they are considered old enough to avoid predation—by rats, dogs, etc.—by closing up in their shell, and are released on the appropriate island.

A map in the entrance area shows what feral animals remain, or did before removal, on each major island: goats, pigs, cows, horses, donkeys, dogs, cats, and black rats. Goats, pigs, dogs, and cats are shot. Black rats seem to be the most difficult to eradicate; traps are used because poison would kill native animals as well. Some 80 New Zealanders were imported to shoot goats from helicopters and on the ground (as deer are shot in New Zealand to reduce destructive overpopulations).

The plane that carried me back to Quito was taking me to some of the richest birding in South America. Here I joined the Audubon Naturalist Society group, led by Mark Garland, an excellent all-around naturalist, and Gustavo, a local guide. We spent the first few days on the western slope of the Andes, working from 10,000 feet down to 1,200.

In the northern Andes, hummingbirds and tanagers steal the show. By the end of our trip we had seen 50 species of hummingbirds and 70 species of tanagers. At our highest stop we parked

Our birding group on the west slope of the Andes

the bus and walked a 2-km trail, along which are five humming-bird feeding stations. Our target was the Sword-bill Hummingbird, which we saw at the last two stations. "Tremendously long bill!" I wrote in my notes. "Longer than its body. The Hooded Moun-tain-tanager and Variable Hawk were especially nice too."

Ecuador has many lodges catering to ecotourists, and we stayed at several. When I stepped out of one after breakfast, "a half hour netted 13 species of hummingbirds, all beautiful and interesting. I particularly liked the Purple-throated Woodstar, a small one that doesn't land on the feeder but hovers like a sphinx moth, raising and lowering its tail."

Restaurant owners, too, have learned about the attraction of birds. In the Milpa area, around 3,000 feet, we stopped for lunch at a restaurant "with lots of feeders that attracted many tanagers to bananas. The Green Honeycreeper, actually a tanager, was espe-cially beautiful. Another birding group, of Brits, was there, but we had the table nearest the window and got the best show."

"That afternoon we went to the Refugio Paz de la Antpittas, es-tablished by some farmers who discovered they could attract ant-pittas to the trails in their forest and birders who would pay to see them. But first we went down a steep forested slope to a blind they had built. Here we hid while a guide tried to call in a Cock-of-the-rock. After an hour we had a distant view of two bright-red Cocks. Then back up the steep trail to a spot where we watched as the guide tossed out worms and called in a Moustached Antpitta, of which we had fleeting views."

After several days in forests, where diversity of birds is great but views of them often brief or obscured by foliage, I was look-ing forward to the open paramo, the South American version of alpine tundra. We visited this environment twice. First we traveled up to a communications station at 13,000 feet. We were looking for Seedsnipe, but saw something much more exciting. From our van-tage point high above an open area with scattered bushes, we saw a large dark form enter that area from the left. It was an Andean, or spectacled bear. Slowly it ambled across the landscape, sometimes disappearing in bushes and then reappearing, until it went out of sight down a slope. Our local guide, now Xavier, said it was only the second one he had ever seen.

Our second stop on the paramo was the private Antisano Eco-logical Reserve, an area of about 20,000 acres owned by an Ecua-dorian family for four generations. On the higher land they have horses roaming free and 10,000 sheep, guarded by shepherds night and day—night in corrals to protect them from predators such as pumas (an animal of North and South America also known as mountain lion, cougar, panther, and catamount). We had lunch in the hacienda, and above our table the skin of a puma hung on the wall. Birds on the reserve included many Black-winged Ground Doves, Carunculated Caracaras, and Andean Gulls.

Next, we went down the Napo River, an Amazon tributary, by motorized boat, and up the much smaller Rio Arunga by paddled dugouts to the Napo Wildlife Center. The center, with attractive thatched buildings, on a lake in the forest, was created by local villagers. Around the lodges, there was lots of noise from Yellow-rumped Caciques and Russet-backed Oropendulas, whose nests hung communally in the palm trees.

Banks of clay where parrots congregate are a big tourist attraction in South America. Parrots eat the clay for minerals that counteract the toxins in some of the fruits they eat. We visited two clay banks near the Rio Napo. The first was typical of such places: "We hear the parrots screeching in the trees overhead for quite some time before they venture down. [There were] great numbers of Dusky-headed Parakeets, smaller numbers of Blue-headed Parrots. The show ended when an Ornate Hawk-eagle attacked but caught nothing."

Our departure down the narrow Rio Arunga was enlivened by the sight of a large fer-de-lance coiled around a branch over the water.

Along the Napo River we saw signs of the development that is eating away at the Amazon forest. At one place trucks were being ferried across the river to a road that had been built to oil wells in a national park. As so often happens in the tropics, people had settled along this road, taking more bites of the forest. At another point on the river a "port" was under construction where a planned road across the Ecuadorian Andes from the Pacific coast was to end and shipment continued down the Amazon River system toward Europe.

"The two weeks with Mark have been memorable," I wrote in my notebook. "Mark has done an outstanding job as leader, looking after everyone's welfare, livening up conversations, and spotting and identifying almost as many birds as our Ecuadorean guides, who were remarkable. I especially liked Mark's little discussions about tropical ecology." Mark Garland, now a free-lance tour leader, was formerly a naturalist with the Audubon Naturalist Society in Washington.

On this trip to Ecuador I added 334 species to my life list.

Newfoundland

Scotland, with its mountains, lakes, and seacoasts, is one of my favorite places on Earth, but Newfoundland goes it one or two better—it also has extensive forests and friendly, humorous people. I drove around Newfoundland twice, once in late June-early July, 1998, and again in April 2005. Below are highlights of these experiences, pulled from my copious notes.

On the first trip I sought nature chiefly, but the lives of the people were also intriguing. I looked more into that on my second trip—especially how they responded to the collapse of their most important natural resource—codfish.

In June, an overnight ferry boat ride took me from North Sidney, in Nova Scotia, to Argentia, on the southeast coast of Newfoundland. One of my first stops was at St. Vincent's Beach on the Avalon Peninsula. Hordes of capelin, a small, slender, smeltlike fish, were on their way to this beach at the head of a cove to spawn, and their predators were feasting on them. Gannets, a large white seabird, were diving from high above to seize them underwater. Humpbacked whales, some only 100-200 yards offshore, made their slow descent to get a mouthful. They seemed more casual about it than the gannets; one just lay on the surface, throwing its flippers side to side. I could hear some of the whales blowing. Down below, remnants of the once-huge codfish population pursued the capelin. On the beach local people were fishing for the codfish. The many female capelin that reached the beach rode the surf ashore and dropped their fertilized eggs in the sand and gravel, to which they attached. Most of the capelin would die after spawning.

Across St. Mary's Bay at Cape St. Mary, an ecological preserve was established to protect the thousands of seabirds nesting there. I walked the one-mile trail from the Interpretive Centre with a guide and a political science professor from Florida Southern University. We passed sheep grazing on the Barren and smelled the guano of seabirds. The trail ended at a cliff edge just yards away from free-standing Bird Rock, which was white with 6,000 pairs of nesting gannets. "Most were sitting on eggs, but some were still building nests and performing courtship rituals like neck entwining and billing. There was constant coming and going of these great, elegant birds." As ornithologist Roger Tory Peterson wrote, "the birds...swirl past the cliff face like a blizzard of snow." Our guide said 10,000 pairs of Common Murres, 10,000 pairs of Black-legged Kittiwakes, 1,000 pairs of Thick-billed Murres, over 100 pairs of Razorbills, and some 20 pairs of Black Guillemots nested on nearby cliffs or rock islands.

Driving toward St. John's, Newfoundland's capital, I passed through Barrens, a tundra-like or moor-like landscape that occupies much of the Avalon Peninsula. A big chunk of it is preserved in the Avalon Wilderness Reserve. Some 6,000 caribou wander about in or near this reserve, feeding mostly on lichens (called caribou moss by the Newfies). From my car I saw about 20 of these animals, most of them far off, but two young ones near the road stared at me. (Many other herds are sprinkled around Newfoundland, totaling in all around 70,000 caribou.) As I drove, I mused about camping and following the Avalon caribou.

At Bay Bulls, near St. John's, I took O'Briens' boat tour around the bay. Our first stop was at cliffs topped by soil and grass where many thousands of puffins nested in burrows. The grassy slopes were dotted with the white beasts of puffins outside their burrows. Kittiwakes nested on the cliff ledges below. Our guide told us the gruesome (from a human standpoint) story of how the kittiwakes are preyed on by large gulls. Herring Gulls take their eggs and chicks. Great Black-backed Gulls do too, but also take adult kittiwakes and puffins. They often work in pairs to catch the kittiwakes; one chases the bird off its nest and the other grabs it by the wing, carries it down to the water and drowns it. At the next island we watched thousands of kittiwakes and Common Murres coming and going, smaller numbers of Razorbills and Thick-billed Murres.

Then we circled around two blue and white icebergs for photo opps. Nearby, at another iceberg, a covered barge with a crane was taking giant scoops of ice. There is a popular novelty: putting pieces of thousands of years old glacier ice into drinks (and paying for them).

At Gros Morne National Park, on the west coast, I climbed Gros Morne, on a nine-mile loop trail. The ascent involves 2,000 feet of elevation. "Up through fir and black spruce forest, then more and more tuckamore [stunted fir and spruce beaten down by snow and wind]. Final part of the ascent is up a scree slope with big rocks. Pretty slow. I was being careful to avoid twisting an ankle or knee. Much use of hands and sometimes knees.

"Near the summit [2,644 feet] movement to my left caught my eye—a pair of Rock Ptarmigans [a grouse-like bird]. The male still had a white belly from his winter plumage and some white in the wing. A guttural clattering sound, the female a quieter sound. She was gray-brown all over—summer plumage." This was a life bird for me, my main reason for climbing the mountain. In her loving publication about the park's beauty, wildlife, and fringing small settlements, *Gros Morne: A Living Landscape*, Pat McLeod wrote this warning about the hike: "Both weather and temperature can change with little warning." She was right. A light rain suddenly ensued and followed me all the way to the bottom.

Now Henry Green was waiting for me at Ventureland, a bit farther up the West Coast, for some salmon fishing. I had met Henry in Virginia's Shenandoah Valley on a Christmas Bird Count and learned about his passion for salmon fishing. "I decided not to get married, to retire as early as possible, and to save as much money as possible so I could salmon fish." He *had* retired early, and now spent his winters hunting ruffed grouse in the Appalachians and his summers in Newfoundland and Nova Scotia.

I had brought chest waders for my first attempt at this sport. Henry had engaged Ralph, a required guide, who showed me what to do. "Fly cast out to the side and let the current carry the [wet] fly down." We were fishing in Portland Creek, which flows out of a lake just upstream and into the ocean a short distance downstream. Others were fishing here but having no success. Everybody was praying for rain so the river would rise and prompt more salmon waiting at the mouth to go upstream to spawn. Most were grilse (one-year-olds). Portland Creek has become a grilse stream, because grilse beget grilse. (Salmon go back to their natal stream.) Other streams could have 1,2,3, or 4-year-olds. An afternoon of hopeful casting yielded nothing. And I slipped on the rocks underfoot and fell, letting water flow in through the top of my waders. I fished the rest of the day with water nearly up to my knees.

The next day was better. We started fishing shortly after 7:00 a.m. "I had a strike from a 3-4-pound salmon, but missed it. After escaping it jumped out of the water," which seems to be how salmon celebrate such good fortune. "This morning I carried a stick made for wading in fast rivers and had no spills." During the afternoon I had another strike and momentarily hooked the fish, but it threw the hook and jumped. Ralph, who was standing beside me, said I should have jerked my rod straight up, not sideways. He said it was 5 or 6 pounds—a good one. He was very unhappy that I missed it. Henry had no strikes today," but he had plenty of time. Only one salmon could be kept, and he wanted at least a 5-pounder. I left the next day and soon headed for home.

I was hooked on Newfoundland now and contemplated writing a book about it. In early April 2005 I drove to the tip of the Northern

Peninsula, through increasingly snowy landscapes. I had in mind first looking for Ivory Gulls, most likely found there. On my first trip I had seen just one life bird—the Rock Ptarmigan. I had missed skuas on the long ferry trip to Argentia; no Boreal Owl answered my amateurish imitation of its call in Terra Nova National Park; I saw no Black-headed Gulls where they were said to be; and it was the wrong season for Dovekies (a small seabird) and Ivory Gulls.

Just a mile from L'Anse aux Meadows, where Vikings had established a settlement in 1000 A.D., I checked in at the Viking Nest B&B and began my hunt for Ivory Gulls. This small, pure white, rare gull breeds in the High Arctic and comes southward in winter with the pack ice, often feeding on carrion. Birders sometimes put out a seal carcass in hopes of attracting them. So I thought my best chance was to go out into the pack ice on a seal hunter's boat. At nearby St. Anthony I stepped aboard Dale Dicks'Glace Bay Lady, explained my Ivory Gull mission, and asked if I could go with them on the seal hunt during the two-week season. He said yes,but they would be out for six days. I didn't have that much time. Ivory Gulls sometimes appear along the shores, so I looked where people said I was most likely to see them. No luck. I ended up writing an article about the bird and my fruitless hunt.

Ivory Gull

During my remaining days I roamed about the Northern Peninsula, much of the time asking people how they had adapted to the cod collapse, due largely to overfishing, and the moratorium on offshore cod fishing by large trawlers that scraped the banks clean. Many families had moved to mainland provinces seeking work. Many single young men had gone to the "oil patch" in Alberta. Fishermen who remained at home sought other kinds of seafood, especially snow crabs, shrimps, lobsters, shellfish, and various kinds of fish. In spring they hunted seals during the short season allowed, which produced an important part of their yearly income.

The couple who owned the Viking Nest B&B—Alonzo and Thelma Hedderson—managed with the B&B income and Alonzo's hunting and fishing. Alonzo had gone seal hunting at the end of March. He and two partners had taken his 23-foot open boat 19 miles out into the Strait of Belle Isle to reach the pack ice. "We shot 219 seals—the dark young ones [during a two-day season there]. They go from white to dark in three or four weeks. Their mothers have left them by that time. [It used to be legal to kill the little white ones, but this was stopped after an uproar, mostly from people beyond Newfoundland.] They must be shot in the head so they don't escape into the water." They skin them but usually leave the carcass, unless some meat is wanted. The three men received $3,000 apiece for the pelts. The year before it was $10,000, during a six-day season.

"I'm a fisherman," Alonzo said with some pride. "The next season begins May 1, for lumpfish 'caviar.' We may be able to sell the fish as well." Later he would gill-net flounder, turbot, and haddock, long-line for cod. He was allowed to take 3500 pounds of codfish, under a quota that varied by shoreline location around Newfoundland. In the fall he would hunt moose for home consumption. He had a permit for one moose either sex. Had never been able to get a caribou permit—"must be many fewer of those animals." The Newfoundland moose population was around 200,000.

During my stay with the Heddersons they fed me moose, seal (slight fish taste, lighter than moose meat), "turr" (murre), and eider duck (a little drier than turr). Thelma said turr was her favorite meat.

Alonzo is a small-boat fisherman—he goes out for just one day at a time. Dale Dicks, on his 65-foot Glace Bay Lady, with a crew of six, goes after sea creatures that require a trip of several days. First it's seal hunting in the spring. "At the end of the first day of hunting, each boat radios in to Oceans and Fisheries how many seals they got. If the quota is not met, each boat is given an equal share of the remaining quota." There was still public opposition to the seal hunting, and sometimes boats from organizations that oppose it tried to block the seal-hunting boats. Like many other seal-hunters, Dicks said they were just trying to make a living to feed their family. "How is it different from killing cows and chickens?"

Next he goes out for snow crabs, a two-foot wide crustacean that was thrown away before the moratorium on codfish. He sets the pots, baited with squid, in 150-220 fathoms. Snow crabs now bring him more money than his next target—shrimp—after the crab season ends in July. He had to trawl on the bottom for shrimp. "You can't trawl them above the bottom. If bottom trawling was stopped [because of the damage to the sea bed] I'd be out of business."

On April 14 I learned something about neighborliness in small Newfoundland settlements. A blizzard had hit and the front doors of my four-wheel-drive Ford Explorer, parked at the B&B, were frozen shut. I got in through the rear door.

> Then got stuck in the driveway. Even 4WD low wouldn't move it. A lady across the street lent me her shovel and I dug down to the ground—a foot or more—but still couldn't move it. Then Thelma's brother showed up—she'd called him—and he dug all the remaining snow out from under. Tony Blake had meanwhile showed up and the two of them pushed while I backed up in the driveway. People help each other up in this country!

Like many women in Newfoundland, Thelma Hedderson made jam from local kinds of berries. At the Dark Tickle Shoppe, partway down the west coast of the Northern Peninsula, I met a woman who had made a business of it. [A tickle is a narrow saltwater entrance to a harbor. This tickle was dark because of the adjacent hills.] She and her husband had worked at the nearby fish-processing plant, but after the moratorium on offshore codfishing it closed. They found a demand from tourists for jam made from partridgeberry, bakeapple, and other berries.

> Then we began buying berries from local people to make the jam. Now around 100 families supply us with berries and we make jam from April to October. We sell it wholesale throughout Canada and to the U.S., and some to Germany, France, Switzerland, and Japan. To tourists in the summer.

They didn't have to leave Newfoundland.

Heading south, I stopped at Rocky Harbour, a town surrounded by Gros Morne National Park, and checked in at the Evergreen B&B, run by Sarah and Carson Wentzell. I had an interesting talk with Carson, who was a Forest Technician at the national park. He and another man managed the woodcutting blocks in the park. "People who live in the area that became the park have this right for two generations, which will probably end around 2050, if rules don't change sooner."

A pulp and paper company had a lease immediately east of the park.

The park is trying to work out a cutting scheme that is not detrimental to pine martens, which are scarce in Newfoundland. The present practice is a 10- or 30-metre-wide clearcut strip alternating with same-width strips where some trees are left. Martens apparently will cross these strips.

Newfoundland's present wildlife is partly a mixture of arrivals, extinctions, and deliberate introductions. Moose were introduced to Newfoundland in 1878 and again in 1904. The last known wolf in Newfoundland was killed in the early 20th century, but some biologists believed it was just a matter of time before some wolves would manage to reintroduce themselves to the island. They could cross the Strait of Belle Isle from Labrador or Quebec on ice floes. "The first coyotes," Carson said, "apparently arrived in Newfoundland in March 1985 on an ice floe. A military man I know said while at sea he saw what he believes were those five coyotes. They fed them." Coyotes are now widespread in Newfoundland.

As we chatted, I sometimes glimpsed, at the bird feeder outside the window, northern birds I seldom see: Purple Finches, redpolls, Pine Siskins, Pine Grosbeaks. It was much more springlike here than at L'Anse aux Meadows: robins, too, were around.

When I left Newfoundland, I wondered how its dependence on natural resources would fare, and what else might bolster its economy and general well-being. As of 2017, four oil fields had been found off the coasts of Newfoundland, some on the Grand Bank, former home of vast hordes of codfish. This oil has boosted the provincial income, but is small in quantity compared with the fields in the North Sea and Gulf of Mexico. Long-term, Newfoundland will have to depend on its other natural resources, such as forests, mining, and the fisheries that remain, including the inshore cod fishery.

General tourism and eco-tourism should grow. As a West Coast resort owner said, We've "got something the world wants: a place that hasn't been ruined yet."

Newfoundland remains in my memory a beautiful, intriguing place with abounding natural wonders, fishing villages that still live, and plenty of room to breathe. (But only one life bird.)

To the Antarctic Peninsula

As I approached my 86th birthday, I wondered if another foreign birding trip was feasible. If so, which destination, if the last, would be the most memorable. I considered Australia and the Antarctic. When Elizabeth discovered that Quark Expeditions had a 40 percent discount on an eleven-day cruise to the Antarctic, that decided it. On November 15, 2017, at Ushuaia, in Tierra del Fuego, I boarded the *Ocean Endeavor*, bound for the Antarctic Peninsula. The trip turned out to be memorable in more than one way.

There were 190-some passengers, from all over the world—the British Commonwealth countries, U.S., China, South Korea, and other nations. My cabin mate was from Taiwan. The ship's staff was equally diverse, including people from Italy, South Africa, Chile, France, Russia, and China, as well as the native English-speakers. It didn't take me long to discover that, though everyone was eager to see the wildlife and land ahead of us, I was the only serious birder among the passengers. I would have to identify birds with the help of the staff ornithologist and a very good book describing what I might see on this particular trip.

The first leg was out the Beagle Channel toward Cape Horn. I wondered what Charles Darwin had seen as he sailed this route aboard the *Beagle* in the 1830s. My guide book described various birds that could be seen here, but most would be on or near the shore. Our course was far from the shore, and night was approaching. Nevertheless, at this stage of my trip, *anything* would be exciting. When a large black and white bird flew away before us, I saw through my binoculars that it was a Black-browed Albatross. And when I swept the water closer to us a pair of Magellanic Penguins came into view, passing in front of our bow on the way, perhaps, to a shoreline colony. That was enough to make me very happy as I went off to sleep that evening.

Crossing the Drake Passage to the Antarctic Peninsula can be very rough, as westerly winds from the Pacific have a long way to build up heavy seas. Our crossing was just medium rough, and allowed me to spend much of the day at the stern, braced against a post, watching the seabirds that followed us. Always present were a dozen or more mottled black and white Cape Petrels wheeling back and forth, up close. Next in abundance were the larger, generally dark brown Southern and Northern Giant Petrels, sometimes accompanied by the similar White-chinned Petrel, whose white bill—rather than white chin—stands out. Five albatross species were the stars: I picked out the Black-browed, Grey-headed, and, largest of all, Wandering Albatross. Fabrice Genevois, our French ornithologist, showed me a Southern Royal and a Light-mantled Albatross, along with Southern Fulmars. The assemblage of these and other seabirds behind us, often close, far surpassed anything I had ever seen in the North Atlantic. It was a wonderful show of slow gliding, fast flapping, high and low arcing of birds over the heaving waves. One of the staff guides told me these species follow ships to pick up pieces of fish chopped up by the ship's propeller. Many other species—some rare—wander those vast oceanic expanses and are much less-often seen by one-time shipboard observers like me.

Cape Petrel

Antarctic landscape

Three days out, in Antarctic late spring, lines of snow-covered mountains appeared on the horizon, announcing our approach to the South Shetland Islands, a foretaste of the Antarctic Peninsula itself. In a cove of Half Moon Island we dropped anchor and piled into Zodiacs for cruising and landing. As my Zodiac rode small waves in, two Gentoo Penguins popped out of the water ahead of us and waddled ashore, where they joined other Gentoos already there. What they all had in mind I don't know, because the breeding colony on this island consisted of Chinstrap Penguins.

Assisted by two ski poles, I followed the trail in the snow made by our guides earlier toward the colony. A cold wind blew and snowflakes fell. I saw what appeared to be a large, smooth gray rock in the snow and walked up to inspect it. The Weddell Seal raised its head. A nearby guide said, 'don't get close, they can bite.'

At the foot of the slope up which the Chinstraps nested, two Brown Skuas landed and ate something they had taken from the colony, probably an egg. At the top of the slope I found many of my shipmates, just a few feet from the penguins, intently watching the close-packed birds on the rocks. They were early in their breeding cycle, with some lying on their pebble nests. Some pairs stood face-to-face, bills pointed skyward, cackling loudly—a territorial statement. Other pairs bowed to each other in courtship. And still others chased away interlopers who had tried to steal a pebble from their nest. Fabrice, our ornithologist, pointed out a lone Macaroni Penguin, with its golden eyebrows, standing amid all these Chinstraps. What was *it* doing here, with no reproductive possibility?

As I walked back down the slope, an Adele Penguin, which had earlier walked up to the colony, now stumbled through the snow on its way down—another mysterious nonbreeder. Newly arrived Chinstraps struggled up the hill from the shore. Overhead, a Kelp Gull looked for prey. Not far away, Antarctic Terns, Antarctic Shags (cormorants), and chunky Snowy Sheathbills completed the avian picture. It was one I would cherish, because this would be my last trip ashore.

When we returned to the ship, we had to step into a bootwash tub to remove any contaminants, as we had when leaving the ship, to protect the pristine Antarctic. I may have been a bit tired from my walk ashore, and when my size 14 gumboots caught the edge of the tub, I fell, and my right side hit an iron bar. People helped me up and I went to see the ship doctor, Simon Bryant. He suspected I had fractured ribs and gave me a heavy dose of Tylenol and some codeine for the pain that would ensue. It did, in spades. Dr. Bryant's care and medications got me through the rest of the trip. Twice he said I was "a tough old bird." Henceforth I did my birdwatching from the ship. Trips ashore on bouncing Zodiacs would have been too painful, and probably inadvisable..

After several stops for landings, then continuing southward along the Peninsula, we came to unexpected "fast ice" that covered all the visible expanse ahead. The captain nudged the ship into the ice and we gathered on a stern deck for a Mongolian barbecue as the lowering sun lit the snowy peaks around us, and a few Gentoo Penguins standing on the ice watched us.

The captain and our expedition leader changed plans and we headed back north. At the first of the South Shetlands, Deception Island, we entered the still waters of the harbor, which filled the caldera of an ancient volcano. Large flocks of Cape Petrels, which appeared to be nesting on the cliffs here, rested on the water. A courting pair ignored our ship as we slowly moved by them. On the shore, remains of a Norwegian whaling station and a British scientific site that functioned until 1967 came into view. Snow had collapsed the roof of one building. Snow Petrels, a lovely pure white bird that was my most-wanted, was known to nest here but none were seen.

As we sailed away from Deception Island, Fabrice went to the bridge with me to look for Snow Petrels, but none appeared. I saw what looked like a large insect flitting across the water. Fabrice said it was a Wilson's Storm-Petrel. Compared with the other seabirds out here, it seemed small enough to be an insect.

In Bransfield Strait, between the Antarctic Peninsula and the South Shetland Islands, we had great whale-watching. First was a small pod of Orcas, including a young one. The captain expertly kept the ship near them, and they seemed curious about us, coming quite close. Most of the passengers were on deck, switching to port or starboard as the Orcas moved around. In a spout I saw a rainbow.

After a long look at the Orcas we continued northward and encountered two Hump-backed Whales, some of the first arriving from farther north. For one and a half hours we watched the slow sequence of spout, back, fin, and, if deep-diving, the raised flukes disappearing downward. Humpbacks often investigate ships and sometimes even scrape themselves on the ship's bottom. As these two came by I could see their white flippers underwater. By now we had chosen whales instead of a planned landing—just another penguin colony.

Our dinner hour was graced by six Fin Whales, the second largest species after Blue Whale, flanking our ship. Compared with the earlier whale sightings, the long back of these behemoths seemed to show above the surface for a long time before submerging. I think we were lucky. This was late November. The larger whales are not usually expected in Antarctic waters until December.

And now back into the Drake Passage. High swells began to roll the ship, but I wanted to see what was following us. Anything new? Yes! As I made my way to the stern, in spite of back pain, hanging on to anything handy and then bracing against the usual post, I glimpsed a flash of dark brown and striking white bands along the slender wings. It was an Antarctic Petrel, usually associated with iceberg-coated waters, but sometimes following ships northward. It swung back and forth behind the stern, as if making sure I saw it. Beautiful! And low above the water flew a large group of small, bluish-gray birds that seemed to disappear against the bluish-gray waves—Antarctic Prions, our ornithologist said. Thus, two petrels ended my seabird list, and I assumed I wouldn't add to it. So I spent little more time at the stern.

Instead, more comfortably, I sat, reading, listening to lectures, eating the very good food we were offered, and sleeping as we crossed the Drake Passage. I thought and read about the Antarctic and human involvement there.

The most pristine area left on earth. Will we keep it that way, as intended in the Antarctic Treaty? Early in the 21st century, 100,000 albatrosses were drowned each year when they swallowed baited hooks let out by long-line fishermen. Fortunately, new management measures are rapidly reducing these losses. Krill fishing, the largest fishery in the Antarctic, is reducing that food source so important for Antarctic wildlife. It needs to be better regulated and moved away from areas around penguin colonies. Climate change is warming some of the Antarctic waters, which breaks up sea ice and causes changes in the food available. Both effects appear to be reducing some penguin populations, as shown by cameras monitoring them. May mineral extraction never be allowed, as stated in the Antarctic Treaty.

When we docked at Ushuaia, Dr. Bryant accompanied me to a clinic, where x-rays showed I had two broken ribs and maybe a third. Next day, sitting on the front porch of my hotel, I watched for birds I'd missed when first at Ushuaia. Yes, a Chimango Caracara flew by! Scanning the sky, I saw a Turkey Vulture being harassed by a Southern Caracara, "a brute of a bird," says *Antarctic Wildlife*. At the airport I walked outside to see what might be on the Darwin Channel shore. Yes, a pair of Kelp Geese, the all-white male and the blackish and white female.

The trip gave me 33 life birds, an unforgettable look at the beautiful, majestic Antarctic Peninsula, and broken ribs.

PART III

Living Abroad

Ten or so years after Elizabeth had to resign from the Foreign Service because of getting married, a (successful) suit was brought against the State Department arguing that that was illegal discrimination against women. By that time we had three half-grown children and my aged mother was living with us. If my wife returned to the Foreign Service we would have to uproot our children from their schools and friends and settle my mother in a retirement community. Because Elizabeth had wanted this career since the eighth grade, I thought she should have it. I could write about nature and environmental issues wherever we went. So we decided to take the leap.

Thus began a 25-year period of life abroad mixed with assignments at the State Department and training for Elizabeth, 7 ½ years abroad with her mixed with years at home working for the park service and doing freelance writing for me, and some time abroad but mostly school and college in the U.S. for our children.

Overseas, I had a year or more in four of Elizabeth's five foreign postings: Malaysia, Nigeria, Turkey, and Azerbaijan. It was a wonderful opportunity to expand my understanding of other cultures, the nature in which they were imbedded, and the environmental issues they faced.

12

Malaysia

In August 1981, as we stepped off the plane at the Kuala Lumpur airport with our three girls, we felt a hot, wet blanket of air that would be a permanent part of our environment for the next two years. Fortunately, the State Department put us in a house with air conditioning and marble on the first floor that felt wonderfully cool on bare feet. Most days had predictable weather: 70 degrees at dawn, rising to 90, then an afternoon thunderstorm that temporarily broke the heat. I found that walking any distance in the open was extremely enervating, and that Harp beer was a necessary coolant.

Our human environment, aside from the diplomats and other expatriates, consisted of Malays—the natives—who worked in agriculture, government, and --a few—in business; Chinese, predominantly in business; and Indians, a smaller minority, also largely in the commercial sector. I thought that if the Chinese in China were anything like the Chinese in Malaysia, they would someday rule the world economically. A Chinaman in Malaysia could make a living growing things on an abandoned tin mine.

Elizabeth had selected the economic "cone" as her type of work in the Foreign Service and was assigned palm oil, rubber, oil, and tin issues to follow. We enrolled Eleanor, 14, Libby, 13, and Molly, 10 in the Kuala Lumpur International School. There were many kids from Texas and Oklahoma whose fathers were in the oil business. In spite of the hot, humid weather these fathers had persuaded the school to include American football in the sports program, complete with an announcer and cheerleaders at games. They played teams as far away as Jakarta. Libby, our best scholar, was academically far ahead of the grade she was put in, so we arranged a lot of special assignments for her. One was a paper on tropical forests, which I enjoyed helping her with and taking her to Taman Negara National Park for first-hand observation.

As was happening in so many tropical countries, Malaysia had replaced much of the rain forest that originally covered most of the country with palm oil and rubber plantations. Both plantations and elephants do best in lowland areas. Mountainous terrain can support few elephants. Unfortunately, elephants love young oil palms, and the authorities were having great problems keeping them out of the plantations. With a go-ahead from *International Wildlife* magazine, I looked into the matter, driving an old, trucklike Land Rover. (*International Wildlife* said my resulting article was "too thin," but revised and expanded *Defenders* magazine published it.)

Moats, electric fences, bags soaked with tiger urine, and even witch doctors, who communicated with elephants, had been tried, but the wild Asian elephants, of which 700 to 900 still existed in Malaysia, had sometimes found a way in. Now the strategy was to capture the invaders and transport them to a large forest area in northernmost Malaysia. With permission from the government I spent eight days with the Elephant Capture Unit near a forest harboring elephants that were marauding an oil palm plantation.

Malaysia had a massive program of settling poor families in remote forest areas, under the Federal Land Development Authority. I was visiting the Gunong Besout scheme, 22,000 acres of formerly forested low hills and valley 80 miles north of Kuala Lumpur that had been converted to an oil palm plantation. The Gunong Besout scheme lay next to the Cawang and Erong forest reserves, which were also scheduled to become FELDA schemes. Chain saws were already cutting. Twenty percent of the Gunong Besout scheme had been denuded of young oil palms by elephants. "We plant all this and no return," the manager mourned.

The capture unit's technique was to locate and follow elephant tracks on foot into the forest. If the unit caught up with them by early afternoon, one was singled out and tranquilized with a dart fired at close range. This was sometimes dangerous. On one occasion an elephant charged the men and was shot, falling to the ground just a few yards away. Under normal circumstances, when a tranquilized elephant lay on the ground, two men were dispatched to camp to bring back two tame elephants. When the wild elephant regained its feet it was roped between the two tame ones, which calmed it, and was walked back to camp. After a day or two, it was hauled by truck to the northern forest and released. Sometimes it took weeks to find and capture a single elephant. I was surprised and pleased at the effort the government made to move wild elephants, but wondered how they fared in a new environment with elephants already living there. I don't think anyone knew.

The tame elephants were walked each day for exercise, and one morning Mohammed Nawayai, the 27-year-old leader of the capture unit, asked if I'd like to ride one. They seemed docile enough, so I said yes. The mahout told the elephant to lie down and I crawled up its flank. The elephant rose with me on its back and the mahout on its neck and we ambled off. During the walk we passed several gardens of local people. At each one the elephant reached into the garden with its trunk and broke off stems that looked good to eat until the mahout commanded it to move on. I don't recommend riding an elephant bareback because you sit on its spine. After two hours my seat was very sore and I requested a descent. When the elephant lay on its side I slid down and walked.

Early next morning we piled into two jeeps and drove muddy roads through the swampy Cawang Forest Reserve until we came across elephant tracks. "It is within our capacity," Nawi said. "Probably a young bull." We parked the jeeps and the nine men—four with .458 rifles, two with shotguns, one with the drug gun, two with ropes—and I followed the tracks. At a brisk pace we went wherever the tracks led, through thick vegetation, chest-deep water, or open ground beneath towering trees whose canopy closed out the sky. It was hard going. These guys were in their twenties and I was fifty. Finally around noon Nawi called a halt and I flopped on the ground, exhausted. Looking up, I saw a 12-foot python wrapped around a branch. It brought to mind a photograph I'd seen of the body of a man inside a cut-open python. He had been walking at night through a forest on the way to a meeting and the python had dropped on him, squeezed him to death, and swallowed him. I reassured myself that the man had been small and the python above me was not big enough to swallow me.

After the rest we set off at a trot, trying to catch up with the elephant before two o'clock, when there would be time to bring in our tame elephants and walk the wild one out before dark. Unfortunately, we did not catch up with it and had to quit. But I had gained great respect for these men who could do this day after day and maybe not capture one elephant for weeks on end. No elephant was caught during my eight days with the Elephant Capture Unit. (Between 1972 and 1991, the capture team translocated 240 elephants, about one-fourth of the Peninsular Malaysian population. Such admirable efforts may not be enough, however. Malaysia's elephants were under the double threat of forest clearance and an uncertain future in the northern forest, where they were poached by Malaysian Communists and Thai Muslim separatists who had taken refuge there).

Malaysia has two states in the northern third of Borneo: Sarawak and Sabah. These beckoned me with a host of subjects I was keen to investigate: among them forestry operations, shifting cultivation, orangutan populations and rehabilitation of confiscated pets, and the Niah Caves, where nests of swiftlets are collected for birds'-nest soup. After a couple of nights in Kuching, Sarawak, in a hotel where a sign on the front door read: "No Durians [a smelly fruit] are Allowed in This Hotel," I went to Bako National Park, on an offshore island.

It didn't take long to see interesting wildlife, as my notes record-ed. "At a small stagnant stream near HQ," I saw "a green snake draped on a branch over the water. Rather heavy, with triangular head, and speckled light green—attractive and scary at the same time. They said it had been in same spot for a long time, apparently waiting for a bird to land nearby." Later I concluded it was some kind of viper. Following a riverine trail I saw crested leaf monkeys.

> One had an orange-furred baby clinging to its belly. Far-ther up trail great racket made by Long-tailed Macaques. Don't know whether they were yelling at me or each oth-er, jockeying for best spot in the tree to spend the night.... Up on the ridge ran into a troop of proboscis monkeys—orange-furred, larger than L-T Macaques. I saw about 5 through the binoculars, though seemed there must have been 10 or more from all the noise.

Next was a visit to the Sawai Forest Reserve, where the Bintulu Lumber Development Company was working. There I watched a small man with a chain saw cut down a giant tree, which fell with a thunderous roar, taking down with it smaller trees and a tangle of lianas (vines). One of the managers led me to a little motorized conveyance that ran on a narrow, undulating track through the for-est. We passed a workers' camp and stopped at stacks of huge logs waiting to be hauled out.

The forest officer, Bernstein Daud Rajit, hosted me. He said he picked his "Christian" name from a list because it sounded different or interesting. He told me that, on average, two workers were killed each year. I soon learned by personal experience how dangerous the work was. A little logger who wanted to give me a slice of wood as a memento began to cut down a tree relatively small in diameter but tall. It started to fall away from us but got swung around wildly by the lianas it was hooked to and fell directly toward us. We dove sideways to the ground to escape being crushed. He cut a thin slab from the trunk as my souvenir.

The forestry visit showed me what was happening to the rain forest in many parts of Malaysian and Indonesian Borneo, often at the expense of tribal villages that depended on the forest for their livelihood and culture. The tribespeople were complaining, but with little success, against the money represented by their trees.

My next stop acquainted me with the lives of some of those people. I had letters of introduction from a forest officer who had grown up in the longhouse of the headman of an Iban village farther down the road. The headman, Councillor Denis Mujang, who spoke English, welcomed me to the wooden longhouse where his family lived. It consisted of apartments along one side and a covered deck, in front, along the other. I noted hanging from the ceiling of the deck a mesh rattan basket containing a skull of a man from another tribe Mujang's great grandfather had killed around 100 years ago. Things were much more peaceful now.

Mujang ushered me into his apartment and a stuffed chair, where as a guest of honor I was supposed to sit. Soon his wife spread a rattan cloth on the wood floor and began bringing out the items of our dinner. I moved to the floor with them and began sampling the offerings. One was a small white object that was crunchy and sweet. This was a delicacy, Mujang said, grubs his wife had dug out of the heart of a small sago palm. I should have continued eating this delicacy but my cultural notions about food stopped me.

During the night, according to my notes, there was

> periodic barking and howling of dogs on the deck, where they sleep along with the tethered fighting cocks, and sometimes a dog fight erupts. Early in the morning the cocks begin to crow, after first a flapping of wings. It sounds as if it starts at one end of the deck and progresses down the line. The flapping of wings sounds like someone knocking on a door, so the effect is of a person going down the porch knocking on each door. The result is the same, too. It wakes you up.

After a night sleeping on a floor pad I followed the villagers a couple of miles to the ripe hill rice on Mujang's sister's farm. To harvest it, each person, including me, had a bag slung over the shoulder and a small knife that fitted onto the fingers. Mujang showed me the proper one-hand way to use it, but I didn't get the

Picking hill padi rice

hang of it. "Mujang said cut it any way I could, which ended up being two-handed, held with left, cut with right." We formed a long line and began walking up the hill, cutting off the rice heads and throwing them in our bags. This particular hill was very steep and I had a hard time remaining upright, but the others talked and laughed as they worked, having no trouble with the incline. "Everybody else picked about 3 heads to my one."

At the tea break Mujang explained to me their agricultural system. In earlier times, when populations were less dense, the shifting cultivators of Sarawak and other parts of Southeast Asia ranged over larger areas, clearing a patch of rain forest, raising crops on it for a couple of years, then moving to another piece of forest when the shallow fertility in the first ran out. (Shallow because rain forest soils are easily leached of their nutrients.) In 20 or 30 years, when forest had substantially regrown on the first area, they could return to it and get another few crops from the renewed fertility. Now, because these farming groups were larger and close together, they had much less forest area to work with. My hosts had to clear a patch after only seven years of regrowth. Because this provided minimal fertility, they had to apply government subsidized fertilizer to get decent harvests. A little spirit house constructed down the slope, they hoped, would ward off any threats to their crops.

A different life, however, was on the horizon. The Sarawak government was trying to move shifting cultivators to schemes with settled agriculture and very little shifting cultivation, and the villages led by Councillor Mujang were soon to move to one such scheme. I described this in an article for *The Asia Magazine*:

> Twenty longhouses will join together on this 20,000 to 30,000 acre [cocoa] scheme. They will still live in longhouses, but these will be clustered together, with a school, clinic, and stores. For the first time, they will have electricity. Each family will have ten to fifteen acres of cocoa and 300-400 pepper plants.
>
> But old ways will not be entirely abandoned. Each family will have a small bit of hill padi—one to three acres each year—clearing, burning, and planting as the Ibans have done for centuries. Appropriate rituals will be observed to keep the rice spirits happy. And on the porch of Councillor Denis Mujang will hang, no doubt, the skull taken by his great-grandfather.

The land they had been using would return to forest, probably for timber—managed wisely, I hope. Tribesmen living higher up in the watersheds would probably resist moving to schemes for some time.

My next destination in Sarawak was the Niah Caves, where the nests of swiftlets are gathered for birds'-nest soup, a subject I was writing about for the Malaysian Airlines magazine. A young Canadian was currently in charge of the reserve, as that country's version of a Peace Corps volunteer. He directed me to the cave. Walking among tumbled rocks, I entered a huge, high-ceilinged room. Looking up through the gloom I saw a rickety bamboo structure the nest-collectors ascended. No one was there as it wasn't the nesting season, but I wasn't sure I would want to watch, because of a fear of heights. The men who do this are following a tradition handed down from one generation to the next. There is a certain pride in it, and perhaps a decent income, that outweighs fear of the occasional fatal fall. All this so that restaurant owners can sell expensive birds'-nest soup, made from the saliva-like substance that holds the nests together.

Later I tried this soup and found it uninteresting. And wondered how anyone had ever imagined the saliva of birds' nests would make interesting food.

In Sabah, the other Malaysian state in Borneo, I went to see the orangutan rehabilitation center in the Sepilok Forest Reserve near Sandakan. This was established to prepare orangutans confiscated from pet owners—keeping them as pets was illegal—to return to a life in the wild. I watched them clumsily trying to climb trees. They were fed, and came back to home pens for the night. Many had been captured when babies, after their mothers had been shot, and had not learned much about normal orangutan life. They were not afraid of people, a trait that did not bode well for a future free life.

Amid, a half-grown orangutan that was missing an arm started following me up a path. Uncertain how an encounter would turn out, I climbed the stairs to a door of a building to escape. The door, however, was locked and Amid came up the steps. He hugged me with his one arm in an iron grip, an act of friendship I suppose, but it was a bit scary. I extricated myself as soon as possible and walked off, hoping I hadn't offended him by this rejection.

After growing out of childhood the orangutans were taken to an extensive forest area where food was put on a platform to supplement what the animals found on their own. The hope was that they eventually could do without the supplementary feeding and would assume a normal orangutan life among whatever wild orangutans were already out there. How those residents would react to them was unknown. And could they find food and learn what they needed to learn without parents to teach them? I don't know if any follow-up studies were conducted to answer these questions.

The squeeze on tribespeople, orangutans, and other inhabitants of Borneo's rain forests continues, as the primary forest shrinks.

From Sandakan I returned to Kota Kinabalu to visit Mount Kinabalu National Park. At the park I went birding with Peter Coe, a gung-ho birder from Britain. Like several other birders I've known or heard about, he was traveling around the world building his life list. Already he'd been to Sri Lanka, and then Thailand, where he'd seen 550 species. Sabah had netted him 250, so far. Then it would be Indonesia, Australia (where he would build up his finances working as a book binder), New Guinea, the Philippines, China, and Japan (where he wanted to see wintering birds from Siberia). In another forested part of Sabah he'd competed with a friend to see who could find the most species of birds in a morning. Both ended up with around 100. On our day-long walk he identified many unseen birds by their calls, which I didn't know.

At 13,455 feet, Mount Kinabalu, Borneo's highest, offers a diverse vertical range of habitats, from tropical rain forest to cloud forest up to 11,000 feet or more, and mostly bare rock above that. A road extends to the 8,000-foot level and from there you must walk, in groups with a guide.

My notes convey the climb up Kinabalu better than my memory.

Started up the mountain this morning, fortified only by coffee and the first of several peanut butter sandwiches. A guide named Tulaad was assigned to a rather horsey but genial, blond Scots girl, an Iban boy named Sylvester, and me. I told them I'd be slow, and after the first rest stop didn't see them again until I reached Burlington Hut, the night's quarters.

It was a 7-hour climb for me, a real job. Mainly getting my breath. I would pause every 100 feet or so, it seemed, the guide patiently waiting behind me. I felt pretty ancient seeing younger people going by in both directions, in good spirits, while I hardly had the energy or inclination to smile or speak. When we reached Carson Camp at noon, 9,000 feet, it started to rain. After lunch, during a lull, I started up again.

Didn't see my guide until the next morning. The last 3 ½ hours and 2,000 feet [of altitude] was in continuous rain and increasing wind. The trail here as below was mostly roots and rocks, with the rocks gaining dominance upwards. It was like walking up a rocky stream. I had on rain suit over short-sleeved shirt, but still got very wet. I just thought about the next little pitch—what I could see—and hoped that around the corner it wouldn't be so steep. But usually it was.

After stopping briefly at a hut,

I set out on the final short leg growing increasingly cold from the wind and rain, stumbling over rocks and roots, and cursing. Finally saw the brown wood Burlington Hut. Found empty bunk, pulled off all clothes, soaking, put on dry ones, crawled into my down sleeping bag, and shook with cold for half an hour [perhaps in the first stage of hypothermia].

Next morning,

up at 3:00 a.m. for the 'final assault.' We go in darkness

at 4:00, with flashlights. I hadn't expected the route to be so steep. It was steeper than yesterday, almost straight up ladders in places....Much hard breathing by me. My guide stays right behind me, because my flashlight has gone out permanently and he shines the next footstep.

Out onto rock faces finally, where ropes help the ascent and indicate the route. Shortly past the Sayat-Sayat huts at 12,500, for the umpteenth time I sit down to get my breath. Tulaad says, 'You O.K., mister?' I say, 'O.K., just slow.' Later I leave him $20—twice what I owe—at the park office for his extra attention and good humor.

For some distance above the huts,

> the way now visible by dawn light and the many rocky projections of the summit—Donkey's Ears, Ugly Sisters, and others—looming black above us. The wind, as one curves higher on the smooth glaciated rock, becomes stronger, until it becomes downright inimical. The temperature is perhaps in 40s. Yesterday two people suffered from hypothermia, and one, a man, had to be carried down on the back of a ranger. Going up the rough, jumbled slope of Low's Peak, the highest point, we encounter small patches of snow among rocks and a film of ice on the pools [this in July].

After two minutes on top, looking briefly at the view, I started down. The mountain usually clouds over by 9:00, making it hard to find your way between cairns on the smooth rock. Most people go back down the mountain on the second day, but I elected to stay another night at the Burlington Hut. Walking around in the forest that afternoon, I "saw Mountain Blackeyes, Mountain Bush Warbler, and a couple of UFOs [unidentified birds]."

The walk down to 8,500 feet took me six hours. On the way I met an American girl walking up. She asked, "Is it worth it?" "I said, 'It is if you like mountains.' " [reverse quotes] Then the easy 2 ½ miles to park headquarters and a dinner of Anchor Beer (large), mushroom soup, minute steak, and coffee—heaven after three days of peanut butter sandwiches.

After I spent 12 days of sickness in a Kota Kinabalu hotel, Elizabeth flew down from Kuala Lumpur and we took off for Lahad Datu, site of a Weyerheuser forestry operation. H. H. (Sandy) Bill, son of Harthon Bill of the U.S. National Park Service, showed us around. This was hilly country, and logs were moved to collection sites by high-leading, a network of cables strung up through the forest, thus reducing the roads needed. Albert Ganing took us through the tree plantations, where various species were being evaluated as sources of wood. Tree plantations were seen as a partial substitute for logging natural forest.

I talked to many people about land use and wildlife in Sabah. In 1982 the government policy was to keep about 53-54 percent of the state in permanent forest, since timber was the major source of state income. Thirty percent of the land—mostly lowland—was classified for agriculture.

One interviewee was willing to talk about the difference between plans and reality.

> Only a small part of the 30 percent is in agricultural use.... [Timber] concessions are supposed to be on an 80-year rotation, and are supposed to cut 1/100 of the area each year, figuring the non-commercial area will be about 20 percent of the total. But in practice companies cut as much as they can handle in one year. The Forest Department is supposed to regulate and check the work of companies, but in practice there's not much control. Concessions are handed out as a political matter, and the Forest Department doesn't want to make the politicians mad.

He thought it likely that the Danum Valley, a lowland area with magnificent primary forest recommended by some for a wildlife sanctuary, would be logged within the next 25 years.

He thought the government was making some headway in getting people to move to schemes (like my Iban friends in the longhouses). But the shifting cultivators "like their independence, farm where they want to, take a few days off to drink rice beer. They want the modern conveniences, but don't want extra work or regimentation. Moving to a scheme is a difficult adjustment for them."

In Sabah, as in other parts of Malaysia, lowland primary forest was going to agriculture, forest reserves elsewhere were being logged, though usually not clearcut, the remaining primary forest was on steep, high hills and mountains where logging is difficult or impossible. Professional foresters and wildlife scientists had good ideas about how to maintain productive forests and wildlife populations, but wildlife and forests were losing out to settlers and forest concessioners. Creation of national parks was generally opposed by political leaders.

***

Every ten years, beginning in 1961, a World National Parks Congress has been held. In 1981, when I attended it, it was held on the island of Bali. The setting, of course, was gorgeous. Our cottages, on the edge of the sea, were shaded by palm trees. At low tide a coral reef appeared offshore. A field trip took a busload of us past Bali's trademark bright green terraces, to a small volcano, which we climbed as we talked about the world's conservation issues.

With attendees from many countries, the Congress produced reports on advances and retreats in the development and management of protected areas, as well as on other important conservation programs, such as a Mediterranean cleanup effort. Two opposing themes appeared in presentations: the fortress mentality of some of the old guard, which emphasized protection of parks from incursions of poor local people; and the attitude that parks should be managed in a regional context, trying to find ways to accommodate the needs of the people who surround them. In subsequent years, I believe the latter view has prevailed.

I was there to learn and to meet and interview people. I became acquainted with the current directors of the National Park Service, the National Parks and Conservation Association, the Sierra Club, the Isaac Walton League, and with Bob Cahn, a prominent conservation writer who had been one of the first members of the President's Council on Environmental Quality. I interviewed people from the International Union for the Conservation of Nature, an organization based in Switzerland that does studies on protected area issues and other conservation needs while its sister organization, the Worldwide Fund for Nature, educates the public and conserves critical natural areas and wildlife.

I was particularly interested in talking with the Chinese delegation to learn about conservation issues in their country, but at first they were reluctant. Finally , after deciding on their party line, I suppose, they sat down with me and presented a brochure on the subject. I don't remember anything memorable or useful being said. I think the Chinese would be more talkative on the subject today.

My other interviews yielded articles about national parks in Southeast Asia, mangrove conservation in Malaysia, and some reporting for *The New York Times* science editor, a classmate at Amherst. The trip was eminently rewarding, and I felt, maybe for the first time, like a real member of the world's conservation community.

Back in Kuala Lumpur, I looked for other things to write about. Early on, I had met two British ornithologists—David Wells and Chris Hails—who were teaching at the University of Malaya. They had briefed me on various good birding spots, especially the abandoned road along the top of the 7,000-foot Gentong Highlands behind K.L., where you could look down on the forest canopy and its birds, and hear the booming calls of Siamangs, a large gibbon. Chris told me he had been hired for three years to recommend how to get more birds in Singapore.

This led me into one of the most fun articles I wrote for the newly started *Asian Wall Street Journal*. As Prime Minister of Singapore, Lee Kuan Yew had almost dictatorial powers. He had ordered the city to be beautified with more trees and flowers, and it was beautified. He wanted to create a Garden City. Then he said the island state had too few birds and needed more. Thus the above mentioned hiring.

I flew down to Singapore to follow the story and took a room in a rundown old hotel. I tried to interview the Prime Minister but his aide said he was out of town. I talked with Chris Hails and followed him around. He had established sixteen 1-kilometer routes in various habitats on the island and was recording birds along those routes. He was also recording the associated vegetation, to try to understand why those birds were there. He planned to collect insects on sticky tape to get an idea of the food available.

So far he had found that many of the trees planted in Singapore were not native to the area, and thus local insects might not have become adapted to using them. More native trees might need to be planted. Also, he had discovered that the large, forested Catchment Area in the center of the island was lacking some birds that formerly bred there. They weren't likely to return because of distance from the Catchment Area of present populations of those birds and unfavorable intervening habitats. But bringing some in might restore breeding populations of those species.

Chris was also studying how to reduce the numbers of nuisance birds, such as crows and mynas—something Lee Kuan Yew also wanted.

During the two weeks I was there I made counts of birds in various parts of the island and joined walks with Chris, his wife, and friends. I collected information about Singapore for another article, but that one didn't happen. Maybe I'll return to Singapore some day and see if the Garden City is full of colorful birds and their bubbling song.

Thanks to a ticket from Malaysian Airlines, payment for a previous article, I flew to Medan, Sumatra to investigate Gunung Leuser National Park, in the northern part of that island. This park, about 800,000 hectares (3,089 sq. miles) in extent in 1982, is very mountainous. Eighty-eight percent is above 600 meters (2,000 feet) elevation. The lowland "tropical" Dipterocarp forest, with a closed canopy 30 to 40 meters high, gives way upslope to montane forest with canopy only 10 to 20 meters high, and finally to a subalpine zone above 2,500 meters (8,202 feet), a mixture of small trees, shrubs, and grassland. Gunung Leuser, at 3,381 m (11,093 feet), is the highest point.

The park, according to the Indonesian Nature Conservation Department, was used by 100 tigers, 50 Sumatran rhinoceroses, and an unknown number of elephants out of an estimated 1,500 in Sumatra. The orangutan population in the park was estimated at 930 by one researcher, 2,000 by another. They live in all undisturbed forest up to 1,800 m., though sparingly at the higher elevations. The Draft Management Plan stated that the park had 105 species of mammals, 313 birds, 76 reptiles, and 18 amphibians, about 54 percent of the Sumatran fauna. The park staff—20 administrators and 80 in the field—had many challenges in protecting this wildlife and the habitat that supported it.

Orangutans in Borneo and Sumatra have been declining for decades, but several rehabilitation centers have publicized their problems and reduced the taking of baby orangutans for pets. One—the Bohorok Orangutan Rehabilitation Centre—is in Gunung Leuser National Park, and I was eager to see it. Its director, Dr. Suharto Djojosudarmo, took me up there from Medan in his jeep, along with his wife, little boy, and the driver.

On the way, he briefed me about his work. He had come in 1979, having earned a Ph.D. at the National University in Jakarta and worked with Dr. Birute M.F. Galdikas on a study of orangutans in central Borneo. Between 1973 and 1982, 86 orangutans had gone through the rehab process at Bohorok and had been released into the wild. Twenty-four were being worked with now.

> First they go through one-month quarantine. We check feces, blood, saliva. Usually we give a rabies injection, sometimes TB, polio. They are fed bananas, corn meal, nonfat milk. They are given leafy branches to eat and make nests on a wooden platform in their cage. When they are

two years old we start letting them out each day to climb in adjacent trees.

From my notes:

Today Desi—female—3 years old spent much time in tree eating leaves, etc., then climbed down and went through window of house to search for food. Had bright look in her eyes. Seemed to be deliberating about whether to make friends with me....Meri—female—5 years old built nest in tree near house, 20 feet off the ground last night. 'She's ready to go to the forest,' Suharto said.

If they appear capable, they are taken to the platform area 1 km away in the forest when three, but some are not ready until they are five or so. The orangutans may range 1 km from the platform. Don't always show up for feeding (8:00 a.m. and 3:30 p.m.). They hang around for 3 months to 3 years, depending on the time they were in captivity. Suharto can recognize all of them. 'Every orangutan is different,' he says. 'Sometimes they come to the platform just to see people and don't eat.'

Up to fifty visitors are allowed to watch.

One morning Suharto went with me for the 8:00 feeding. He had labeled 40 trees along the path with wooden signs painted green and white. On the way he pointed out the sounds of argus pheasant, gibbon, siamang, long-tailed macaque, and rhinocerous hornbill. And showed me tiny claw marks where a bear had climbed a tree to get honey from a hive. "I want to know everything in the forest," he said.

Today only nine orangutans showed up. Two stayed away. Youngest of the nine was 3 years old, a little fellow or girl clambering fearlessly in the treetops. The oldest was 8 years old. Sat on the platform with hands on its head. Its dark face looked morose, but Suharto said, 'Just relaxing.' When the two rangers first went on the platform they were surrounded by a moving mass of red hair eager for the milk/cornmeal/bananas. After the food was gone, some left, others just sat quietly on the platform with the rangers, seemingly enjoying their presence. When the rangers left, three orangs continued sitting there, and still remained when S and I left. One orang was up in a treetop, dismantling an old nest and dropping the pieces.

At the Ketembe Research Station, just inside the park on the Alas River, I met five Dutch researchers—Carel Van Schaik and his wife Maria, who were doing Ph.D. research on the ecology and behavior of long-tailed macaques, a couple doing Masters level research on macaques, and a person studying bird populations and species distribution.

Van Schaik was concerned about lack of enforcement of regulations in the park.

> There's much illegal logging, clearing for crops, fish bombing and poisoning....The PPA people [Conservation Department] are mostly from this area. They don't want to make enemies....The Army has strong influence on local and provincial government. The general apparently calls many of the shots. The Indonesian government is trying to reduce the influence of the Army on government. There needs to be pressure from someone high in government to protect the park.

He said that few Indonesians, other than researchers or those in training, came to Ketembe. "Indonesians don't have much interest in coming to see nature [though the orangutan rehabilitation centers were popular]. Most of the people who go to parks, for instance in Java, go for a picnic or to climb a mountain."

A road had been cut through the northern part of the park, and the Army wanted to improve it. He said that might have been to speed Army forces to Aceh Province, at the northern tip of Sumatra, which has independent, separatist tendencies. "There is definite movement of elephants, rhinos, and tigers across [this road]. Clearing all along it would effectively cut the park in two, and separate many species into two populations."

A rehabilitated orangutan around 18 years old, named Binjai, hung around the research station with 7-year-old Ans, her first youngster, born of a wild father, and Ellen, just 1 year old. Ellen, I wrote, is a "cute little thing with big round eyes staring out from behind her mother." One morning when Binjai and her baby were back in the tree in front of my cabin she tried to get my underwear off the laundry line, but the staff people chased her off. Van Schaik said she eats clothes—a recent development.

Nasori Djajalaksana had been the park warden for 1 ½ years. He switched from the Forest Department to PPA "because my heart is not in the cutting of forest." He loved the natural forest. "My main problems are 1) encroachment, 2) hunting, and 3) depredations of tigers, elephants, and pigs in village areas around the borders."

There were no forestry concessions in the park, but 51 around the borders. Forty-four of these were small—up to 100 ha (247 acres) and seven large—up to 10,000 ha. (38.6 sq. miles). There were 34 saw mills around the whole park. "Maybe 40 percent of these saw mills have no concession. I want to close these [because they get much of their wood illegally from the park]." Suharto had told me that villagers around the park cut trees as much as 5 km inside the park and drag them out with one or two water buffalos. "They cut only for their stomachs," he had said, meaning just to get money to buy food. The main form of encroachment seemed to be people clearing a patch of park forest to grow crops. Nasori said he first gives them a warning. If the man makes more ladang he would be taken to court. But in his 1 1/2 years here he hadn't done that. (Niko J. van Strien stated that "fields occupy an area 1 to 2 km inside [the park].")

After saying hunting was one of his biggest problems, Nasori added, "But hunting is not too big a problem now." Soldiers and police had hunted in the park, but that lessened when a "nature reserve" was established where hunting of deer and pigs was allowed. Poaching of rhinos for their horns had been happening, but there had been no evidence of traps or shooting of rhinos in the last three years. Three of the local *pawangs*—men believed to be able to attract rhinos to a trap by magic—had been hired as rangers to stop rhino poaching.

Problems with elephants, tigers, and pigs occurred mainly at villages around the edge of the park. When elephants went into agricultural areas, the practice was to chase them out with fires, carbide cannons, and yelling. Tigers were a more serious matter. In the open northern part of the park and an area outside it, 20 people had been killed by tigers in three years. If pigs were present, a problem in itself, that attracted tigers.

The above description of Gunung Leuser National Park and its management issues was typical, I think, of the situation of "protected areas" in Southeast Asia in 1982.

Subsequent information about forests in Sumatra and Malaysia suggest that national parks and other preserves may provide the last stand for rainforests in that part of the world. In Sumatra an undated report stated that "about 12 million hectares of forest have been cleared in the past 22 years, a loss of nearly 50%."[1] The tropical forest area in Malaysia decreased by 78,000 ha. from 1990 to 2000, and by 140,000 ha. from 2000 to 2005.[2] In terms of percentages, those from Malaysia are smaller than in most other Southeast Asian countries, but the numbers show that the loss was increasing. Most of the remaining forest outside of protected areas is in mountains too steep for logging.

Toward the end of our two years in Malaysia I researched and wrote an article about the effects of selective logging on wildlife in rain forests for *Ambio,* an environmental journal published in Sweden. Pulling together information from people who had studied the matter, and from my own observations, I concluded that a high proportion of the primate and bird diversity found in primary tropical rainforests could return after selective logging, though possibly taking many years, and if there was primary forest nearby to act as a source of the species displaced by logging. The effects on other vertebrates and plants had received little study. The subject needed, and probably still needs, book-length attention; tropical rain forests are extremely complex ecosystems.

13

Nigeria

We arrived in Nigeria in 1983 without children, who were now in boarding schools back in the states. The American Embassy was then in Lagos, a rather chaotic city with dense traffic and few traffic lights that often were ignored. Electric power went off for a while nearly every day. People would say, when this happened, "NEPA [the National Electric Power Authority] done quench." We lived in a duplex on a short street where most of the houses had been robbed. We avoided that misfortune, but the Irish ambassador next door didn't. And one day when workers were cutting vines off our house with machetes one cut our telephone line. Such events seemed typical in Nigeria. Elizabeth continued reporting on economic matters, especially oil, and I began exploring the country.

The vegetation in Nigeria grades from rain forest in the south northward to savanna and then semi-desert, as the climate becomes drier and cooler. Christianity prevails in the south and Islam in the north, a situation sometimes causing bloody clashes. With Mark, my young assistant from Ghana, I began driving about in a new white Land Rover, much easier to drive than the old, trucklike Malaysian one.

My intention in Nigeria was to write a book about Nigerian wildlife and national development, the thesis being that wildlife conservation depends on level of development. To that end I would have to travel all over the country, talk to many people, and read whatever literature on the subject existed. As it turned out, after I had done a considerable amount of research, the book didn't happen. The Oxford University Press turned me down because "the Nigerian market is depressed." I didn't propose it for the Nigerian market, rather for the international conservation community, but oh well, the research was interesting and worthwhile.

One of my more frequent destinations was Kainji Lake National

Park, in the west central part of the country near Kainji Lake, which was formed by a large dam that provided half the country's electricity. The Kainji Research Institute studied the biology of the lake and surrounding lands. I visited the head of the institute to learn about their studies. Such visits, especially one after dark, aroused the suspicions of the Nigerian security people. I learned later that they had been following my travels, and had interrogated the Kainji research chief for some time. But they gave me no trouble.

Quotes from my article in *Defenders* magazine (Jan.-Feb. 1985) will give you a sense of the park. On my first trip to the park I was

accompanied by my assistant and houseboy Mark Boachi and a park guide known to me only as Yusuf. From the town of Wawa we bumped down a track in my Land Rover past small farms lying idle during the dry season. Long before we reached the park boundary, the farm patches gave way to fairly dense savanna woodland with trees up to 30 or 40 feet high. Near a pool of the Oli River, a tall Fulani herdsman watched over his dirty-white zebu cattle. In the custom of the nomadic Fulanis, he had driven his cattle south for the dry season and would return northward after the rains began.

In the days that followed we explored much of the 1,600-square-mile Borgu sector of the park—rolling country, mostly covered with close-spaced trees, that sloped down on the south to the Oli River. The Oli's remaining pools in the western and southern parts of the park provided the only dry-season water other than Kainji Lake at the park's narrow east end. We saw buffalos, warthogs, a few hippos in the deeper river pools, side-striped jackals, and a lovely civet cat. Because it was their breeding season, male kobs in their territories near the river tended small bands of females and their young. Troops of red patas monkeys sometimes crossed the road, and baboons often did. We saw a few tracks left by elephants, now scarce in the park, and many fresh lion tracks [though we never saw a lion]. We walked by the river, taking care to look first for any leopard or python that might be lying concealed in the dense foliage overhead.

Birds of many species abounded. Brilliant blue rollers, multi-colored bee-eaters, iridescent starlings and other small birds foraged near the road, while here and there a

Secretary Bird
(photo by Kent Minichiello)

hawk or eagle watched for prey from a treetop. Occasionally, too, we passed a black, turkey-sized hornbill, and once I
was startled to see a tall, grey Secretary Bird stalking down
the middle of the road.

The park's wildlife, though nowhere near the spectacle seen in
East African parks, was the best that Nigeria had to offer. But many
people said it *could* have five times its present density of wildlife.
The problems and possibilities were easily discovered. Hunting
had been the chief problem. People in villages around the park relied heavily on hunting for food, both legally outside and illegally
inside the park. This was mainly for the family pot. Hunting gangs
did the more serious damage. Groups of five or more men would
camp in the park for weeks, killing most of the game in one area,
then move on to another area. They sold the "bushmeat" under
cover of darkness to local dealers, who in turn sold it to markets up
to 300 miles away.

Poachers, if arrested, even for severely wounding a park ranger,
were given light fines and released. But when Kainji Lake was up-
graded to a national park (the only one in Nigeria), the act creating
the national park provided for fines of 500 to 2,000 naira (officially

$650 to $2,600) or four months to three years in prison for illegal activities. In one year 40 people were arrested, 30 were convicted, and fines and jail terms up to three years were handed down.

"Poaching is decreasing," J.S. Ibeun, the park superintendent said. "If a whole village has to collect 1,000 naira to pay a fine, they will discourage poaching in the future." Heavy fines also reduced the damage Fulani cattlemen caused. And those driving livestock through the 25 miles of the main, Borgu sector were required to do it in one day on one dirt road. Nature may have encouraged quick passage. One morning we saw fresh lion tracks on top of cattle tracks. "It is a mighty one!" Yusuf exclaimed. Lions sometimes follow cattle out of the park, he said, and may kill one when they settle down for the night.

Citizen interest in the park was beginning to grow. Those who come to the park like it very much, Yusuf said. A Nigerian who drove a German family to the park from Lagos saw a beautiful group of kobs near the road. He put his hands to his head, exclaimed "wonderful!" and ran into a tree. Under the circumstances, the Germans forgave him. Local villagers were less enthusiastic about the park, but job opportunities and visitor spending were helping to soften resentment. At the much older Yankari Wildlife Reserve farther east, time had boosted Nigerian visitation and awakened pride in local people that their former hunting land was now a popular preserve.

Yusuf was a very nice fellow. His eyesight was threatened by parasites transmitted by the bite of a river fly, and he hoped he could save enough money to have a corrective operation. I always wondered what happened to him and felt a little guilty that I hadn't contributed to his savings for the operation. I did help him through a dry patch when he didn't get paid because the government was replacing the old currency with new, and I always paid him to guide us in the park.

The best rain forest near Lagos lay to the east in a forest reserve. Large patches of the reserve were being logged, but one section of primary forest, designated the core of the Omo Biosphere Reserve, was so far undisturbed. Biosphere reserves—an international program of UNESCO-- typically have a core area that remains natural, for comparison with the surrounding area, where various kinds of use are practiced, supposedly sustainably, and studied. I don't know if this biosphere reserve had that kind of management, but I at least wanted to see the core area.

I had with me a letter from the government official responsible for biosphere reserves allowing me to visit it. The chief of the nearby village, who was the local guardian, would not be able to read my letter, but he would recognize it by the drawing on it of an elephant and palm trees. I stopped first at the office of the forest reserve manager, a Scot, who explained how to get to the village. The track got rougher as I progressed, with loose planks over rivulets, but my new Land Rover negotiated everything and I soon arrived at the bank of a river, across which lay the village.

I yelled, and two men appeared out of the brush opposite and paddled a dugout canoe over to get me. A third, apparently just curious, lay on a large rubber ball and paddled himself across. They gave me dinner (local fish I think) and I gave them canned food I'd brought. I was ushered to a room of the chief's house where I spent the night. Next morning the chief escorted me to the protected forest. I was allowed to walk around its perimeter but not into it—they took its protection very seriously. I noted a few birds and the impressive size of the trees, but I had to conclude that getting there had been more interesting than this outside view of the forest itself.

I would visit no more primary rain forest in Nigeria. I would, instead, explore savanna and semi-desert to the north.

Yankari Game Reserve, in the central part of Nigeria, lies, like Kainji Lake National Park, in the savanna zone, with tree cover of varying density. Savanna is the zone that holds the most visible wildlife—or maybe the most wildlife—in Africa. And Yankari was a popular destination for school kids and tourists—mostly Nigerian. (Unlike many other countries in Africa, Nigeria is not exactly an international tourist magnet.) From my one visit to Yankari I recall, primarily, a nearby herd of elephants browsing among thick trees near a river, broad patches of their grey hides visible through the green foliage. This reserve seemed fairly well protected and a good advertisement for conservation.

One Nigerian journey, however, surpassed all the rest for absorbing interest and excitement. Mark and I left Lagos early one February morning for a long swing through the northern tier of states, stopping first at Kaduna to pick up some motor oil. My oil level was low, and I didn't want to run out in the back of nowhere. Finding some proved complicated and costly, because of a current paradoxical shortage in this oil-rich country. A "foreign service national" in our consulate in Kaduna knew somebody who knew where oil could be obtained. He rode with me to this somebody's house, and that person joined us on the way to the owner of the oil. The two quarts cost me $60, but I could travel with an easier mind.

We arrived in Kano in mid-afternoon on a Friday, just as the mosques were letting out. Driving down a major avenue I saw coming toward us a river of white-robed men. It was harder than getting through a big herd of sheep—in fact impossible. I backed out of the situation before I had an incident on my hands.

Shortly thereafter I did have one. An old man riding his motor scooter on the shoulder ran into the side of my Land Rover when I made a right turn into a driveway. He sat on the ground, stunned, as a crowd began to gather. I had heard that crowds in Nigeria sometimes took the law into their own hands in such situations, so I asked the federal wildlife officer we had collected here what to do. He examined the man, found that he wasn't hurt, and told me to give him $20 to fix his bent handlebars. I did so, and the man and crowd seemed satisfied.

Traveling eastward, we stopped for the night in a large concrete agricultural storage building near a small village. That evening a man came from the chief, offering us food. We had plenty but sent our thanks for his hospitality. It was rather cold at this time of year, this far north of the coast, and we were in dry country that loses heat rapidly at night. In the morning I crawled out of my sleeping bag early to walk some warmth into my body and saw a large, light-colored bird sitting on a fence some distance away. Drawing closer, I found it was an Egyptian Vulture, my first. Here it was in its winter range, having flown, perhaps, from somewhere north of the Mediterranean. Later, in Turkey and Azerbaijan, I would frequently see this species, soaring above dry mountains.

Waterfowl dominated our next stop, an area of lakes, marshes, and irrigated fields. Hundreds of pintails, Garganeys, and other ducks from the north dotted the lakes. Later, the Nigerian Conservation Foundation, at the request of the International Council for Bird Preservation, headquartered at Cambridge, England, bought land for a reserve here. It used money that an American company (Boos, Allen, and Hamilton) couldn't repatriate and so donated to the NCF. (I had argued, unsuccessfully, for buying a piece of rain forest.)

Here in this dry country we encountered the first of several primitive forms of water management. Buckets on the end of long poles mounted on pivots were dipped into a river and swung around to dump water into small channels between rows of plants. Closer to Lake Chad we saw brushy dams across streams. In this dry season the streambeds were mostly mud, but fish flopped in the pools behind the dams. At Lake Chad the local farmers had planted crops in the wet soil left where the water had receded. They would mature before the soil became too dry or the water rose in the next rainy season.

Our reason for coming to Lake Chad was not agricultural, however. I wanted to see the elephants that lived here in the marshes, elephants that over centuries, I was told, had developed broader feet—an adaptation to the wet substrate. By now we had added to our entourage Baba Grema, a Senior Game Warden in Borno State, a tall, competent fellow. He kept asking villagers if the elephants had been seen recently. After a series of "no's" we drove farther around the lake's edge and stopped for a look. Climbing to the top of the Land Rover to see over the fringing reeds, we spotted large dark objects way out in the marsh. We floundered through bushy swamps until we found the boatman we'd engaged, climbed into his plank canoe, and when it grounded in shallow water walked until we were within several hundred yards of the elephants. We were close enough to hear the rumbling in their bellies as they fed. Then we noticed a large bull following a female, quickening his steps whenever she did. He mounted her and they copulated, a sight I'd read was seldom observed by humans. After a brief encounter, the female resumed feeding but the male started walking toward us. This made us nervous, as we were now some distance from our boat. When we reached it, our boatman began poling urgently back toward shore and the bull slowed his advance. Probably he was just telling us to get the hell out of there, which we were happy to do.

Along the road away from Lake Chad, near the Cameroon border, I was looking at some bird when I saw a truck full of soldiers approaching. Instantly I tossed my binoculars into the car, because of an earlier experience with the military (described below). The truck stopped beside us, but our two Nigerian wildlife officers said the right things and we were not bothered. Incursions from Cameroon--in a border dispute I think—made the military suspicious of anybody in the area.

We now had to get back to Maiduguri, the state capital, across a vast, flat plain, and the sun was sinking. This was a unique black soil area where cotton was grown. It looked like a giant checkerboard, treeless except for a few spots on the horizon where trees announced a village. It was surreal out there as we followed one track after another, sometimes no track at all, asking anyone we met which way to go and generally heading toward the sun. A man on horseback wearing a cape and carrying a lance appeared ahead of us, like a chess piece on this board. Somehow we came out exactly right and entered the tree-lined streets of Maiduguri as the sun set.

Baba took us to the home of a relative, where we first sat in a circle and passed around a bowl of water, each taking a sip—the Kanuri custom. It seemed to me a religious ceremony, like the wine of a Christian Eucharist, but here it was water, in this dry country where water was life itself.

The next day Baba directed us to a game reserve that was a seasonal destination for a herd of elephants that, unlike our Lake Chad elephants, wandered around the state. We saw no elephants, but had a distant view of ostriches running through the acacias. I was so impressed with Baba that later, as he requested, I recommended him for a grant to study wildlife management at New Mexico State University. I hope he got it. And I hope the militants now operating in his area have done him no harm.

Several times in my life my use of binoculars has gotten me into trouble. One incident happened in Benin, next door to Nigeria. We had gone to a Hilton Hotel on the beach near the capital city for a short holiday after Christmas. In swimming shorts and T-shirt, armed with binoculars for birds, I walked up the beach. At first my attention was drawn by fishermen up ahead, but then I noticed a bird on a sand dune, far away at the inland edge of the wide beach, in front of trees screening an airport. I walked far enough to see that it was a Grey (Black-bellied) Plover, then turned back toward our hotel. I saw a soldier between me and the hotel and dropped down the steep bank to the water, hoping to be out of sight of the soldier, as he looked like trouble. Might want to lift my binoculars.

When I was opposite him, he appeared at the top of the bank, yelling something. Then he yelled at another soldier, who came running. That one was tall, had a large tumor on his neck, and carried a rifle. They marched me to their barracks beyond the trees, where I tried to explain to the sergeant in charge in my meager French that I was birdwatching. But I couldn't remember the French word for birds (*oiseaux*). Apparently they thought I had been spying on the airport. The sergeant said they were going to put me in jail. The troops gathered around, enjoying the predicament of the foreigner standing there in his bathing suit. I said something about the U.S. embassy and the Marines they would send looking for me (in English that they no doubt didn't understand). Fortunately, a compromise was reached in which they would take me back to the hotel and inspect my papers. I climbed on the back of a motorcycle and we roared off to the hotel. The manager looked alarmed when three armed soldiers in fatigues and a white guest in a bathing suit came through the front door. Elizabeth looked equally surprised when she opened the door to our room. The soldiers wrote down particulars from my diplomatic passport and ID papers and left.

Meanwhile, my binoculars—8 x 23 Nikons that I'd bought in Singapore—had been confiscated. I figured they would immediately be sold, but miraculously they were returned to me a month later in Lagos. Our ambassador in Benin had achieved this.

Though I did not write a book about wildlife conservation in Nigeria, I did join the Nigerian Conservation Foundation, established by Mr. A.P. Leventis, a wealthy Lebanese with long-term family business involvement in Nigeria, and a few other influential people, including a prominent tribal chief and businessman, Chief S.L. Edu. Leventis asked me if I'd serve as the foundation's executive director, but I demurred, saying a Nigerian would be more effective. A retired Nigerian diplomat, Ambassador Olu Adesola, took the job and did well, I think. I wrote most of the foundation's first two newsletters, as well as a script for a slide program on conservation in Nigeria.

I hope some of the country's oil money found its way into conservation projects, but, considering recent Nigerian history, that is not likely.

14

Turkey

Six years of diplomatic service in Istanbul and Adana made Turkey Elizabeth's favorite foreign country—then and now. Her Istanbul years were filled with high-level associations and activities, interesting friendships, taking on the duties of the consul-general when he was away, and memorable car trips to archeological sites and other places around the country. As Principal Officer at our consulate in Adana, she followed the Turkish army's conflict with the Kurdish PKK, American activities at the nearby Turkish Incirlik Air Base, business developments in southeastern Turkey, for which she received a coveted award, and helped American citizens in trouble.

I caught only glimpses of her life in Istanbul during two visits from the U.S. My experience of Turkey was much broader while living with her in Adana for a year and a half (after I retired from the National Park Service).

American tourists going to Turkey for the first time usually go home with glowing tales about the rich history, shown in a multitude of archeological sites, and the hospitable people. I enjoyed both. But when out birding I tried to avoid the country people, who inevitably would invite me to their home for tea and thus curtail my birding. Unlike most tourists, I spent a lot of time also enjoying Turkey's natural wonders, which include the Mediterranean coast, bird-rich marshes and lakes, high mountains, and environments that range from semi-desert in southeastern Turkey to grassland on the central plateau, conifer and hardwood forests on many mountains, and alpine tundra on the highest peaks.

I visited all such kinds of places, usually alone, driving a rented car. My first car came to me through Yildirim, a "foreign service national" who worked at our consulate in Adana. He knew an old man who lived near Incirlik Air Base who had an old car he would rent for an attractively low price. The price was right but the car wasn't. On my first trip it failed just a few miles out of Adana. A truck driver saw I had trouble and worked on the car's wiring with my pocket knife. The car came back to life, but my knife didn't come back to me. *Hediye*, the trucker said, "present." I returned to home base. On the next trip the battery gave out. I bought a new one, finished my trip, and then rented a newer car, from someone else, for twice as much. Thankfully, it worked fine.

On many of my excursions, I explored the lagoons and marshes along the Mediterranean coast. Those near Adana, in the Cukurova Delta of the Ceyhan River, were full of waterbirds. From fall through spring particularly, the lakes thronged with shorebirds, waterfowl, flamingos, herons, gulls, and terns. A British couple—Geoffrey and Hilary Welch (Hilary wrote the Turkey section of *Where to Watch Birds in Turkey, Greece and Cyprus*)—periodically helped survey the wetlands in Turkey, and one year I joined them in the Delta. We counted some 100,000 waterbirds.

Better known to birders is the Goksu Delta, farther west. More than 330 species of birds—around three-fourths of all those recorded in Turkey—have been seen here. A large lake and marshes, near the inland edge of the delta, is the main attraction. The Society for the Protection of Nature in Turkey (initialed DHKD for its Turkish name) has an office here to watch over and study this Special Protected Area, so designated by the Turkish government. One fine December day I borrowed a canoe from the representative of the DHKD and paddled through the marshy Akgol Lake, putting up Pigmy Cormorants and masses of coots and surface-feeding ducks from the shallow water, while Marsh Harriers and two Lesser Spotted Eagles quartered overhead, watching for infirm prey. Returning toward land I looked in vain for the place where I had emerged from the marshes into open water. That's a disturbing feeling—not knowing the way back—but somehow I muddled through the reeds.

The Goksu Delta is a hotspot for rarities. On other visits I often saw the endangered Purple Gallinule, or Swamphen, and Marbled Teal, the latter then under study by Andy Green, from the Donana Biological Station in Spain. Poking through the reeds I spotted my one and only Baillon's Crake, a small rail. And at the mouth of the Goksu River I saw the rare Audouin's Gull, an adult and a juvenile sitting on the beach. Only a few of this species remain, mostly farther west in the Mediterranean.

An even rarer sight was bestowed on me as I drove through the scattered bushes on the flat, dry outer delta. Suddenly a black-and-white-winged bird appeared, doing strange somersaults in the air over the bushes as it sang. Not large, it had a longish bill and long legs. I followed it on foot, marveling at its antics. My field guide showed it was a Hoopoe Lark, so named for the common Hoopoe of Europe, which has a slightly similar wing pattern. Checking further I found it was native to North Africa and had never been seen in Turkey. Apparently it had overshot North Africa on its spring migration, crossed the wide Mediterranean, and landed on this lonely delta. I looked for it the next day but couldn't find it. The experience is described in my article for *Sandgrouse*, journal of the Ornithological Society of the Middle East.

The Turkish government listed the Goksu Delta as a Special Protected Area not only for its endangered species but also for its rare dune vegetation and its nesting loggerhead turtles. This last feature led me to park my car one moonlit night and walk out to the Mediterranean shore. It was beautiful: the night, the wide sandy beach, the great sea, and just me. I walked a long way, saw many turtle tracks, but no nesting turtles.

The DHKD made protection of such turtles and their beaches a priority, especially at Dalyan, on the Aegean. Here the tourists were required to stay out of the nesting area at night, but were free, and excited, to watch the turtles, from a short distance, crawl up, dig their nest hole, bury the eggs, and lumber back to the sea. Foreign and Turkish visitors took the turtles' needs to heart and conscientiously complied with the rules. In Malaysia I had stood beside a huge leatherback turtle as she laid her eggs, so I knew the awe of this experience. (Apparently, the nearness of watchers didn't deter leatherbacks.)

Among the many historical sites in Turkey are medieval castles. One of my favorites was the Snake Castle, not far from Adana. It sits atop a high hill overlooking cultivated plains and the Ceyhan River, flowing by far below. Its design suggests it was built by the Armenian Crown Prince Leo sometime before 1266, when he was captured by the Arabs. One legend says the castle got its name because it was full of snakes, but I never saw a snake there.

The place *was* full of birds. Besides the many species on the surrounding slopes, I found two of special interest right at the castle. In February 1997, as I approached the battlements, I spotted the usual Black Redstarts and a Blue Rock Thrush on the rocks and walls. Then, near the castle itself something different flashed from one rock face to another. My first Wallcreeper! In winter plumage, it had a pale grey head and throat that contrasted with dark wings that turned black, white, and red when the bird flew. I watched in fascination for some minutes as the Wallcreeper hopped restlessly about, flicking its wings and probing crevices with its decurved bill. Then it flipped out over a wall and went where I couldn't follow. In a month or two it would be back in alpine heights, nesting.

Spring was well advanced when I last visited the Snake Castle, on April 28. My hoped-for bird was the Little Swift, found in Turkey primarily farther east but known to nest in the castle, perhaps its westernmost breeding site in the country. I hadn't seen it in mid-April. This day, however, two pairs were careening around the east end of the castle, in courtship flight, their white rumps conspicuous when they turned. They would fly close together, then veer apart and go solo for awhile. One briefly glided with wings held vertically as a pair zoomed right past me. It was all a splendid farewell to the castle for me—the swifts exhuberantly cleaving the air with Barn Swallows and Red-rumped Swallows, the plain spread all around below, under benevolent blue, white-clouded sky.

Southeastern Turkey is the driest part of the country and home to a number of bird species not found elsewhere in Turkey. I found some of those birds, but of most interest to tourists was the very rare Bald Ibis. There is no question about *finding* the Bald Ibis because all those in Turkey nest at a station near Birecik on the Euphrates River, in nest boxes erected for them or on adjacent cliffs, and are fed pans of ground meat and corn. This is a strange-looking large black bird with red face, long curved red bill, and long feathers flying off its nape. In the late 1990s these birds and a few in Morocco, to which Turkish breeders in the past migrated for the winter, were all that remained of the species. The station, operated by the Forest Department, was manned by two wardens working in 12-hour shifts around the clock.

Entering the station through a gate in a high fence, Davut, a guard at the U.S. consulate in Adana, and I passed by a large watchdog on a chain. Ibises were perched around the nest boxes or sitting on eggs. Late nesters were flying in from across the river with sticks in their bills. "We have 50 birds this year," one of the wardens said, a number encouragingly higher than the mere handful a few years earlier. "Last year they raised 30 young but 20 flew away and never came back. In June and July we will get the birds into cages for the rest of the year," hoping to do this before any young took off.

Turkey is a land of mountains. Almost everywhere you see mountains—close or far away. As a mountain lover, I had some of my most interesting experiences on them. From Adana, on a clear day, we could see the snow-capped Taurus Mountains to the north, which run west, paralleling the Mediterranean, for several hundred kilometers. My favorite birding place in these mountains was Demirkazik, at 12, 323 feet (3,697 m) the loftiest peak in the Taurus. To reach Demirkazik you drive up a lovely mountain valley with a perennially rushing stream flanked by poplar groves and apple orchards to the village of Demirkazik and the Mountain and Ski Centre. Here you have two choices: walk up the open slopes to the south of the Mountain Centre—my usual route--or up the deep, narrow gorge to the north of it.

One bird I was hoping for was Radde's Accentor, a scarce bird, and in mid-March I saw it, foraging under barberry bushes in a gully, right at the snow line. A shy bird, it mostly remained hidden but occasionally came into sight, showing its black face and crown and prominent white supercilium (eye stripe). Sparrowlike, it was not impressive but gave me joy because I had been hunting it for so long.

Radde's Accentor breeds in the subalpine zone of high mountains from the Taurus of central Turkey to eastern Turkey and the highlands of Armenia and Iran. It requires scattered low bushes, grass, patches of bare ground, a nearby water source, and rocks or large boulders for shade. It nests only in juniper or barberry bushes. The main threat to it is heavy grazing and the burning and cutting of bushes. Since sheep and goats graze most of the year on the slopes of Demirkazik, I wondered how they and their herders might be affecting the bird. Sheep avoid such plants, but I worried about the unparticular goats until I watched one approach a barberry bush. It took a couple of small nips near the top, avoiding the thorns, and then walked away. Perhaps goats were not a big threat. Firewood was scarce on the mountain, and I hoped the herders weren't cutting barberry bushes for fires. (Grazing and browsing by sheep and goats are a serious ecological force in the Middle East.)

On my last May 10 in Turkey I finally walked up all the way to the high rock wall of Demirkazik's peak. Snow Finches flashed white as they fled over the bushes. As I watched them a Golden Eagle came flying down a gully low and right over me. It probably had been perched on a rock, watching for sousliks (a ground squirrel). At the foot of the mountain's rocky crags, a spring pipe spouting water had created a green basin where Alpine Choughs and Water Pipits were feeding.

I was contemplating this magnificent scene when I heard the croak of a raven. Following it through my binoculars I saw it swerve and dive at a Lammergeier, which took evasive action into a gorge. When the raven passed on, the Lammergeier lazily glided along the walls of the gorge, its shadow easier to follow than the bird itself. It was an adult, its head and underparts buffy-rufous, its wings long and narrow and tail long and wedge-shaped—more like a falcon in appearance than a typical vulture. Later it dove at a Griffon Vulture, flew alongside it for awhile, then rose on a thermal and glided westward. It seemed to crown the scene, to epitomize this dramatic, remote terrain.

I could not find Caspian Snowcocks, my most-wanted bird, on Demirkazik, so I tried a 10,000-to-12,000-foot section of the Taurus Mountains known as the Aladaglar—the westernmost end of the snowcock's range in southern Turkey. The party I organized for this expedition was rather unusual. It consisted of Erdogan, our Turkish friend from the consulate in Istanbul, a former Commando in the Turkish army and three times heavyweight boxing champion of Istanbul; Huseyin, our household cook; Cavit, our stocky, gray-haired guide; a donkey that carried our gear, and me.

The route looked steep and a long way up. As an out-of-shape sexagenarian with an unease about heights, I worried about what my guide book said: This route "is not recommended if you are unfit, unsteady on your feet or nervous of heights." However, there was no sheer drop off along the path, and if you fell you wouldn't slide very far. More discomfiting was the thunderstorm that descended on us as we neared our camping place. We came over the final rise to see the tents of villagers from the valley below with their sheep and guard dogs. Cavit knew one of the women in this group and we ducked into her tent.

It was rounded, framed with long curved branches and covered with plastic and canvas. The rain had found a hole in the plastic and dripped onto the dirt floor at the front of the tent. Around the edges were piled the accoutrements of transhumant life: pots and pans, bags of small sticks and large gnarled pieces of juniper for firewood, a pile of wool and a spindle of spun yarn. Against the side of the tent huddled a week-old lamb. It peed, fortunately on the dirt part of the floor. A kangal—a large and ferocious dog used for guarding sheep—I knew never to go between a kangal and its sheep—walked stiff-legged past the round opening of the tent, eyeing us.

When the rain stopped, we put up our tents nearby and Huseyin spread a feast on a carpet. We were in a grassy swale at 9,000 feet, with peaks all around us. Our neighbors would be up there all summer grazing their sheep. We would be there one more day, looking for large, gray-brown, grouse-like birds that spent the night in the crags above and in the morning flew down a gully and worked their way back up, feeding.

As darkness settled, from our tents we could hear the cries of a baby, the scolding voice of a woman, the barking of dogs. Many sheep and a few goats had been milked and now were being driven by the men and boys down across a deep valley and up onto the far green mountainside. Faintly the sound of their bells came across the yawning space.

Next day we were out at dawn, stationed on a rise that gave us a good view down the ravine we had climbed the day before. For a long time we watched for the white in wings of a flying snowcock. Erdogan saw one, I didn't. But we could hear their calls from the distant cliffs: "kek-kek-kek," chuckling sounds, and then a loud "ooo-leee!", a call like that of curlews on northern European meadows.

As the morning wore on the others went back to camp and I decided to go look for the calling birds up in the ravine. It was maddening. Nearby, "ooo-leee!" would sound from the rocks and echo all around, but I couldn't spot the caller. I started picking my way farther up, admiring the small lavender, red, and yellow flowers huddled among the rocks. In some places the rocks were half covered with green plants, and I noticed one such green patch far upslope, near the head of the ravine, lit by a shaft of sunlight. I was looking at it through my binoculars when a snowcock walked into my field of vision! It pecked around among the plants and rocks, apparently unaware of the two-legged creature down below. I kept moving up a few more yards and watching the bird, which stayed in the same patch, disappearing for minutes at a time, then magically reappearing. It sat on a rock and preened, then moved on.

At the next advance, I saw small birds following the large one. Three chicks, only a fifth their mother's size, were pecking around like her, getting their food as they had since breaking out of the shell. Now the mother saw me and became alarmed. "Oo-lek!" she called. I knew she would herd her chicks higher up, away from me, so I turned back down. But I had seen snowcocks, in a way I never expected—in a glimpse of their daily family life. "Thank you, God!" I exclaimed.

Nemrut Dag is a 7,000-foot mountain in southeastern Turkey north of Adiyaman. Atop the mountain rises a tumulus where Antiochus—"the Great King, God, the Righteous, Epiphanes, the Romanophile and Hellenophile," as he called himself— probably is buried.

Elizabeth and I were driven to Nemrut Dag after lunch with the district sub-governor, escorted by a truckful of gendarmes. (The Kurdish PKK had been chased out of the area but the regional security people weren't taking any chances with official visitors.) We stayed at a hotel part way up the mountain, with four guards who mostly played cards, and rose next morning at 3:30 a.m. to go to the top.

There we found a crowd of people, shivering in a cold wind, waiting for the sunrise—the most dramatic moment on Nemrut Dag. Soon the sky reddened in the east and the sun broke over the dark mountains. It took the edge off the chill and lit the awesome scene around us. We stood on the east terrace, which was the principal sanctuary of the *hierothesion* because it faced the rising sun. Behind us, at the foot of the tumulus, sat on thrones a row of five colossal statues representing a mixture of Greek and Roman deities, including Antiochus himself, deified as *Theos Epiphanes*, "the God made manifest." The heads of all except Tyche had fallen off over the centuries and lay scattered below them on the terrace.

Amidst all the people, rocks, and ruins, a pair of anxious Rock Thrushes came and went, feeding young in a hidden nest. Bird song floated in the air, so I walked around, looking for the sources. Snow Finches, conspicuous in this now-snowless place, flashed away. I admired the clean black and white plumage of a male Finsch's Wheatear perched on a rock. Then I walked past the remains of the north terrace to the shaded west terrace, where another row of the gods and Antiochus sits. When the other visitors departed, I stayed. I wanted to be alone in this place.

It was an eerie experience. Here most of the statues and all the heads had fallen down, shaken perhaps by earthquakes. The seven-foot-high heads had been placed upright, facing toward the sea of mountains to the north. Though the staring eyes were stone, I felt the presence of these gods, in these barren mountains. Time had gone back two thousand years.

Then I had the notion to walk down to our hotel, not ride, and look at nature rather than history. A Shore Lark flew off as I climbed around the side of the tumulus. Along the stone path small alpine flowers bloomed and Crimson-winged Finches got up. It appeared that sheep and goats had been kept off, allowing the low native plants to flourish on the rocky mountainside. At the teahouse Rock Sparrows flew into crevices in the walls where they probably had nests. Inside, I noticed a cage holding a Chukar, a favorite game-bird. I had been told that the caged Chukar, when placed in Chukar habitat, calls and attracts its fellows to a snare or waiting hunters.

Continuing down, I saw a pair of Cinerous Buntings, carrying food for their young. This species, described as "rare and local" in one of my field guides, was a first for me. So also were the Tawny Pipit and White-throated Robins. Soon I began seeing Red-tailed Wheatears, the males black-throated and grey-backed with a rusty rump. Here they were at the western end of their range but surprisingly common. From distant slopes came the "poo-poo-poo" of a Hoopoe, that amazing bird with the flashing black and white wings and enormous crest of brown feathers.

The 3 ½ -mile walk was totally satisfying—good birds, no sheep or goats, and hardly any humans, just a few on horses or donkeys, come up here to gather grass for winter fodder. Scattered bushes but no trees gave a wide open view. It was a high point of all my days in Turkey.

Sultan Marshes

Turkey has lost, and continues to lose, many of its wetlands through drainage for agriculture. But many remain and harbor great numbers of waterbirds. Waterfowl from the north come in winter; breeding waterbirds, such as flamingos, move in from the south in spring, and migrating shorebirds and others pass through in spring and fall. The wetlands are magnets for an impressive array of smaller birds as well. The Sultan Marshes, south of Cappadocia, one of the best, with 120 species of breeding birds and more than 130 other visiting species. This site deserves its fame among nature lovers.

Coming from the south, you cross a low ridge with volcanic deposits eroded into turrets like those of northern Cappadocia, and see before you a broad valley backed by the majestic mass of snow-capped Erciyes Dagi. Within the valley you glimpse the water of lakes and, in the growing season, the green of marshes.

My first visit was in mid-April. Most of the birds I saw were flying, a small suggestion of the many that were undoubtedly hidden in the wetlands below them. Garganeys, Red-crested Pochards, and Mallards circled and dropped down out of sight. In more direct flight, Glossy Ibises, egrets, Purple Herons, Pygmy Cormorants, and a few shorebirds swept from one part of the marsh to another, while Marsh Harriers and an occasional Black Tern quartered over the reeds. High above the Sultan Marshes my first, two-toned Booted Eagle was soaring. It all suggested an even more exciting morning the next day, when I would take a boat trip into the marshes.

However, I had heard that ordinary tourists are apt to treat this as a lark, with radios blaring, and serious birders, unless they're the first of the day, are likely to get minimal rewards. This is in keeping with a common approach to nature in Turkey—as a place to picnic, have fun, test your physical skills, but not to enjoy nature itself.

So I took an early-morning boat trip, hoping to see waterbirds before they were scared out of their concentration areas. I climbed into a flat-bottomed boat poled by a small boy. Just ahead of us, another boat filled with Dutch birders pushed away from the soggy landing. We had no blaring radios, but our boatman kept up a constant chatter with the boatman ahead, and wouldn't slow down when we wanted to get a better look at something back in the reeds. Further dampening our spirits, a light rain settled in. Huddled under raincoats, we passengers tried to train water-spotted binoculars on passing birds as the two boatmen poled us ever deeper into the marsh through winding channels. The rain kept getting heavier and the wind stronger, and finally we decided there was no point in continuing.

In late October I came back and followed the strategy recommended by birders: work around the fringes, using what roads are available. Again it was raining, so I drove slowly to avoid sliding off the muddy tracks. This time I got good looks at Moustached Warblers picking insects off open vegetation mats in the marsh. This is a reddish-brown bird with dark brown cheeks and forehead and white eye-stripe that breeds locally in marshes from the Caucasus to the Mediterranean coast of Spain. This was also a better-than-average day for raptors. Besides the expected kestrels, Long-legged Buzzards, Marsh and Hen Harriers, I came across a group of Red-footed Falcons hunting grasshoppers from telephone wires and a Peregrine perched in a bare tree near the road.

In a small restaurant near the marshes I warmed up with a cup of coffee and flipped through a book of notes written by visitors. In addition to Turks, there were French, Germans, British, Dutch, and Americans. I read an entry by Jim Clement, from California, who identified himself as the author of *Birds of the World: A Checklist.* I later bought a similar book, intending to find out how many of those species I've seen, but so far the effort to find my lists from the

countries I've lived in or visited has been only partially successful.
Soguksu National Park

Driving north through the center of Turkey, you eventually leave
behind the dry, rolling steppe land and cross a succession of mountain ranges paralleling the Black Sea coast.   Each range is better
clothed with vegetation than the one before, and each is greener on
the north side than on the south. When you reach the north slope
of the last range, you find truly luxuriant forests—deciduous at the
lower elevations and coniferous higher up, with alpine meadows
and snow much of the year above about 2,500 meters (8,300 feet).
The vegetational richness here is due to substantial year-round
precipitation caused by eastward moving low-pressure systems
along the coast in winter and moisture-bearing northerly winds off
the Black Sea in summer. A rain shadow on the south sides of the
mountain ranges produces the sparser vegetation there.

Turkey has several natural national parks. My favorite was
Soguksu National Park, in the mountains north of Ankara. It is
small (1,050 hectares. 2,310 acres) but richly forested with oak,
pine, beech, and willow at the lower elevations and aspens, fir, and
Scotch pine farther up. A 16 km (10-mile) loop road runs from the
park headquarters up through this forest. The park's name refers
to hot springs, two of which feed swimming pools at the *Cam* (pine)
Hotel near the park entrance.

With Davut, the bodyguard, at the wheel, John Christie, a Scot-
tish family friend, and I arrived in mid-May and checked into the
hotel. We found we were the only guests, except for members of the
Turkish Olympic wrestling team, who were training for the Olym-
pics in Atlanta two months hence.

As a retired U.S. National Park Service writer, I wanted to learn
something about the management of the park, so with Davut as
interpreter I visited the superintendent. He was a short fellow, very
serious and dignified, with a small, trim moustache (as opposed to
the bushy moustaches of so many Turks). He ran his park, I learned,
with eight employees, although a private contractor handled trash
pickup and security. The hotel was government-owned but was
managed by a private firm. "People come here mostly to picnic or
swim in the pools for health," he said. (Not like me, to enjoy the
forests and look for birds.) The mammals, seldom seen, included
bears, wolves, wild boars, foxes, jackals, and rabbits, he said, but
no deer as in some of the forests farther west. I was relieved to hear
that hunting was not allowed.

Early next morning John and I hiked up the loop road. Grape Hyacinths and other spring flowers were blooming along the roadside, a stream rushed somewhere below, twisted old Black Pines rose against the sky, where clouds opened and closed. Now in mid-May the leaves of deciduous trees were just half open, light green and fresh.

The world holds promise on such a day. I accepted with thanks the appearance of Hawfinches, Kruper's Nuthatches, and Redstarts, among other birds. But the best came later—one of the rare birds I'd been seeking. John was well out of sight ahead when I approached a picnic shelter on a high ridge. Suddenly, from behind the ridge, two giant Black Vultures came soaring, perhaps disturbed from their roost by John. They circled low right above me, displaying their long, broad wings, wedge-shaped tail, and unpatterned blackness, then disappeared back over the ridge.

When I returned a year later, in early April, there were few signs of spring, other than a few swelling buds, some tiny yellow and lavender crocuses, and the songs of Chaffinches, Blackbirds (a thrush), and Mistle Thrushes. The oak trees still held dead brown leaves, and patches of snow remained in sheltered places.

On the highest part of the road, around 5,000 feet (1,500 meters), I encountered continuous snow and ice, so parked and walked. Bands of Coal and Great Tits, occasionally accompanied by a Short-toed Treecreeper, provided most of the avian action. A Great Spotted Woodpecker drummed loudly in the pine forest, and a few European Siskins and Common Crossbills fed on pine seeds. Below the most elevated saddle a goshawk rose from the forest and circled until it was high overhead, then disappeared behind a ridge.

But this day mammals provided even greater interest—some the superintendent had mentioned. I soon discovered from its tracks in the snow and mud that a brown bear had walked the road, probably during the previous night. A particularly good set of tracks in mud clearly showed the 5-by-5-inch front feet and the larger hind feet, about 5-by-6 inches. Perhaps it had been checking trash cans along the road, as park bears often do. Another set of tracks, about 4 inches long, looked like wolf or large dog.

Farther up, from a side road, I spotted a fox trotting along a track in the valley below. With its thick grey coat, bushy white-tipped tail, pale face and black muzzle, its colors matched those of the grassy slope it began to investigate. I was only about 200 yards away, plainly visible, but so intent was the fox on its hunting that it didn't see me. It sniffed and searched and then suddenly jumped to a certain spot. It had sensed a rodent that dove into its tunnel. The fox began digging, pausing now and then to stick its nose in the hole to locate the direction of the prey. Finally I saw a thrust of the head and jaws working to kill and swallow the little animal. Then the hunt resumed. I walked down the trail until I was only 75 yards away and then the fox saw me. It froze, staring at me, then ran down the hill.

The next morning I took the counterclockwise route up the loop road. At a young oak forest the small, round-toed tracks of a wild pig crossed the muddy road. Nearby I saw rooting and a couple of water-filled wallows. High up, in a saddle between peaks, I again parked the car and walked, because snow filled the road ahead. A light snow was falling—the vanguard of a rare, widespread April snowstorm—as misty clouds swirled through and a hazy sun appeared.

Once again, the mammal world intruded. Something had followed the road for a long way, leaving 4-toed, 4-inch-long hind tracks and 3-inch-long front tracks in the foot-deep, crusted snow. It was heavy enough to once in awhile break through the crust, as I was frequently doing. Pine marten, I concluded. It would have been hunting rodents and red squirrels, such as the one I'd seen on the way up, its red tail gleaming against the snow as it bounded into the forest.

The snow kept falling, and I considered returning to my car, not wanting to get snowbound up here. Fortunately, however, I continued, and a few minutes later a Bullfinch—my first—flew across the road into a young aspen. It was a male, deep rosy red below, with a black cap. Like a Christmas tree ornament it glowed amidst the white flakes. I felt lucky, because the Bullfinch occurs through most of Europe, but it's not easy to find in Turkey, being restricted to some of the mountain forests in the Black Sea coastlands.

Two days later I was farther west at Abant, beside a snow-and-ice-covered crater lake surrounded by fir, spruce, and Scotch pine forest. At 6:30 a.m. the thermometer by the hotel entrance read 10 degrees F. The air was still and now snowless, but when I returned from my brisk walk down the valley road snowflakes were again falling. And in a tree on the hotel grounds four Bullfinches—three males and a female—were eating buds. I think I will always associ-

ate Bullfinches with falling snow.
Kizilirmak Delta

The Kizilirmak, one of the major rivers of Turkey, empties into the Black Sea near Samsun, forming a delta some 30 kilometers (18 miles) wide and 25 kilometers (15 miles) deep, the largest and most intact wetland on the Turkish Black Sea coast. The best birding is in the lake-dotted, marshy eastern half, offering the birder 500 km2 (300 sq. miles) to explore.

I won't detail *my* explorations there, because, although I did see various waterbirds, my time was depressing because of getting lost and having a flat tire during three rainy days. Instead I'll describe some of the problems this important conservation area is up against, as are so many other valuable wetlands in Turkey. Sunay Demircan, one of the DHKD staff members at Kirzilirmak, told me that DHKD expected to close that office in 1997, after five years of studies, management planning, and educational campaigns.

He said there were five main problems.

(1) DSI (the state water institute) had developed an irrigation/drainage plan that would destroy much of the wetland, but DHKD had gotten them to change the plan so that most of the wetland would be preserved.

(2) Two dams built in 1990 and 1992 on the Kizilirmak River south of the delta reduce sediment reaching the coast, which results in coastal erosion.

(3) From April to November 1,000 cattle and 3,000 water buffalos grazed on the eastern half of the delta. The water buffalos, especially, fed in the marshes.

(4) Illegal building of holiday houses along the shore continued, some of it in the wildlife-rich forest area. People cleared and burned some of the forest, then showed the Forest Department there were no trees, and the department allowed them to build.

(5) Sewage, fertilizers, and pesticides were polluting wetlands. Conservation efforts would have to continue if the natural riches of the delta were not to be gradually destroyed. (As of 2018, more than 350 illegal summer houses had been demolished, allowing regrowth of forest there.)

After the three days of rain and difficult birding, late on the last day I did get a reward. Along a drainage channel, its yellow head and breast glowing in the grey light, a Citrine Wagtail flew by. It lifted my weather-born depression and lit up my day. This gorgeous wagtail breeds from Russia to northern China, and is mainly an uncommon migrant in Turkey. After much looking, I had finally

seen it.
Caucasian Black Grouse

The north side of the coastal range was aflame with mid-October orange, yellow, and red deciduous trees as I drove along the coastal road. Ruins of ancient fortresses crowned a few seaside hills. Wherever streams came rushing down mountain valleys to the sea, gulls bathed at the mouth. Fishermen in small boats plied their meager trade.

West of Trabzon I turned up a road beside the Iyidere stream, headed for the mountain village of Sivrikaya. Along the way, women were cutting winter fodder for their animals. Neat rows of tea and hazelnut bushes broke the surrounding forest. A man fly-fished—a sport of the affluent that I hadn't noticed elsewhere in Turkey.

At Sivrikaya, you have passed above the tea and hazelnut zone and entered Swiss-Alps-like country, where log houses are perched on steep mountain meadows, the high-altitude spruce forest has become scattered patches, and nearby snowy peaks form the backdrop.

I was looking for the Caucasian Black Grouse, which lives in and around bushes in alpine and subalpine meadows. Although an estimated 70,000 inhabit the Greater Caucasus of Georgia and Azerbaijan, only a few hundred are left in the Lesser Caucasus of Armenia and Azerbaijan, and similar numbers remain in the coastal range of northeastern Turkey. It is a prize for birders in that country.

Having missed the bird at one place where they were said to occur, I sought the help of Mustafa Sari, a local guide who one book said "knows the mountains and the bird well." I finally found him as he came down a trail leading a small horse loaded with firewood. Mustafa was thirtyish and genial. With one of his neighbors we conferred about the Caucasian Black Grouse. "They are difficult this time of year," Mustafa said. "Hiding." But he was willing to give it a try.

We got in my car and drove to a chained side road. He unlocked the chain and we proceeded up the dirt road, switch-backing ever higher up the open slopes, getting stuck momentarily in rocks where a stream crossed the road, and stopping a couple of hundred yards short of the first rhododendron patch.

"You stay on the road," Mustafa indicated. "I call if I see black-cock," pronouncing the name as if it were one word. He climbed the slope swiftly and soon was entering the top of the low rhododendron thickets. Almost immediately I heard a yell, looked up, and saw four male grouse, their long black tails streaming behind, flying high and fast, out across a deep valley and disappearing over the next ridge, a kilometer away. Perhaps only birders understand the excitement I felt at this sight—the difficult quarry, its wild flight, the special bird found after long travel and doubt, in this wonderful open mountain space.

Some guides and some birders might have considered the quest finished at that point. The bird had been seen. It was safely on the life list. But fortunately Mustafa didn't give me time to consider that option. If four black grouse were good, more would be better. "Come," he said. So we continued walking up the road, then followed cow paths along the green slopes. Some flowers were still blooming: yellow buttercups, blue harebells, a white daisy-like flower. When we came to rhododendron patches, Mustafa sent a few rocks tumbling down, but they scared up no grouse. He pointed out two plants the grouse like to eat, one with berries still on the bushes. He showed how the grouse sleep at night, in a circle, beneath the thick, two-foot-high rhododendrons.

Finally we worked our way over the next ridge, where more rhododendrons covered the north-facing slope. We were part way through this when we heard wings below us. Four male black grouse—quite possibly the same four—went sailing down and again disappeared over the ridge beyond.

By this time I was limping along pretty slowly on a knee I had strained several days earlier. This, and two grouse sightings, apparently convinced Mustafa that we had achieved enough. He sat down for a smoke before the return hike. With his few words of English and my few of Turkish, aided by my pocket dictionary, we talked about grouse, local animals, this place in the mountains. The grouse are supposed to be protected, Mustafa said, but men from Trabzon come up here and hunt them with dogs. "The police do nothing," he added disgustedly. In winter the black grouse go down into the spruce forest, he explained, where the snow isn't so deep. The snowcocks, which summer on the high crags, can feed through deeper snow. He thought in winter they go lower but not into the forest.

I asked about animals around here. "We have polecats [pine martens]. Sometimes they catch the blackcock. And sometimes foxes do too." (I love the Turkish word for fox—*tilki*. It so beautifully conjures up the pert little ears and nose and the dainty step.) There are usually four or five wolves around, he said. "People shoot them if they can." And one or two bears roam the area.

He talked about his village, too. It was obvious he loved Sivri-kaya. I could tell it was a hard life up here, but a beautiful place to live it. We could see a house or two down below, a patch of forest across the main valley, snow-covered peaks above. White clouds drifted in a blue sky.

When we reached the village, I asked how much I should pay him, but, as usual in such situations, it was up to me. I gave him 3 million Turkish lira (about $30 then). This seemed to please him mightily. He invited me to the tea house. As we sipped glasses of tea at one of the tables surrounding a wood-burning stove, he described to the others our day and, I surmised, told who I was and where I came from. Among the nine men was one, inexplicably formal, in a grey suit and tie. He wanted to know if I spoke German. (No.) A young man in a jacket and khaki trousers—the village schoolteacher—looked nonindigenous. No doubt sent here from some city, he appeared, and probably felt, rather alien. A stray horse wandered down the road and one of the men intercepted it and brought it to the door. The horse tried to walk in. Everybody laughed.

When I left, I thanked Mustafa profusely, embracing him with the traditional two-cheek hug. Then I drove up to the pass, parked the car, and walked out across the rocky alpine meadow. No one else and no bird was there. Just the cool wind, the sky, and the peaks. I gave thanks to God/Allah, or whoever or whatever directs the course of things, for the day I had had. Like the day on Nemrut Dag, it was one that would always stand apart.

Migration Bottlenecks

Spring and fall, hundreds of thousands of raptors, of some 35 species, migrate through Turkey, along with up to 800,000 or so storks and lesser, but still impressive numbers of other large soaring birds such as White Pelicans and cranes. Turkey is a funnel for such birds going to or from Eastern Europe and Russia around the eastern and western ends of the Black Sea. Most of them do not cross the Mediterranean because they are incapable of a long overwater flight; they require rising air, which usually does not occur over large water bodies. The flight matches or exceeds the numbers crossing at Gibraltar, which channels most of the West European and Iberian trans-Saharan migrants. Smaller crossings of certain species capable of direct sustained flight occur in between, such as over Malta, Crete, and Cyprus. Most passerines, on the other hand, can cross anywhere.

In Turkey, migrating raptors and other large soaring birds are concentrated at three bottlenecks: the Belen Pass area at the northeastern corner of the Mediterranean, the Bosphorus at or near Istanbul, and the Black Sea coast around Hopa, in the northeastern corner of Turkey. In the fall, most migrants coming around the west side of the Black Sea, on their way toward the east end of the Mediterranean, take the easiest, most direct route across the Bosphorus. Those coming around the east end of the Black Sea find the coast turning westward when they enter Turkey and so look for the lowest mountain crossings, especially in cloudy weather, to direct their flight southward. These crossing areas occur along the Coruh River valley and in the vicinity of Hopa. Many of the latter migrants, and most of those crossing the Bosphorus, go through the Belen Pass area, on their way down the rift valley that runs from there on through Israel and into East Africa. It is assumed that raptors take various routes between the Bosphorus and the northeast corner of the Mediterranean, including passes in the Taurus Mountains such as that north of the Goksu Delta.

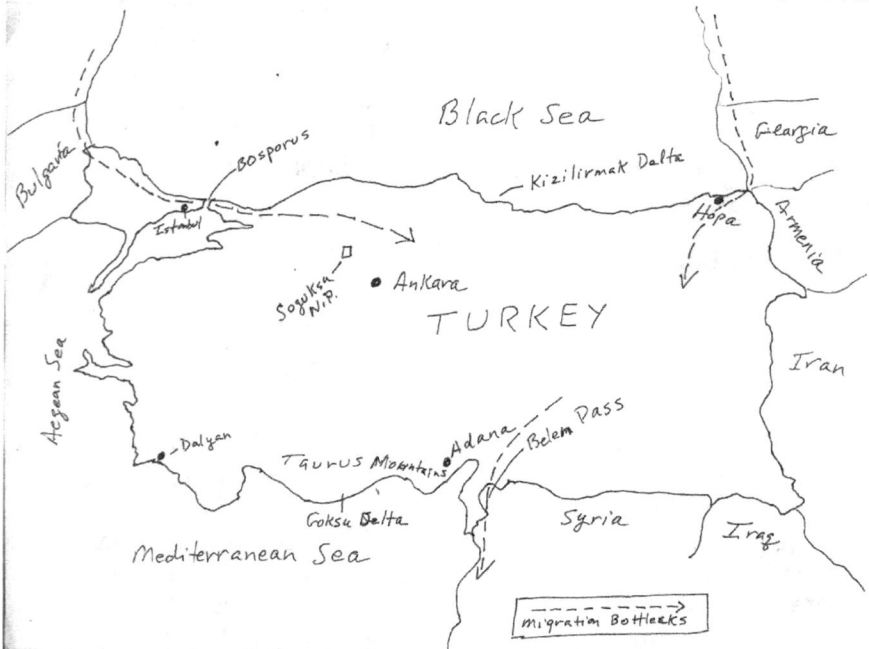

In spring, the birds follow these routes in reverse, although in smaller numbers and with some differences of species. The most numerous species in early spring is the Common Buzzard, most of which are Steppe Buzzards, an often red-tailed subspecies that breeds in Russia. In late spring Honey Buzzards and Levant Sparrowhawks predominate. The timing of the various species correlates with their feeding and nesting requirements in the breeding range. For instance, Honey Buzzards and Levant Sparrowhawks, both of which feed heavily on insects, may migrate later because their prey is more abundant in late spring. Common Buzzards, on the other hand, feed mostly on rodents, which are in good supply earlier.

During my last spring in Turkey, I finally fulfilled my vow to check out the migration at the Belen Pass. March 26 was sunny with scattered clouds, but a stiff north wind was blowing. Relegating to the subconscious my wife's warning about PKK activity and a recent jailbreak in this area, I stationed myself on a dirt road leading off to the south side of the pass and scanned the skies. In spite of the north wind, a lot of storks and a few buzzards were moving. Some birds flew low, perhaps to avoid the wind, working their way up to the pass. Some of the White Storks got part way up and then turned back. Most of the storks and buzzards, however, circled up in thermals over the wide, flat rift valley running north beside the Amanus Mountains, and when they had gained enough height, glided over the pass on the higher, snow-dusted mountains. Between 9:30 and 12:00, I counted 685 White Storks, 25 buzzards, 2 unidentified harriers, and a juvenile Spotted or Lesser Spotted Eagle.

The Belen Pass was relatively close to Adana, our home, so I made three more trips that spring. On April 18 there was decent weather, with some blue sky showing between white clouds—the clouds helpful as a backdrop to dark birds high up. A pattern seemed to be emerging. Some 1,200 White Storks went over between 10 and 11 o'clock, then the flight of storks dropped off dramatically the next couple of hours. The same sort of thing had happened March 26, and did again April 28. I thought perhaps many storks spent the night out in the rift valley fields nearby and therefore didn't have far to go to the pass the next morning when the earth had warmed sufficiently to create rising air. April 28 was also enjoyable for a flock of 15 white Spoonbills and a sprinkling of raptors, including buzzards, Lesser Spotted Eagles, Eurasian Sparrowhawks, a Common Kestrel, an unidentified harrier, and my first Hobbies.

The flights were tapering off by May12, my last visit to the pass. Between 9:30 and 12:00, I tallied 436 White Storks, 8 Black Storks, and 24 raptors, including my first and only Honey Buzzard. (I never caught one of those big Honey Buzzard days, in spring or fall).

When raptors or storks weren't moving, I just enjoyed the scene from this high point: the mountains running north and south, the broad valley below, and local villagers passing by: some boys with shotguns carrying a Woodpigeon they had shot; a man with a donkey laden with firewood. Two old men stopped to see what I was doing. One looked through my telescope. He was surprised when I said the birds were coming all the way from Africa. The other said something about Amik Golu, a large lake in the valley that held great numbers of waterbirds before it was drained for agriculture in the 1960s.

My numbers of birds in spring were enjoyable but not nearly as impressive as those seen by others during the fall flights at the Belen Pass. W.J. Sutherland and P.J. Brooks, who made systematic counts in 1976 between August 20 and September 23, recorded 26,755 raptors of 22 species. Two-thirds of these were Honey Buzzards and Levant Sparrowhawks. Storks, most of them White Storks, were even more abundant—86,190. Besides all these, 6,203 White Pelicans and 586 Spoonbills were seen coming through the pass. It must have been quite a show.

In the fall of 1996 I planned to drive up to Istanbul to catch the migration phenomenon there, but circumstances kept me from going at the peak time—late September. On the phone Ali Ilhan Tirali, a young man who worked at DHKD, told me excitedly about the great numbers of Levant Sparrowhawks, Honey Buzzards, Common Buzzards, and Lesser Spotted Eagles that had passed over after being held up by several days of rain. I hoped that when I got there some of the show would still be on.

It was October 5 when I finally got to Istanbul. The best raptor-watching points are Sariyer Hill, west of the Bosphorus and now difficult of access because of a military installation, and two hills just east of Uskudar—Buyuk Camlica and Kucuk Camlica. I arrived at the top of Buyuk Camlica, the higher of the two eastern hills, at 8:30 the next morning. Tour buses full of American, German, French, and Japanese tourists were already arriving, along with local citizens up for a Sunday outing. They all headed for the tea house and the tree-shaded tables beside it. I headed for the open lawns where views were best. The sky was clouded over and a cool north wind was blowing. I kept looking out to the west, where tall communication towers rose, but no raptors appeared, just some flocks of swallows and swifts, and once a bunch of bee-eaters flying, inexplicably, north.

At 10:30 I gave up on Buyuk Camlica and took a taxi to Kucuk Camlica, where the top is more open and did not have a tea house. I sat on a wall and waited, enjoying the distant view of the Bosphorus and lower Istanbul. About 11:30 the clouds began to separate and some blue sky appeared. At noon the first Steppe Buzzards came over, sailing past and then grouping to catch a thermal and circle higher before the next glide eastward. The buzzards were easy to identify by their red tails. The Lesser Spotted Eagles, only slightly bigger, had wings of more uniform width, looking more squared off at the tips, and they held them angling slightly downward, as opposed to the slight upward tilt of the buzzards' wings. As the eagles turned in the sunlight, I was often able to see the contrast between the lighter brown wing coverts and the darker flight feathers, a pattern that is reversed in the very similar Spotted Eagle. Once in awhile a sparrowhawk flew over, and a few small falcons that I never identified seemed to be hunting in the area. It was a riveting afternoon, with only short breaks in the action.

Around 4:00 they stopped coming. I had seen some 300 raptors, along with a late White Stork and several more flocks of bee-eaters. I walked happily down the hill through tall twisted pines and past clusters of picnickers, all undoubtedly oblivious to the drama overhead.

I was totally content with my afternoon's tally, but some days can be much more spectacular. Dave Gosney, in *Finding Birds in Western Turkey*, says that during the peak period, usually between the 20th and 25th of September, "if conditions are just right, you might see up to 6000 Buzzards, 5000 Lesser Spotted Eagles, 2000 Black Storks, 800 Short-toed Eagles, 150 Red-footed Falcons and 100 Booted Eagles in a day. Late August would be better for White Storks (up to 50,000 in a day), Honey Buzzard (up to 8000) and Black Kite (up to 400) and mid-September would be better for seeing swarms of Levant's Sparrowhawks (up to 2000 per day). All these species should still be seen in smaller numbers during that peak September week."

So great is the number of storks that hardly anyone can fail to notice them. An American friend of Elizabeth described this phenomenon in a letter: "From my office...overlooking the Bosphorus, I used to see the flocks of storks going past at certain times of the year, and I found it quite wonderful, quite other-worldly. The Turks would stand at the windows, silent, watching, and when the birds had gone out of sight, they would say what good luck it was to see the storks flying."

The migration point in northeastern Turkey is not as well known as the Bosphorus crossing, but the one relatively complete count, made in 1976 from August 17 to October 10 by J. Andrews and others, produced some 380,000 migrating raptors of 28 species. A complementary count the next year, from October 11 to October 25 by M. Beaman, recorded a little over 7,000 birds of prey of 18 species. Common Buzzards and Honey Buzzards constituted over 90 percent of the two-count total, with Black Kites a distant third. The latter count had higher numbers of Steppe Eagles, and one species—Merlin—that was not seen during the earlier count, perhaps indicating that these two species migrate through distinctly later than the others. The counts here showed some interesting differences from those at the Bosphorus: There was a much higher total of individuals but very few Levant Sparrowhawks and Black Storks, and no White Storks at all, although White Storks and good numbers of Levant Sparrowhawks pass through in spring. I haven't seen any explanation for this seasonal difference. One species seen in modest numbers in the northeast but not at all at the Bosphorus—Steppe Eagle—has a more easterly breeding range.

There are two practices at the northeast bottleneck that are seldom seen at the other two bottlenecks: shooting of raptors and capture of sparrowhawks for falconry. The shooting is done for sport or to feed the shrikes used to lure sparrowhawks into nets. Falconry is an old tradition in Turkey, going back at least to the time of the Crusades (11th and 12th centuries). But by the mid-20th century, it had faded nearly everywhere in Turkey except in the northeast. There it continues to flourish. Because of the high toll of raptors and decoy shrikes taken by this practice—all totally illegal under Turkish law—Gernant Magnin, a Dutch ornithologist who worked for DHKD, conducted a detailed study of the situation. The description that follows is based on his report (Falconry and Hunting in Turkey during 1987).

Having crossed the Black Sea, Common Quail migrate through northeastern Turkey from about the beginning of September until mid-October. Trappers capture migrating sparrowhawks, small bird-eating Accipiters used by falconers to hunt quail, during the whole month of September. They, or others—often young boys— begin the process back in August by pouring soapy water into holes where mole crickets reside, forcing the insects out. A cricket is placed in a wire cage, which is set out where Red-backed Shrikes, which pass through in August and probably the first part of September, can see it. When a shrike goes into the cage after the cricket, it trips a spring shutting the cage. The decoy for capturing sparrowhawks is now in hand.

Falconers build blinds of leafy branches and other natural materials and repair them at the beginning of each fall migration season. These are positioned in the coastal hills between Rize and Hopa, often in bushes or a forest clearing, and in a place with a good view to the north or northeast, the directions from which migrating sparrowhawks usually come. The trapper carries to his blind a net fastened to bamboo poles, one or more shrikes, and a shotgun. He sets up the triangular or rectangular net beside the blind and watches through an opening in the blind. When a low-flying sparrowhawk appears, the trapper holds out behind the net a stick with a blind-folded shrike attached to it and jiggles the stick, causing the shrike to flutter up and down. If interested, the sparrowhawk dives at the bird and is caught in the net. (This is somewhat similar to the method frequently used in other parts of the world by hawk-banders.)

The sparrowhawk is kept at home by the trapper for several days to accustom it to humans. It is fed bits of meat and eggs and frequently stroked. When the bird has calmed down in human presence the trapper sells or gives it away or takes it out himself for hunting. Falconers hold the bird in their hand and when a quail is flushed fling it javelin-style toward the quarry. The sparrowhawk carries its prey to the ground and sits on it. The falconer then takes the quail or, if the sparrowhawk refuses to give it up, places a dead quail beside it to distract it. Few sparrowhawks, apparently, fly off during hunting. Most falconers or those who keep sparrowhawks just as pets release them during the last week of October.

This falconry and pet-keeping exacts a heavy toll on Red-backed Shrikes, raptors shot to feed them, and on sparrowhawks. Magnin estimated that each trapper kept an average of 2.5 shrikes and that there were about 4,000 trappers in the Rize-Hopa coastal zone. Of the 9,000 or 10,000 shrikes released in mid-October, after the trapping season, he believed that most would have lost their migratory urge, would have had a hard time finding insects or other suitable prey during the winter, and would perish. He concluded that the total number of sparrowhawks trapped each year could be conservatively estimated at 15,000 and the number dying as 10,000 — shot to feed decoys, dying of disease, or released after the quail season too late to proceed with migration, in a region already saturated with normally overwintering sparrowhawks. Probably 15,000 other raptors were shot to feed the decoy shrikes.

This tradition is carried on simply for pleasure or sport. A relatively small number of quail is actually caught this way. Those who hunt quail for food use the much more efficient shotgun.

Another Run-in with Gendarmes

The day I went to this northeastern bottleneck area, hoping to watch the late migration of raptors, brought something else.

I had taken the winding mountain road to the small town of Borcka, walked 5.5 km (3.3 miles) up a rough dirt road to a knob with a good view north down the Coruh River valley, south up the Coruh valley, and west to snow-covered peaks of the Kackar Range glistening in the sun. Down at the foot of the mountain the Coruh River wound through Borcka. Behind me the small dome of a village mosque rose above the trees.

It was a beautiful day—too beautiful. My bird-finding guide had warned me about this: "For good numbers of birds in autumn, rain and cloud are essential; on clear, sunny days the [raptors] fly high and pass unseen." This day was totally cloudless. I trained the binoculars repeatedly in all directions, including straight up, and saw nothing—nothing except a lone sparrowhawk, probably local, chasing a crow. From time to time I heard shooting down below. I assumed it came from the gendarme camp by the river—a target range probably—but even through binoculars I couldn't locate the source.

Around 1:00 I gave up and started the return hike. Immediately I saw four local men ahead, obviously curious about what I was up to. When I came abreast of them one insistently motioned me over. This man, with a lean dark face and wearing a purple wool cap, questioned me vehemently. My few words about *kuslar* (birds) and *kartal* (eagle) didn't seem to satisfy him. He imitated my looking all around with the binoculars. Eventually the others got through to him that I didn't understand what he was saying. The men then remained silent. One with white hair and mustache just squatted on the ground and smiled.

Then a young, black-bearded man wearing a white sweater invited me—insisted rather—that I come to his house for tea. I was curious about this little community on the ridgetop and gladly accepted. We passed the mosque, whose call to prayer I had heard earlier, and the schoolhouse beside it, and proceeded to the last house on the road, the home of the *imam* who was leading me.

Inside we took off our shoes and I was ushered into a small parlor where books were piled on all the chairs. I noted a television set, radio, a camera, some quinces on the floor, and on the walls three framed quotations in Arabic, I assumed from the Koran. He set his two small boys to making tea, motioned me to the sofa, and we tried to make conversation. I learned that it was cold there in winter and the snow was sometimes three feet deep. I tried to explain that I was from the American consulate in Adana and had been birdwatching. In my field guide I showed him pictures of the birds I had seen on the way up, and in my pocket notebook my list of those birds. But he didn't seem very interested in the birds. He turned on the television and flipped from one channel to another, usually coming back to some sit-com in Turkish.

As we sipped tea, he yelled out the window at one of his neighbors and phoned somebody. I thought I heard the word *turist*. Soon people came wandering in. I recognized the smiling white-haired man, now with his grandson, the man in the purple wool cap, this time making a friendly gesture, I suppose because I was a guest in somebody's home. During the ensuing conversation I heard the name Mohammed several times. I wondered if they were talking about a neighbor or the prophet. When the room was nearly full, the *imam* cleared off a small table, pulled up two chairs, and brought in soup and noodles. He and I were eating when another young man came in carrying a walkie-talkie. I inquired if he was the local *ogretmen* (teacher). He shook his head and smiled. Then another man in the room placed two fingers across his upper arm. Comprehension began to dawn and I asked the young man who had come in if he was a gendarme. Still smiling, he pointed out the window, where four gendarmes with automatic rifles stood around a military jeep.

After I finished my soup and noodles, everyone filed out and I was escorted to the jeep. Cramped in the back of it, I waved sardonically at the *imam*, who I thought looked a little ashamed or even guilty for turning me in. As we bounced down the road, the young corporal looked through my day pack—bird guide, mosquito spray, rain jacket, and all—but was disappointed to find nothing incriminating. We came to a hairpin curve and the driver asked him to look out and see if we were going to make it. If not, there was nothing for a thousand feet down to stop us. The corporal nodded O.K. I held my breath as we proceeded.

Now it occurred to me that the earlier conversation about Mohammed might have revolved around the question whether Mohammed the prophet would approve of the *imam*'s having me arrested. Was this the sort of hospitality one should extend to a stranger? And I wondered what would happen at the headquarters below.

Fortunately, the episode in Borcka wasn't quite so traumatic as my experience on the beach in Benin. The corporal thought he had a live one—somebody spying on the gendarme camp from above. At headquarters I was surrounded by suspicious gendarmes, one of whom thought I had a camera concealed in my binoculars (the same pair, incidentally, that had been taken from me in Benin). He took them outside to look through. Then they woke up the young man who spoke the most English and I explained to him how lots of Europeans (an exaggeration) came here to watch the raptor migrations. This conversation and my consulate identity card, in Turkish, seemed to turn the tide. The captain told them to let me go. I was offered tea or coffee in apology. I declined but as I walked out the door thanked the corporal for the ride down the mountain.

Later I wrote Hillary Welch and Dave Gosney, in Britain, about the dangers of following their advice here. Moral: do your birding out of sight of anything military.

Nature Conservation in Turkey

During the 1990s, while I was living in Turkey, I attempted the following assessment of the country's conservation efforts. I go into considerable detail on Turkey because Elizabeth was posted there for six years, I lived there for a year and a half, and we have a continuing relationship with the country.

In 1990, about 41 percent of Turkey's population was rural—about 23 million people. Although the percentage and total number of rural people have declined over recent years, with heavy migration to cities, the number of rural inhabitants remains higher than the land can sustain without damage (at least under present practices). The consequence has been smaller farms (children inherit land equally) used more intensively, and increased planting of marginal lands. Herds of cows, sheep, and goats have grown well beyond the capacity of rangeland to support them without degradation, and they graze illegally in forests, removing ground cover and reproduction of trees. According to TEMA, a private conservation group, 90 percent of the country's rangeland is seriously overgrazed. The result of overgrazing and current farming practices is moderate to severe erosion on 80 percent of Turkey's land area.

This erosion not only reduces the productivity of the soil and silts up rivers and lakes, but also decimates the flora and fauna. Turkey has some 8,800 species of vascular plants, of which more than 30 percent are endemic (found nowhere else). Some are wild relatives of crop plants such as wheat, barley, lentil, and apple and thus contain important genetic resources. Others have medicinal or horticultural value. The natural vegetation taken together provides habitat for thousands of species of animals, from micro-organisms to mammals. The intense use of land has eliminated the native vegetation from large areas, along with animals, from butterflies to bears, that are dependent on these plants and plant communities.

The same sort of thing is happening to seas around Turkey. Overexploitation, added to the severe pollution from land sources, is reducing fish populations and other sea life. Fishermen feel they have to fish all the harder, and often disregard regulations, in order to make a living.

Air and water pollution are escalating because of growing urbanization and industrialization and increased use of fertilizers and pesticides in agriculture. The pollution control laws are inadequately enforced and financial resources for pollution control are low. Our city of Adana, for instance, with a population of 2.2 million, had no facilities for sewage treatment other than collection pools where organic waste is oxidized. The rest went untreated into the lower Seyhan River or directly into the Mediterranean. A project to build proper facilities *was* underway, however. Other Turkish cities on the Mediterranean also lack adequate sewage treatment.

Wildlife, my chief concern here, suffers from all this pollution and loss of habitat. It also faces an enormous amount of unregulated hunting. "Turks are hunters," one DHKD official told me, and this tradition begins early in life. "Everywhere in the countryside you see small boys with slingshots or homemade bows and arrows. With adolescence they graduate to .22 rifles and shotguns." Developed areas are not immune to their hunting: I once saw some boys with a .22 walking along the main highway through Adana looking for birds to shoot. According to Gernant Magnin, "In Turkey some two million people possess a shotgun and the required license to possess it. Another one to two million people keep a shotgun without a license. Of the registered shotgun-holders, some 1.2 million people also possess a hunting license, and of this number 14,000 — 16,000 are considered fur-hunters, the rest are mainly bird-hunters."

Turkey has quite detailed hunting laws, including huntable species, protected species, seasons, daily bag limits, allowed hunting methods, areas where hunting is prohibited, fees and fines, as well as special regulations for foreign tourists. The police, gendarmes, people from the Forestry Department, and "voluntary hunting inspectors," are responsible for enforcement of the laws. In some areas, enforcement is fairly strict, but in many others, little enforcement takes place. The result, to a dismaying extent, is people hunting whatever, whenever, and wherever they like. Rare species, like Dalmatian Pelicans, fall to the gun, and Protected Special Areas are often hunted.

In view of all these problems, where does Turkey now stand in the protection of nature and the environment? As suggested above, the country's environmental and hunting laws could go a long way toward conserving its natural resources if the laws were better enforced. A number of government agencies have responsibilities in environmental and natural resource protection. Chief among these are the ministries of Environment and Forestry. The latter has jurisdiction over all areas considered forestland (about 26 percent of Turkey) and conducts extensive tree planting in these areas. The Authority for the Protection of Special Areas comes directly under the Prime Ministry. At the local level, municipal governments have considerable influence on environmental matters.

Private conservationists frequently mention two problems having to do with governmental management of natural resources: These agencies tend to make decisions without conferring with the local people directly affected; and they have difficulty cooperating with each other. Management plans such as the one for the Goksu Delta will require overcoming both of these problems.

National parks, nature parks, nature conservation areas, and natural monuments fall under the jurisdiction of the General Directorate of National Parks and Wildlife, which is a subdivision of the Ministry of Forestry. Most of these areas are relatively small; they total about 865,000 ha.(3,339 sq. miles), slightly more than 1 percent of the total land area of Turkey. If Protected Special Areas and other lands with some legal protection are added, the total would probably approach 2 percent. Conservationists often propose 10 percent of a nation's land area as a rule-of-thumb minimum for reasonably adequate protection of biological diversity. Among OECD (Organization of Economic Cooperation and Development) countries, of which Turkey is one, six had surpassed the 10 percent level by 1989 (Austria, West Germany, Luxemburg, New Zealand, Norway, and the United Kingdom). So Turkey has a long way to go.

As of 1995, Turkey had established 31 national parks ranging in size from 264 ha. (0.91 sq. miles) (Yozgat Pine Grove) to 88,750 ha. (305 sq. miles) (Beysehir Lake—mostly water). Most are smaller than 40,000 ha. (137 sq. miles). A management plan is required for each national park, but as of 1997 only about six or seven had well developed plans.

Although hunting, grazing, and woodcutting are prohibited in national parks, shortages of staff make enforcement difficult. Perhaps not surprisingly, and assuming no hunting, plants and animals flourish best on military bases, which are well protected from intruders. Botanists, I am told, are tempted to search in such places.

Interpretation of national parks, in the form of literature, signs, and guided tours, seems to be better in the cultural than in the natural national parks. In a natural national park you may be able to obtain a descriptive brochure if you ask for one, but there probably won't be a highway sign saying you are entering the park or any signs or exhibits pointing out natural features. As for seeing and understanding the flora and fauna, you're on your own.

Between 1988 and 1990, 12 Specially Protected Areas were declared and established by the Cabinet of Ministers. These are areas with unique natural or cultural values based on national and international criteria. Those values are to be protected, and agricultural and other development is to be planned and conducted so as not to diminish those values. The Authority for the Protection of Special Areas was established to study, plan, and protect these areas. Nine of the 12 SPAs are on the Mediterranean or Aegean coast. Many inland sites, especially wetlands, would seem to merit similar protection. Two SPAs in particular—Goksu Delta and Belek, which has 25 km of sandy beach used by nesting sea turtles and also intense touristic development, with condominiums and golf courses—will be good test cases for the accommodation of development to natural values. They will show whether the SPA designation has any lasting benefit.

As noted earlier, Turkey's natural heritage includes many species—plants especially—that are wild relatives of important food species. These include wheat, barley, lentil, chickpea, pear, apple, plum, cherry, walnut, olive, pistachio, chestnut, and hazelnut. The country also harbors unique adaptations of pine, fir, and cedar found nowhere else; wild relatives of aromatic, spice, and industrial crops such as anise, coriander, oregano, and poppy; and herbaceous and woody ornamentals, including tulips, daffodils, snowdrops, and Cedar of Lebanon.

A World Bank project begun in the mid-1990s through the ministries of Forestry, Environment, and Agriculture and Rural Affairs, with the assistance of foreign experts, established pilot Gene Management Zones (GMZs) to conserve such valuable genetic resources, with emphasis first on the food plants. Preference was given to forest and agricultural areas that were already under some kind of state protection or management. The uses in GMZs were to be managed to protect the species and natural communities of concern. A national plan was developed to extend the network of GMZs to cover the entire country and to protect economically valuable non-food species and "land races"—primitive cultivated varieties.

Some of the national parks and most nature conservation areas were established to protect unique forest ecosystems and rare tree species. The GMZs, if widely created and protected, will extend conservation to wild relatives of crop, medicinal, industrial, and ornamental plants. One would hope that Turkey's total system of protected areas will eventually also encompass other categories of the country's rich biological diversity, and that these areas will truly be cherished and maintained effectively.

One day I lectured a landscape architecture class at Cukurova University about progress on environmental issues in the United States. I touched on forest and wildlife conservation, soil erosion, air and water pollution. At the end I listed what I thought were the main influences in achieving progress: the role of national leaders such as Teddy and Franklin Roosevelt; the role of well-known public figures such as the cartoonist Ding Darling and the actor Robert Redford; the role of religion and culture, such as Native American reverence for nature; the widespread revulsion at flagrant destruction of nature, such as the slaughter of bison and extinction of the Passenger Pigeon, the Dust Bowl, huge forest fires, and deep gullying of hilly cropland; awareness created by books such as *Silent Spring*, television programs, newspaper articles, and education by conservation groups and schools; and the betterment of people's lives through economic development, freeing people to think about betterment of the earth as well.

A student asked me which one I thought was most important. As I fudged an answer, saying all were important, the class's teacher confidently broke in: "economic development of the people." He may have been right, for all countries, not just the United States. Many countries, like Turkey, have good environmental laws that are not adequately enforced, and national parks that are not well protected. For such good intentions to be realized, there must be a citizenry that supports them, and such a citizenry probably does not arise until the general economic level is high enough to allow most people to think of something beyond putting food on the table.

In Malaysia I found environmental awareness and concern mainly among the more affluent urban dwellers. In Nigeria, the leaders of the fledgling Nigerian Conservation Foundation were mostly wealthy businessmen and a few important tribal chiefs. The same general thing appears to be true in Turkey, where members of the upper-middle and upper classes and academics seem to be the groups most conversant with environmental issues. Students, at all levels, are beginning to show interest. But Turkey has only a small (but growing) middle class and a minute upper class, and until these grow considerably, the majority of people will probably rank environmental protection as one of their lowest priorities. Environment is not yet a major political issue; I don't know of any politician who was elected or defeated, even partly, on the basis of his or her stand on environmental issues.

Let's return to my list of factors that triggered widespread environmental concern and action in the United States and see how they apply in Turkey. I am aware of no leading public figures, in or outside of politics, who have championed the environment in Turkey, although a few businessmen of some stature, such as Hayrettin Karaca, founder of the conservation organization TEMA, have been active in this field. As for religion, the Koran says much about care of the earth. In his book, *Green Deen* (green religion), Ibrahim Abdul-Matin says,"I sought out Muslims who are committed to being Stewards of the Earth (k*halifah),* who understand the oneness of God and His creation (*tawhid*), who look for signs of Allah (*ayat*) in everything around them, who move toward justice (*adl*), who seek to protect the delicate balance of the natural world (*mizan*), and who honor our sacred trust with God to protect the planet (*amana*). Happily, what I discovered is that Muslims are involved in every aspect of the stewardship of the Earth."[1] This, however, was in America. Religious faith *could* have an effect on environmental concern in Turkey, but apparently not yet strongly.

Environmental events that made news *have* had an effect on public awareness and attitudes. One day our ambassador to Turkey, Mark Grossman, Elizabeth, and I met with several professors and the Rector at Cukurova University to talk about environmental issues. The ambassador asked if certain events had triggered the beginning of environmental concern in Turkey. Hunay Evliye, head of the university's Environmental Research Center, said yes, that the building of a nuclear power plant on the Aegean in 1980 had aroused opposition. The plant was not used. Also of importance, she said, was the nuclear accident at Chernoble, serious air pollution in Ankara, and the Gulf War and "black rain" that came from burning of oil wells in Kuwait.

The journalist David Tonge wrote that "The first Turkish newspaper article I have been able to trace on the environment appeared in *Cumhuriyet* in 1978...." Now the Turkish print and electronic media frequently carry environmental news. I saw articles in the *Turkish Daily News*, the country's principal English language newspaper, on a great array of subjects. A few headlines suggest the range and tone: "Bears also affected by the April 5 austerity package"; "Turkey joins international movement to save endangered wildlife"[CITES]; "Rising waters threaten bird sanctuary"; "Turkey experiencing 'catastrophic' level of erosion from deforestation"; "Environmentalism and enforcement" [solid waste]; "The environment concerns everyone, but is everyone concerned about it?" [air and water pollution, garbage]; "And Istanbul's hunt for water goes on and on"; "Cycling for the environment" [bicycling]; "World's children in Turkey to discuss environment." Turkish-language newspapers, however, seem to publish fewer environmental articles than the *Turkish Daily News* does.

Private conservation organizations have been springing up in Turkey since the 1970s. Three appear to me to be particularly active: the Environmental Problems Foundation of Turkey; the Turkish Foundation for Combatting Soil Erosion, for Reforestation and the Protection of Natural Habitats (whose acronym for the Turkish name is TEMA); and the Society for the Protection of Nature in Turkey (DHKD).

The Environmental Problems Foundation, headed by Engin Ural, a lawyer, is based in Ankara. It is especially strong in writing environmental legislation and in researching and publishing reports on subjects such as population policy, environmental law, and clean energy sources. It periodically revises its publication, *Environmental Profile of Turkey*, which covers air and water pollution, soil, flora and fauna, energy, solid waste, pesticides, and noise. Among its biological reports are *Biological Diversity in Turkey* (1987) and *Wetlands of Turkey* (1989).

TEMA was founded in 1992 by the industrialist Hayrettin Karaca, a white-haired gentleman now in his 70s who all his life has loved plants and gardens. At Yalova, south of Istanbul on the Sea of Marmora, he created a magnificent arboretum, now one of the three official storage points of seeds of plants endemic to Turkey. He has given 80,000 plants to help establish 26 other arboreta. His love for Turkey's native plants and concern about the threats to them from overgrazing, soil erosion, and poor forestry practices led to his founding TEMA, but he had been outspoken on soil erosion for years before that.

TEMA, based in Istanbul, already has more than 3,000 members and the support of many prominent businessmen. It campaigns through all available media for protection of Turkey's land resources, gives talks to school children, and organizes seminars. With the assistance of a scientific council made up of scientists from various universities in Turkey, it is conducting pilot rehabilitation projects at several locations, showing villagers how to restore and maintain grazing land. TEMA is also working on a soil erosion map of Turkey that will provide the data about erosion on which to base remedial action.

"Are Turkish citizens becoming concerned about soil erosion?" I asked staff members at TEMA headquarters. They said they find that children are very sensitive to the subject. "Adults are not so sensitive, except for the highly educated. We have not had much response from farmers."

DHKD, the Society for the Protection of Nature, has had a similar experience. "The children are more receptive than the adults," said Murat Yarar, then head of the Wetlands Section. "We need one or two more generations for good progress." Which is not to say, however, that progress has not already been made. From the time DHKD was founded, in 1975, until 1985, it had no premises, no staff, and no funds. In 1997 it had spacious offices, a staff of 28 professionals, 7,500 members, and funding from a number of sources, both national and international. From begging the government to listen to their views on environmental issues, they had achieved a stature that caused government officials to *ask* for their views. They had played a significant part in getting the environment onto the national agenda.

DHKD conducts environmental education through many channels—school talks, publications, television, newspapers, and others—but its chief activity is on-the-ground conservation. It began this work in 1986, when plans to build tourist hotels at Dalyan, where there's an important turtle-nesting beach, became publicly known. DHKD succeeded in publicizing this threat and stopping the project. Today DHKD has a Coastal Management Section that is working to protect all 17 important turtle-nesting beaches in Turkey, through cooperative planning with developers, government agencies, and others. Its Bird and Wetland Section is doing the same for Important Bird Areas (an international designation). It produced a detailed publication about some 100 such areas in Turkey and is pressing for protection of these wetlands and other places. In 1992 it began its Indigenous Propagation Project, aimed at protection of wild bulb species, such as snowdrops and cyclamen, through establishment of artificial propagation centers. These supply plants for export to replace the widespread, unsustainable collection of such plants from the wild.

The enthusiasm and professionalism of groups like DHKD, TEMA, and the Environmental Problems Foundation give hope that their concern for the environment will eventually be adopted by large segments of Turkish society. Effective action, however, may depend on the future political direction of the country. When Refah, the Islamist Welfare Party, gained the Prime Ministry in 1996 it filled slots in the bureaucracy, including the ministries of Environment and Forestry, with its members. Often these people were selected solely on the basis of party affiliation, not experience or ability. According to Professor Hunay Evliye, the other political parties at least have stated environmental policies, even if they do little, but Refah didn't even have such written policies. In general, Refah wanted to undo many of the Western-oriented reforms of Ataturk and move toward Islamic government, with a stronger link with Islamic governments elsewhere and fewer ties with the West. For instance, it reduced budgets for symphony orchestras, which mostly perform Western music, and was phasing out the use of English in teaching public high school courses, other than English courses themselves.

Refah subsequently was declared an unconstitutional party because it was based on religion, but Islamist sentiment is not likely to go away in Turkey. Western ideas on conservation, such as national parks, may again come under attack.

Underlying everything, in the long term, the cultural heritage of Turkey may both help and hinder the progress of conservation. Many Turks love nature in general. Witness, for instance, the popularity of picnics in natural surroundings. But conservation requires both a love of nature and a scientific understanding of it. I find Turkish feelings about nature to tend toward being fanciful and sentimental. Major wetlands are called "Bird Paradise." But protection of those wetlands depends not only on caring, but also on knowledge of the ecological relationships involved, including human impacts on the ecosystem.

The scientific approach is tied in with the whole question of Westernization, a process that the majority of Turks seems to favor but one that the cultural heritage seems to hold back. In his book, *The Emergence of Modern Turkey*, Bernard Lewis describes this difficulty:

> The adoption of European science, requiring entirely new attitudes as well as techniques, proved far more difficult [than the adoption of European approaches to history, archeology, language, and literature]....It was easy enough to teach the new knowledge, with a scientific instead of a religious authority behind it. It was quite another matter to inculcate and develop the scientific mentality, without which no real scientific progress is possible. A Turkish psychologist, in a recent appraisal of the progress of Westernization, sees in this the cardinal failure of the whole movement, and warns his countrymen, especially the intellectuals, of the consequences of their inability to master this fundamental element of the modern civilization of the West. Some have held that Western civilization derives from Greek, Latin, and Christian sources, and that therefore the Turks, who do not share its classical and Christian heritage, cannot hope to become full participants in it. To them, he replies that modern Western civilization is, in essence, not so much classical and Christian, as scientific. Therein lies the cause of past failures, and the hope of future success, in the Westernization of Turkey.[2]

What then, is the outlook for the land and other natural resources of Turkey? Turku Altan, a professor of landscape architecture at Cukurova University who has conducted many environmental studies, is pessimistic. Even if Refah goes out of power, he said, government inaction and inflexibility, along with widespread poverty, work against environmental gains. "There's a hard bureaucratic wall. They have blinders on and only see straight ahead. It's difficult to introduce new ideas." As for the countryside, "there's been little governmental help to rural areas in the last 15 years." And such help is sorely needed. "If you have enough money to live, then you will think about conservation. Otherwise, they will take from nature all possible things. Every year we lose more natural areas. There are only a few small lights for the future," he concluded. "It's mostly darkness."

Hunay Evliye is not so pessimistic. She sees environmental awareness gradually growing, among all segments of society, and she believes the citizenry has the power, when concerned enough, to push the politicians toward beneficial environmental action.

The above discussion applies to Turkey around 1995. My request for current information about environmental progress or decline sent to an environmental organization was not answered, perhaps because of fear of retribution. As of 2018, the situation is probably being affected negatively by the administration of President Erdogan, who is gathering more and more personal power. People are afraid to do or say anything that might look like opposition or criticism. Freedom of the press is a thing of the past. Many journalists and academics have been jailed for what they said or wrote. The failed military coup in 1916 led to thousands more people, including military officers, being jailed or fired from their jobs. Environmental organizations may be able to continue their work only if it remains scrupulously apolitical. A major airport being built north of Istanbul in a stopover area used by many thousands of large migrating birds suggests a lack of concern for natural values. The government's main interest in places such as cultural national parks and the country's many important archeological sites is the tourism they can attract. A return to a more democratic government is probably needed to resume the growth of environmental concern and progress seen in the past.

Perhaps we should pause here and make clear the context of the "nature" I've been talking about in this book. It consists of living and non-living parts, and exists in several levels of organization, from the genetic to species and ecosystems. The term **biodiversity** generally refers to all these levels and their variability. And it is in trouble at all levels.

Why does it matter?

> Recent experimental studies on whole ecosystems support what ecologists have long suspected: The more species that live in an ecosystem, the higher its productivity and the greater its ability to withstand drought and other kinds of environmental stress. Since we depend on functioning ecosystems to cleanse our water, enrich our soil, and create the very air we breathe, biodiversity is clearly not something to discard carelessly.[3]

Wild species are also the source of products that help sustain our lives, especially pharmaceuticals. Virtually all biologists and conservationists agree: the only way to save biodiversity with existing knowledge is to maintain it in natural ecosystems.

Many organizations are involved in this effort. Some of the better-known private organizations in the U.S. are The Nature Conservancy, with projects in over 70 countries, and all fifty U. S. states; the World Wildlife Fund for Nature, the Sierra Club, Conservation International, National Audubon Society, and the Natural Resources Defense Council, which works primarily through legal cases.

Two other organizations, one public and one an international financial institution, have a major global impact. The U.S. Agency for International Development (USAID) has a Blueprint for Biodiversity Conservation, with two goals:

1. Conserve biodiversity in priority places, and

2. Integrate biodiversity as an essential component of human development.

One way they work is through Debt for Nature agreements. Under these agreements, a portion of a developing nation's foreign debt is forgiven in exchange for using the funds thus generated for local investment in environmental conservation measures. In one such case, approximately $233 million in Congressionally-appropriated funds were used to conclude 20 agreements with 14 countries to protect and manage tropical forests.

The World Bank, headquartered in Washington, D.C., "works with countries to put policies in place so that biodiversity is valued as a key driver of sustainable development."A recent statement said that beyond implementing grants of $1.4 billion from the Global Environment Facility for biodiversity conservation and management, the Bank has itself committed $2 billion in loans and has leveraged $2.9 billion in co-financing. It has funded over 240 projects in more than 70 countries, the majority of which are in Africa, Latin America, and the Caribbean.

An important factor in all such programs is **sustainability**—the ability to keep something going over time or continuously. Economic development takes place in an environmental context—some part of the biosphere--that must *remain* healthy, and biodiversity is particularly important for creating that sustainability because of the specialized roles each species plays in maintaining ecological balance.

We are in a race with time to halt the loss of species and decline of the ecosystems of which they are a part. The extent and speed of loss on land areas seems to depend in large part on the percentage of land in protected areas. That percentage is currently around 15 percent. In his book, *Half-Earth: Our Planet's Fight for Life,* E.O. Wilson states that extensive research on the relation of sustainable species to the area of their habitat concludes that commonly the fraction protected in one-half the land surface would be about 85 percent, with a higher fraction if the global "hotspots" where the largest numbers of endangered species exist are included. He doesn't try to suggest how the "half-earth" could be achieved beyond building on the best reserves we have now. I suppose my great-grandchildren will get a sense of how far we go between 15 and, say, 90 percent.

15

Azerbaijan

Our two-year tour (1999-2001) in Azerbaijan, where Elizabeth was the Deputy Chief of Mission, put us in a small country where one could drive to any part of it in a day or less. I took frequent advantage of this fact, using our car and driver to reach most of the places that interested me, and a horse to reach others. (Elizabeth could use an embassy car and driver for her work.)

There lay before me a land that is essentially a dry trough between high mountain ranges—the Greater Caucasus on the north and the Lesser Caucasus and Talysh mountains in the south. Subalpine and alpine vegetation occurs on the highest mountains. Forests are restricted mainly to mountain slopes between 1,000 and 2,000 m, southeast and northeast lowlands, and along major rivers. The rest of the extensive lowlands supports semi-desert or steppe grassland. Numerous wetlands lie along the Caspian Sea coast and throughout inland areas.

I scoured these habitats for birds, of course, and wrote about them, as well as about the environmental problems that plague Azerbaijan. It was a productive and interesting two years. Here is a sample of the natural hot-spots I visited.

Red Lake

I soon discovered there was a bird-rich lake right on the edge of Baku, the capital city where our embassy was located. This modest-sized lake was formed by the building of a road that dammed it. South of the road was an oily, salty lake with no birds. North of it was this freshwater gathering place for waterfowl in fall and winter and shorebirds spring to fall. Here and in the adjacent marshes I saw 103 species, mostly waterbirds. Among the more uncommon ones were Long-tailed Duck, White-headed Duck (rare), Purple Swamphen (listed in the Red Book as globally threatened), Broad-billed Sandpiper, Bar-tailed Godwit, and Slender-billed Gull. Wind-blown trash diminished the aesthetics, but the bird diversity blew this trash out of my mind. One day a large falcon flew to the top of a telephone pole, but something momentarily distracted me, and when I looked back it was gone. Number 104—either a Peregrine or a Saker Falcon, which would have been a life bird for me.

Shirvan Nature Reserve and Conservation Area

Farther down the Caspian Sea coast, this area protects 55,800 ha.(215 sq. miles) of mostly flat steppe and semi-desert. Its most famous inhabitant is the Persian gazelle, said to number 4,000-5,000 in 1999. During my several visits I saw small bands of gazelles, but none approaching 100 or 200. Poaching is a threat to them. The manager described dramatic night-time chasing of poachers, and I hope these continued and were successful in protecting the gazelles, but I expect their numbers have declined.

One day as Elnur, our driver, and I bumped along a track across this vast plain in the Jeep Cherokee, we stopped to look at a small bird standing in the road before us. After close study and later reference to my field guides, I decided it was a Richard's Pipit, far from its normal range in Central Asia, and a first for Azerbaijan as far as I could tell. It's really fun to bird in a country where you have more of a chance of a first record than in, say, the U.S.

I believe all the Nature Reserves in Azerbaijan were established while it was a part of the Soviet Union. These reserves most resemble a *zapovedniki*, as described in Philip Pryde's book, *Conservation in the Soviet Union* (1972). They were created for their natural values: plants, animals, forests, scenery, etc., but also strongly emphasized scientific research and, in some, tourism. Research could be done in the Azerbaijan Nature Reserves, and visits are possible, but written permission from the State Ecological Committee is required for entry.

Qizilagach Bay Nature Reserve

Encompassing Qizilagach Bay on the coast in southeastern Azerbaijan, this nature reserve is the country's largest (88,400 ha., 303 sq.

miles)), one of the oldest (1929), and in winter home to Azerbaijan's largest concentration of waterbirds (around 500,000).

In January 2001 I headed down there. Most exciting was the view from the east side of the bay, reached by following the least muddy tracks down a long peninsula between the bay and the Caspian Sea. For four hours I watched an ever-changing panorama of birds: long strings of pink flamingos coming and going, thousands of waterfowl resting, feeding, and flying, dozens of Black-tailed Godwits and Eurasian Curlews. Walking over to the nearby Caspian shore, I saw four Great Black-headed Gulls resting with other gulls. Seeing this impressive and scarce bird, which breeds in Central Asia and winters on the Caspian, Black Sea, and eastern Mediterranean, was always a treat for me. Exploring the tip of the peninsula, I scared up a Short-eared Owl. I thought, wouldn't it be wonderful to camp on this peninsula with all these birds surrounding me, but never did it.

Aghgol Nature Reserve

Later that same January I received permission to visit this reserve, 4,500 ha. of lakes and marshes in central Azerbaijan. Getting there is not easy. With a staff member as guide, I followed indistinct tracks across the broad plain, and, coming to thirty yards of shallow water, gunned the Jeep across. Having brought my own food, water, and sleeping bag, I was allowed to stay at one of the three guard stations.

The birding, as expected, was good. Among the many birds I saw were a flock of Little Bustards, 12 species of waterfowl, 11 species of shorebirds, and a Great Black-headed Gull, here far from its usual winter haunts on the Caspian Sea. The second day, eating my lunch at the guard station, I was offered some meat. It tasted good. I was then informed that it was a Purple Swamphen that a guard had just shot. This bird was on the Red Data Book of globally threatened species, but later I was relieved to learn that among the 115,000 waterbirds counted here in January 1995 were 11,500 Purple Swamphens! This bird, it seems, is locally common in Azerbaijan. The guards at Aghgol made only $6.00 to $15.00 a day and, like guards in some other nature reserves, supplemented their meager earnings with a little local harvesting.

Lake Jandar

The authorities in Azerbaijan didn't like foreigners visiting places on the border of the country. So when I wanted to hike up a high mountain near the border with Iran I asked our military attaché at the embassy to tell the Azeri military where I was going. They didn't object, so I went. When I came back I reported that I hadn't seen any soldiers. The response was, "You didn't see us but we saw you."

Lake Jandar is at the western edge of Azerbaijan, half in that country and half in Georgia. I didn't think there would be a problem, but there was. In February 2001, after driving through bare hills, pastures, and wheat fields, Elnur and I arrived at the lake and set up my scope. Along with many waterfowl we saw three White-tailed Eagles and 65 Great Black-headed Gulls. I was beginning to learn that the latter was more widespread in winter than I thought. About half an hour after our arrival a Jeep pulled up and out jumped a man who said we couldn't be here without permission from the Ministry of Defense. So we left. It was a two-day trip for half an hour of birding.

Pirguli Nature Reserve and surroundings

It didn't take long to find the substantial mountains that were nearest to Baku—1 ½ to 2 hours to the northwest. From dry lowlands one turns up into foothills and then mountains, the highest topped by snow much of the year. My fondest memories from that area are of a winter trip when Elnur and I went searching for Guldenstadt's Redstart. The Collins *Bird Guide* describes the adult male as "*Quite big*, sturdy and broad-chested with large head....Unmistakable: white crown/nape, very big white wing patch, dark rust-red underparts, and black bib." In Azerbaijan it breeds in the Greater Caucasus from 2,200 m (7,211 feet) to over 3,000 m (9,843 feet) This species, along with the Caucasian Snowcock and Great Rosefinch, were the three alpine species I most wanted to see. I hoped to see them on their dramatic breeding grounds, but when I read that this redstart descends to river valleys in winter, I couldn't wait. North of Pirguli two mountain peaks rise to over 2,700 m. I thought maybe Guldenstadt's breeds there and descends to the nearby Pirsaat River valley in winter.

Driving along the partly cleared gravel road, we saw a Rough-legged Hawk, a migrant from Arctic Russia, flying over the snow-covered slopes. That is one of my favorite birds, and it seemed a good omen. Beyond Damirchi Elnur shifted into four-wheel drive along a track that followed the Pirsaat River and crossed it into the village of Zarat Heybari. We parked there and began hiking up the river. Searching patches of thickets, we finally found one sheltering a male Guldenstadt's Redstart. Not as majestic an environment as its summer grounds, but the bird justified the effort.

When we returned to the cottages near Pirguli, where we intended to overnight, with their sweeping view of the mountains, we saw a flock of Yellowhammers flitting around and sitting on fences. Scanning these birds with binoculars, I spotted a male Pine Bunting. Yellowhammers breed in much of Europe and into Russia as far as Central Asia. Most winter on the breeding grounds but some migrate into the Middle East and Transcaucasus, including Azerbaijan. The Pine Bunting is a "sibling species" of the Yellowhammer that breeds over most of the latter's Russian range, often in the same habitats, sometimes hybridizes with it in Western Siberia, and winters in Central Asia and locally west to the Middle East and southern Europe. The bird was totally unexpected and exciting, especially as it appeared it hadn't been recorded in Azerbaijan.

Zakatala Nature Reserve

On the border with Dagestan (Russia) in northwestern Azerbaijan, Zakatala is another of the oldest (1929) and one of the largest (25, 218 ha., 94 sq. miles) in the country. The early recognition of its importance was well-founded. Lying between 650 and 3,646 m (2,133 and 12,712 feet) it protects a mature forest of beech, oak, maple, and other trees, and large areas of subalpine and alpine habitat. Wolves, brown bears, lynx, Dagestan aurochs (a mountain "sheep" endemic to the Caucasus), and many other mammals roam these mountains. Vultures, including the Lammergeier, and many raptors top the bird list. What especially attracted me were birds of the subalpine and alpine zones, such as the Caucasian Black Grouse, Caucasian Snowcock, and Great Rosefinch.

One enters this reserve, with official permission, on foot or horseback. At the entrance a guard met me with an extra horse, from which I admired the forest on the way up to the reserve headquarters. There I was surprised to see cattle grazing. I don't know who owned them, but somebody was getting free grazing from the government.

As evening came on, I heard the barking of a roe deer in the forest down the slope. A flock of Common Cranes flew over, very high up, uttering their guttural call, going north to their breeding grounds in Russia. During the night I was awakened by people shouting and running, and I heard a cow bellowing nearby. Wolves had attacked it, but the men scared them off.

Next morning we saddled up for a trip to the heights. Every spring the staff conducted a count of Caucasian Black Grouse, a generally scarce bird with a relatively large population in this reserve. On the way up, we stopped on a ridge for lunch. I had the rare experience of looking *down* on a Lammergeier as it glided by. From here the going became steep and very rocky. My horse began balking, so one of the guards took the reins and pulled it. When we came to a v-shaped passage through rocks with smooth sides my horse tried to go up, slipped and fell, pinning my leg underneath it. Fortunately no damage was done. This called for a halt and assessment. Clouds were closing in, restricting the visibility needed to spot grouse, so we turned around.

My hope for alpine birds would have to wait for another horseback trip, elsewhere.

Approaching Babadag

I figured Babadag, 3,629 m high (11,910 feet) and closer to Baku, was my best bet for alpine birds. There are two routes up Babadag, one on the east side and one on the west. I decided on the latter and, with Yunus, our cook, and Aslan, our current driver, went to the village of Istisu. Here we engaged guides with horses and began riding the 14 km up the Keshna River toward our camping place near tree line.

I am not exactly comfortable on horses, and when Yunus, an experienced horseman, began galloping off my horse began galloping after him. I felt I was going to fall off and yelled at Yunus to stop, which, thankfully, he did. Every time we crossed the fast Keshna River I wondered how deep it was and if my high rubber boots would fill up with water if we floundered. I would have enjoyed riding through the magnificent beech forest if I didn't have to keep watching for overhanging branches that would knock me off my horse. Stopping for lunch beside the river was a welcome breather. During it we were handed cups of a drink I assumed was Vodka. Yunus told me later it was ethyl alcohol cut with water. When we reached the meadow where we were going to camp my horse, who apparently didn't like me, simply sat down and I had to slide off the back end. So ignominiously ended an uncomfortable trip.

Next morning the chief guide pointed out a trail on the other side of the river that led to a ridge near Babadag and said I could ride a horse up it. Seeing the steepness of that trail and recalling my falling horse at Zakatala and my nervous ride to this camping spot, I decided I'd rather walk up a ridge on our side of the river that led to the main ridge at 3,000 m (9,846 feet). But the going got steeper and steeper and finally near vertical, so I stopped around 2,500 m (8,205 feet) The Lammergeier, Griffon Vulture, Golden Eagles, Alpine Choughs, Rufous-tailed Rock Thrush, and Red-fronted Serins were nice, but not as nice as Caucasian Snowcocks and Great Rosefinches would have been.

I suppose I'll never see those birds.

Writings

After visiting these and other places I decided I should record my knowledge and experience in a small book. *Where to Watch Birds in Azerbaijan*, "The first birdwatching guide for Azerbaijan in English," describes 30 good birdwatching places, tells how to get to them, and recommends the best (sometimes Spartan) lodging near them. My casually drawn map of each place shows roads and landmarks. Of course this hasn't been an international bestseller, but I've enjoyed helping birders going to Azerbaijan, most of them from Britain. The internal market is virtually nil, since I know of no amateur Azeri birders—just a few government ornithologists. My wife gave Haidar Aliev, the President of Azerbaijan, a copy of my book. He looked at it in puzzlement and exclaimed, "You mean some people just *watch* birds!" (and don't shoot them).

A more professional product of my time in Azerbaijan was an article—"Azerbaijan: Environmental Conditions and Outlook"—written for the Swedish journal *Ambio*.[1] Here are the subjects I explored:

The country had separated from the collapsed Soviet Union in 1991, I suppose with a sense of freedom, but their transition from communism to a nominal democracy had drawbacks. With a post-Soviet decline in the economy, the quality of education suffered, and people were no longer assured of a job. Salaries dropped, and many people were unemployed. Our maid had been a microbiologist under the Soviets.

Environmental conditions were a legacy from the Soviet years, one that would present a challenge for many years to come. With an attitude of "meet production quotas at any cost," the Soviets pushed heavy use of pesticides, such as DDT, and fertilizer, and created massive air, water, and soil pollution at Sumgait, an industrial city north of Baku. They ignored the widespread overgrazing that led to soil erosion and degradation of grasslands, and the cutting of remaining forests for firewood and pasture.

By 1999, when we arrived, Azerbaijan had adopted a constitution, which includes environmental considerations; revised its environmental laws; ratified or acceded to several international conventions dealing with environment; started projects for environmental improvement with the help of international organizations; and produced a National Environmental Action Plan. It appeared that organizations such as the World Bank and the United Nations Development Program (UNDP) were making some progress with the problems. Surprisingly, the country had about 60 environmental NGOs, of which about a dozen were particularly active. Twelve "strict nature reserves" established by the Soviets remained, some of which I described earlier, but the staffs were deplorably underpaid; one reserve official moaned, "We don't even have uniforms anymore."

My thinking about the most important factors that environmental progress depends on had arrived at six. Here they are in roughly ascending order of importance:

- Public awareness of environmental disasters.
- Championship of environmental causes by prominent public figures.
- Growth of scientific knowledge about the nation's environment.
- Education of the public by schools, the media, publications, non-governmental organizations, and government agencies.
- Development of democratic institutions and attitudes.
- Development of the economy to the point where most people have their basic needs met and there is a substantial, well-educated middle class.

The first two factors had little or no influence in Azerbaijan. Scientific research had fallen off drastically since the collapse of the Soviet Union. Typical pay for people working for the Academy of Sciences during the Soviet era had been $250 per month. Now it was $30. Academy scientists had to seek research funding and assistance from foreign (especially oil) companies and international organizations. Broad knowledge about environmental conditions in the country was growing very slowly.

Education of the public about environmental issues was underway. With an adult literacy rate of 97.3 percent and 254 television sets per 1,000 people, communication with most of the public was possible. The quality of education in general had declined seriously, but more attention was being paid to environmental issues in some schools and universities. Media coverage of such issues was weak. Fifteen print journalists discussing environmental reporting in June 2001 rated environment well below politics, economic issues, crime, and sports in reader interest and newspaper coverage. However, my ornithologist friend Elchin Sultanov, who frequently spoke about environment on TV and radio, thought environment ranked below only politics and economics.

With an Azeri environmentalist interpreting, I was on national TV one day discussing environmental issues. I was one of the Western journalists teaching Azeri journalists how to write about pollution and other problems of the Caspian Sea. My column on environmental issues in an English-language newspaper may have opened a few eyes. And I helped some NGO members obtain U.S. government grants for educational trips to our country.

Education of the public was a major activity of the environmental NGOs. They did this through educational materials for schools, publications for a general audience, appearances on TV and radio, clean-up projects, tree-planting, exhibitions, art and essay competitions for children, workshops for journalists and others, nature-oriented excursions, and other activities. Some NGOs also conducted research, advised parliament on development of environmental laws, or promoted cooperation among different kinds of professionals on environmental issues. Probably, NGOs ranked with schools as the most important sources of public environmental education.

The government agencies did little or nothing in the way of such education, or of environmental improvement, and I suspect that is still true (2014). Vast amounts of revenue are coming from Azerbaijan's oil and gas fields in the Caspian Sea, but most of this seems to be going to the construction of buildings, "the like of which has possibly not been seen since the dawn of Dubai." They include the Tallest Flagpole in the world, and "dozens of high-rise buildings in ever more extraordinary shapes...one of them, a hotel owned by the President's wife, is shaped like a flame because Azerbaijan is the land of eternal fires." [2]

There is both "go" and "stop" in the effort to develop democratic institutions and attitudes. Azerbaijan is attempting to move from Soviet authoritarianism to democracy, but the weight of the past hangs heavy. The country has been independent only between 1918 and 1920 and since 1991.

One factor pushing the government toward democracy is its wish for closer association with the West, for both aid and as a counterbalance to the influence of Russia and Iran. Partly to gain admission to the Council of Europe and other ties to international organizations, it has taken a number of steps toward democracy. Among these, it has adopted a constitution that grants all people freedom of thought and speech, conscience, assembly, and information; it extends the normal rights and liberties of a democratic society to all citizens.

Other factors are putting a brake on this trend. The country is often described as a khanate, before, during (more secretly), and after the Soviet period, ruled by one family (or, in earlier history, several families). Today, that family and its close associates control much of the economy and most of the politics. By 2000, 40 political parties had been registered. Parliamentary elections held in the fall of that year allowed a *few* members of opposing parties into the legislature. Twice I was one of the many outside monitors of those elections and saw no funny business at the polling stations I visited, but people were skeptical about the results.

Some of the people speak out for citizen involvement in improving society and its environment, but many others are suspicious or afraid of doing so. They wait for the government to do something; and they are nostalgic for the Soviet days, when most people were better off economically and the government did do more for them. This attitude limits the sense of personal responsibility for the condition of the environment. As S. Panahov, UNDP Sustainable Development Policy Specialist, said to me, "Next to apartments is garbage, inside their flats it's clean. The outside is not mine. Only when people begin to participate in society, when all people are involved, can we make progress."

Finally we come to that factor the landscape architecture professor at Cukurova University in Turkey thought most important:

economic improvement of the people. In 2000, 68 percent of Azerbaijan's people had incomes below the World Bank poverty line. (sources in my Ambio paper) The monthly salary of employees ranged from about $23 to $67. Assuming that a substantial middle class, whose members can think about things beyond putting food on the table, I tried to find out the size of Azerbaijan's middle class. A businessman with wide experience in the country estimated it at about 3 to 13 percent of families. He used $200-$400 monthly income, including unreported and illegal income, as the definition of middle class. Government data in 1996, excluding the latter income, suggested the middle class percentage was much less than 1 percent. In a survey of 1,000 adults, only 2 percent said they could buy some expensive items like a TV or refrigerator (which middle-class people presumably could afford; but note the "254 television sets per 1,000 people" above). Although incomes were slowly rising in 2000, it appeared that development of a substantial middle class, and major environmental progress, would take a long time. (One might ask, however, whether outside help could bring about such progress. In 2014, the World Wildlife Fund was planning to establish a program in Azerbaijan to improve the nature and wildlife situation; the World Bank and United Nations Development Program were already at work in the country. As of May 31, 2018, WWF had done critical work in Azerbaijan in the restoration and sustainability of native leopard and gazelle populations, as well as doubling the size of protected areas across the country.)

I tried to do my bit for the environment in all the countries I lived in thanks to Elizabeth's job, but probably I was most pleased with what I did in Azerbaijan, in the company of dedicated environmentalists.

PART IV

Concluding Thoughts

16

Is Nature Sacred?

I would posit that the stronger and deeper the bonds with nature people have, the more likely they are to actively protect it. Those bonds, or lack of bonds, occur as a spectrum in societies and in individuals.

One end of the spectrum might be represented by attitudes of tribal New Guineans. Jared Diamond, who has studied birds and human relations with nature in New Guinea for many years, finds a very "practical" attitude (in Kellert's typology a "utilitarian" attitude).

> New Guineans have detailed knowledge of birds, mammals, other animals, and plants that they eat, use for decoration, or other uses. They have names for a high percentage of the species, including fish, crustaceans, mollusks, snakes, lizards, frogs, plus certain insects, spiders, and worms.

But

> do they exhibit any positive emotional responses to animals as living creatures—responses such as love, reverence, fondness, concern, or sympathy? New Guineans certainly are capable of positive responses to at least one species of domestic animal, the pig, which serves as a major status symbol and with which they live on intimate terms....It is rare, however, to see corresponding signs of New Guineans recognizing individual wild animals as living creatures to which one can form a bond.[1]

A more common attitude toward nature among people directly dependent on nature for most of their basic needs might be described as **respect**. They feel a tie with and gratitude for animals they must kill to stay alive.

A good example are the Koyukon Indians, who live along the Yukon and Koyukuk rivers in the forests of northern Alaska. Anthropologist Richard Nelson lived several years with these people and found they have detailed knowledge of every aspect of their boreal forest environment.

> They also have an equally voluminous knowledge from a realm that lies beyond the senses. Animals, plants, and elements of the physical world possess qualities that are both natural and supernatural. The environment is inhabited by watchful and potent beings who feel, who can be offended, and who should be treated with respect.[2]

The most spiritually potent are the black bear, brown bear, wolverine, lynx, otter, and wolf, but "even a redback vole or a ruby-crowned kinglet is a power to be recognized. No one is ever alone in the wild: no one is ever outside the bounds of moral restraint. 'There's always something in the air that watches us,' a village elder said."[3] Even "elements of the 'nonliving' environment—earth, mountains, rivers, lakes, ice, snow, storms, lightning, sun, moon, stars—all have spirit and consciousness."[4] "Based on the anthropological literature," Nelson concludes, "it's reasonable to suggest that most of humanity—over the span of our species' history and evolution—has conceptualized the natural world according to principals much like those of the Koyukon and other Native American peoples."[5]

The next step up on the spectrum (as I see it) is **love** of nature. This can be a purely emotional response, or an emotional response mixed with varying degrees of interest and study up to the scientist's, whose whole career may develop from an original love. E.O. Wilson, the brilliant and eloquent Harvard biologist, describes the way love enters into the picture for many scientists: "...let me offer the following rough map of innovation in science. You start by loving a subject. Birds, probability theory, explosives, stars, differential equations, storm fronts, sign language, swallowtail butterflies—the odds are that the obsession will have begun in childhood. The subject will be your lodestar and give sanctuary in the shifting mental universe."[6] More generally he asks, "Is it possible that humanity will love life enough to save it?"[7]

In "The Land Ethic," first published in 1933 and included in his classic work, *A Sand County Almanac*, Aldo Leopold argued for the extension of ethics to include "the land"—natural communities—as well as the human community. He argues for this because we are members of the land-community, as subject to its ecological needs as are nonhuman members. "It is inconceivable to me that an ethical relation to land can exist without love, respect, and admiration for land, and a high regard for its value. By value, I of course mean value in the philosophical sense."[8] "No important change in ethics…was ever accomplished without an internal change in our intellectual emphasis, loyalties, affections, and convictions."[9]

Paleontologist and evolutionist Stephen Jay Gould echoes Wilson and Leopold regarding the importance of love in conservation: "We cannot win this battle to save species and environments without forging a bond between ourselves and nature as well—for we will not fight to save what we do not love."[10]

Countless nonscientists have that love. Take birdwatchers, for instance. "Active and committed birders in our studies," writes Stephen Kellert, "are usually distinguished by an unusual degree of appreciation, interest, knowledge, and concern for nature and biological diversity…."[11] Most can be said to have a love of birds and this love often expands to all of nature.

More generally, Kellert found a humanistic evaluation of nature in many people, arising often in children between the ages of six and twelve. "Middle childhood marks a time of rapidly developing humanistic, symbolic, and aesthetic values of nature."[12] The humanistic evaluation is the one closest to love of nature.

What is important here for stewardship of nature is the kind and strength of that love. In some people it does not extend beyond their pets. In others it is a broad and deep passion.

One further step—to the top end of the spectrum—is the attitude that sees nature as **sacred**. In some people this is the most powerful motivation for care of the earth. Michael Soule suggests that this should be harnessed in environmentalism. "Only a new religion of nature, similar but even more powerful than the animal rights movement, can create the political momentum required to overcome the greed that gives rise to discord and strife and the anthropomorphism that underlies the intentional abuse of nature."[13]

What, then, does "sacred" mean. The American Heritage Dictionary definitions range from "dedicated to or set apart for the worship of a deity;" "made or declared holy;" to "worthy of reverence or respect." Its definitions of "holy" are similar: "1. Belonging to, derived from, or associated with a divine power; sacred." I include in this chapter people who fall under any of these definitions.

Rudolph Otto, in his book *The Idea of the Holy*, uses the term "numinous," which excludes the rational, the quality of goodness, and the ethical. It is something that "cannot be strictly defined," and "can only be evoked, awakened in the mind." He believes this ability is a universal *potentiality* of man but is not "in *actuality* the universal possession of every single man; very frequently it is only disclosed as a special endowment and equipment of particular gifted individuals."[14]

A similar caveat is expressed by Jeremy Benstein in discussing human relationships with nature: "...our age is characterized by distance, or downright estrangement, from the divine, the human (both self and society), and the natural. We need to relegate, bind, and bond, and bond not only spiritual connections with divinity (quite likely a possibility only for some) but also, perhaps more accessibly, social and personal connections in the form of nurturing relationships and communities and—not least—connections with the natural world as an ongoing source of sustenance."[15]

Perhaps if we listen to some people who seem to have a spiritual feeling about nature we can sense any sacredness in it. After publication of *The Sea Around Us*, which was broadly acclaimed, a few people were critical. James Bennet, a lawyer in New York City and perhaps a creationist, disagreed with Rachel Carson's account of evolution in the sea and noted her lack of mention of God as Creator. She replied to Bennet:

> It is true that I accept the theory of evolution as the most logical one that has ever been put forward to explain the development of living creatures on this earth. As far as I am concerned, however, there is absolutely no conflict between a belief in evolution and a belief in God as the creator. Believing as I do in evolution, I merely believe that is the method by which God created and is still creating life on earth. And it is a method so marvelously conceived that to study it in detail is to increase—and certainly never to diminish—one's reverence and awe both for the Creator and the process.[16]

However, in quoting this letter in her biography of Rachel Carson, Linda Lear called it "a study in diplomacy....it hides her deeper spirituality and simplifies her concept of both the Creator and the process of evolution." I've found it difficult to discover Carson's concept of the Creator, and perhaps she did too. Perhaps what she says in a letter to her friend Dorothy Freeman will have to do: "part of my trouble [with respect to a deity] is finding anything definite I can really feel is true. But I am sure, there is a great and mysterious force that we don't, and perhaps can never understand."

In his book, *Making Nature Sacred: Literature, Religion, and Environment in America from the Puritans to the Present*, John Gatta, a professor of English at the University of Connecticut, describes "the diverse theologies of Creation that have arisen and found [literary] expression within the primary context of Western religion."[17] He examines the work of many writers, ranging from William Bradford and Jonathan Edwards to 20th century authors such as Rachel Carson, Wendell Berry, and the novelist John Cheever.

About Carson he says, "Throughout her life, [she] insisted in diverse ways on the reality of the spirit….she [argued for the] 'affinity of the human spirit for the earth' and claimed that 'natural beauty has a necessary place in the spiritual development of any individual or any society.'"[18]

She "applauded Einstein's statement that 'the most beautiful and most profound emotion we can experience is the sensation of the mystical,' and that recognizing the impenetrable 'is at the center of true religiousness.'[19] She believed that not only nature but human love and sublime works of music all testified to life's impenetrable mystery and beauty."[20]

In my youth, beginning to have experiences similar to his, I very much enjoyed Donald Culross Peattie's 1941 book, *The Road of a Naturalist*, given to me by my father. Now, rereading it, I find something I didn't absorb at the first reading: someone whose *faith* was Nature, though perhaps a dependable, awesome, but not divine Nature. Perhaps, however, his feelings suggest a reverence for nature, which allows us to put Peattie in the "sacred" camp.

> …the years of common lot that I have so far lived are quite enough to teach any man that, whether he would have it so or not, he is Nature's child and prisoner."[21]
>
> …the discoveries of science are due not to the greatness of man but to the awesome greatness of the order. That order is not inscrutable; it invites to exploration like a beautiful corridor….this leads…into a vast, an infinite temple. Man is born into the order; he is always a part of it, and

whatever indignities he suffers, that order cannot be outraged.[22]

Now, in the cabin on Fish Creek, Wyoming, I had what
most I lacked as I sprinted, that first autumn [at Harvard],
through the Cambridge streets....I have her arms now, and
the arms of our children around me. I have a car, and here
were all the Rockies to visit in it. Here on the table stood
my dissecting microscope; my choice of books lay spread
beside it; and the room with those great white columbines
in the dark corner shone as a chamber does with a bride in
it....My drowsy wife opened her eyes and smiled. If ever
any man has riches, I have, and know it. And I know too,
as I began to guess at twenty-one, that the last of these with
which I would ever part is the one that nothing in heaven
or on earth could take away from me. Call it my faith. My
belief in the Nature of things.[23]

Perhaps we should include here a group of people—some already discussed—whose feeling about nature is rather similar to
Peattie's, who were or are devoted to "Nature worship" that does
not involve a deity. In his book, *Dark Green Religion*, Bron Taylor
wrote: "Henry David Thoreau is often regarded as a patron saint
for such spirituality in America, casting a long shadow and influ-
encing virtually all of the twentieth-century's most important environmental thinkers," such as John Muir, Aldo Leopold, and Rachel Carson. Taylor asserts that dark green religion means "religion
that considers nature to be sacred, imbued with intrinsic value, and
worthy of reverent care." (In this chapter the word "sacred" may or
may not include a link with God.)

Albert Schweitzer's Reverence for Life came to him after a long,
agonizing search "struggling to find the elementary and universal
concept of the ethical that I had not discovered in any philosophy."
He was traveling on a barge up a river in West Africa.

Late on the third day, at the very moment when, at sunset,
we were making our way through a herd of hippopotamus-
es, there flashed upon my mind, unforeseen and unsought,
the phrase 'reverence for life.' The iron door had yielded.
The path in the thicket had become visible. Now I had
found my way to the principle in which affirmation of the
world and ethics are joined together![24]

Arriving independently, I assume, at something similar to Aldo Leopold's Land Ethic, he wrote, "Until now the great weakness in all ethical systems has been that they dealt only with the relations of man to man. In reality, however, the question is, What is our attitude toward the universe and all that it supports? A man is ethical only when life as such is sacred to him—the life of plants and animals as well as that of his fellow men—and when he devotes himself to helping all life that is in need of help." [25]

By profession a microbiologist, Rene DuBos's writings range over the whole purview of biology, including the human species and its relationships with the earth and its fellow humans. In a chapter titled "A Theology of the Earth" (in *A God Within*), he approaches the idea of sacredness in nature:

> Earth is choice, precious, and sacred beyond all comparison or measure.
>
> The adjective 'sacred' may be surprising in a description of the characteristics of this planet, and yet it expresses an attitude which has deep roots in the human past and still persists now. The very fact that the word 'desecration' is commonly used to lament the damage men are causing to the environment indicates that many of us have a feeling that the earth has sanctity, that man's relation to it has a sacred quality. [26]

He also expresses ideas similar to biophilia, propounded later by E.O. Wilson:

> The quality of human life is inextricably interwoven with the kinds and variety of stimuli man receives from the earth and the life it harbors, because human nature is shaped biologically and mentally by external nature. [27]
>
> Men seek contact with other living things probably because their own species has evolved in constant association with them and has retained from the evolutionary past a biological need for this association. [28]

And he sees science as possibly laying the groundwork for a religious perspective on nature:

> Both polytheism and monotheism are losing their ancient power in the modern world, and for this reason it is com-

monly assumed that the present age is irreligious. But we may instead be moving to a higher level of religion. Science is at present evolving from the description of concrete objects and events to the study of relationships as observed in complex systems. We may be about to recapture an experience of harmony, an intimation of the divine, from our scientific knowledge of the processes through which the earth became prepared for human life, and of the mechanisms through which man relates to the universe as a whole. A truly ecological view of the world has religious overtones.[29]

An ethical attitude in the scientific study of nature readily leads to a theology of the earth.[30]

We might include here the 19th century Transcendentalists, who taught that divinity pervades all nature and humanity. In his book *Nature* Emerson writes:

In the woods we return to reason and faith. There I feel that nothing can befall me in life—no disgrace, no calamity, (leaving me my eyes), which nature cannot repair. Standing on the bare ground--my head bathed by the blithe air, and uplifted into infinite space,-- all mean egotism vanishes. I become a transparent eyeball; I am nothing; I see all; the currents of the Universal Being circulate through me; I am part or particle of God.[31]

I note with interest that three chapters in *Nature* coincidentally address three of Kellert's valuations of nature: aesthetic, symbolic, and utilitarian.

John Muir can be described rather like Aldo Leopold once was, as someone "who had the mind of a scientist and the soul of a poet." He studied and wrote about nature—its plants and animals, and its geology—but also reveled in nature and worshipped it. The historian Donald Worster described Muir's first summer in the Sierra Nevada as

a long moment of ecstasy that he would try to remember and relive to the end of his days....He bounded over rocks and up mountain sides, hung over the edge of terrifying precipices...laughed at the exuberant antics of grasshoppers and chipmunks...slept each night on an aromatic mattress of spruce boughs....Each thing he saw or felt seemed joined to the rest in exquisite harmony....more intensely than ever before in his life he felt his own heart beating in unison [with nature]. He experienced, in the fullest sense yet, a profound conversion to the religion of nature.[32]

'God' for Muir was a deliberately loose and imprecise term referring to an active, creative force dwelling in, above, and around nature. Continuously animated by that divine force, every part of the natural world was in constant flux—the earth moving under foot, glaciers moving down mountainsides, plants and animals evolving and spreading. Always the flux was purposeful. Always it moved toward beauty. Always and everywhere it was holy.[33]

Later in his life, having married and become a successful businessman and a leader of the young conservation movement, he seems to have edged a bit toward a Christian view of nature. "His earlier pantheistic tendencies, which celebrated every nodding flower, every zephyr, as divine in itself, became more muted. 'All is beauty, all is God,' he had once maintained. Now he was more careful to reassure his more conventional readers that beauty *is made* by God." But he dropped "only a few casual reassurances to his readers that he believed in a Supreme Being."[34]

John Gatta describes the range of Muir's religiosity:

When assessments of Muir take any account of his religion, they represent him variously as a pantheist, a Transcendentalist, a mystic, an ecocentric evolutionist, an idiosyncratic Protestant Christian, or a post-Christian Romantic....despite the eclectic character of Muir's earth-centered religion, his faith preserved some essential traits of biblical Christianity. His heterodox yet robust piety drew constantly on biblical paradigms of grace, conversion of heart, evangelical poverty, and a loving Creator.[35]

Many poets, of course, have been inspired by nature, and some have seen the hand of the divine in nature. William Wordsworth was preeminent among the latter. John Muir, who had a similar feeling about nature, quoted his work. Donald Worster, in his biography of Muir, said this about Wordsworth:

What Wordsworth put in simple, accessible, and moving words was a new religion that made nature the source of revelation. Put aside your old creeds and dogmas, your theories and libraries, he invited, and go to the mountains. There you will find answers to your most fundamental questions: what is good or evil? How should humans live? Does God exist? Nature says yes to the last question, but no to a deity conceived in the Judeo-Christian tradition.[36]

(However, in his later years, Wordsworth was close to the Anglican Church and wrote some "Christian poems." Muir didn't go this far in his religious views.)

In "The Tables Turned" (1798), Wordsworth wrote:

Books! tis a dull and endless strife;
    Come, hear the woodland linnet,
    How sweet his music! On my life,
There's more of wisdom in it.

And the oft-quoted lines:

One impulse from a vernal wood
May teach you more of man,
Of moral evil and of good,
Than all the sages can.

In "To a Skylark" (1805-07) even nature praised God:

Happy, happy Liver,
With a soul as strong as a mountain river
Pouring out praise to the Almighty Giver,
Joy and jollity be with us both!

If some of Wordsworth's late poetry could be called Christian, all poetry of the Jesuit Gerard Manley Hopkins (1844-89) flowed out of a deep Christian faith. He saw God's work everywhere. His poetic style can be difficult, but "Pied Beauty" to me is accessible and beautiful. Man's landscapes and other works seem to be included in this paean to God's creation.

Glory be to God for dappled things—
For skies of couple-colour as a brinded cow;
For rose-moles all in stipple upon trout that swim;
Fresh-firecoal chestnut-falls; finches' wings;

Landscape plotted and pieced—fold, fallow, and plough;
And all trades, their gear and tackle and trim.
All things counter, original, spare, strange,
Whatever is fickle, freckled (who knows how?)
With swift, slow; sweet, sour; adazzle, dim;
He fathers-forth whose beauty is past change:
Praise him.

Many individuals of various religious faiths have seen God in nature and nature as God's creation. An interesting and articulate example is Thomas Keating, a Trappist monk widely known as a teacher of contemplative prayer and one of the founders of the Centering Prayer Movement. In his book, *The Better Part: Stages of Contemplative Living*, he touches on the role of nature in those stages:

> Religion is not the only way to God. *Nature* [italics mine], spiritual friendship, conjugal love, service of others, art— these are all ways in which God calls people to himself.... Moreover, like the spokes of a wheel, all paths to God tend to come closer to each other as they come closer to God, who is the center and source of them all. For example, it is normal for someone who has taken the religious path to begin to perceive the wonders of God in nature as a further means of uniting with God.[37]

Thinkers both medieval and modern have extended the human relationship with nature beyond just our Earth to the whole universe. For instance, "the cosmos, for William [of] Thierry [1085-1148, a theologian and mystic, and abbot of the monastery of Saint-Thierry] is a sacred image of God and it contains the Spirit of God in its very being."[38]

Thomas Berry (1914-2009) was a Catholic priest of the Passionist order, cultural historian, and ecotheologian. He was deeply influenced by Pierre Teilhard de Chardin (1881-1935), who "observed that the universe from the beginning had a physical and psychic component—matter and spirit were evolving together over time." Berry's view of the sacredness of the universe led him to a theological necessity of care of the earth, our part of the universe.

> The universe is the supreme manifestation of the sacred. This notion is fundamental to establishing a cosmos, an intelligible manner of understanding the universe, or even any part of the universe.[39]

In my view, the first step in achieving any adequate human or Christian activity in saving the planet from further
irreversible dissolution is to recognize that the universe story, the Earth story, the life story, and the human story—all
are a single story.[40]

There is a…component that cannot be neglected, namely,
love of the natural world, without which the human world
cannot function in any effective manner. The entire Earth
was born of divine love and will survive only through our
human and Christian love.[41]

Though such people have spoken eloquently about seeing God
in nature, the Church (all Christian denominations) as an institution has been slow to embrace the non-human part of God's Creation. This has an important bearing on environmentalism because
there are so many people within the Church and a religious impulse toward stewardship of the earth could have powerful effects.

In the late 1960s my wife and I were attending an Episcopal
church in Ann Arbor, Michigan. Parishioners were invited to con-
tribute a short statement about religion for the cover of the weekly
bulletin. I wrote one asking Who is my neighbor? (with regard to
the commandment: Love God, and your neighbor as yourself). I
answered that my neighbor was not only humans but also trees,
grass, rabbits, implying all of living nature. As I remember, no one
commented about this.

For the first Earth Day, April 22, 1970, I organized a seminar at
the University of Michigan on Religion and Environment and invited around 20 local clergy to attend. Only one showed up.

Why was the Church so slow to get involved in earth stewardship? In September 2011 I presented this question to Sam Lloyd,
former Dean of the Washington National Cathedral. He singled out
two main causes. "The scriptures focus on history—God working
within the divine-human saga. The New Testament is an anthropo-
centric narrative—experiencing the kingdom of God, sin and guilt,
healing, and so on. Nature is a backdrop to the story."

The other important cause, he said, is the Bible's "narrative of
dominion over the earth. This is easily understood as ownership.
Earth is there for humans' sake." This view, expressed in the first
chapter of genesis, led historian Lynn White, Jr. to deliver a speech
entitled "The Historical Roots of Our Ecological Crisis," which was
published in *Science* in 1967. "Whether valid or not," DuBos says,
"White's thesis demands attention because it has become an article

of faith for many conservationists, ecologists, economists, and even theologians."[42] Dean Lloyd, however, cited places in scripture, such as Noah's covenant with God to rescue pairs of animals from the Flood, and Psalms in which "Nature is seen as God's presence."

In the 1960s and 1970s, the Church did begin paying attention to earth stewardship. It realized that "environmentalism was in the air," as Dean Lloyd put it, and that the Bible, especially the Old Testament, is indeed replete with passages about God's love for his creation and about the need to take care of it. A small sample: "The Lord God took the man and put him in the garden of Eden to till it and keep it." (Genesis 2:15, a more earth-friendly phrasing than Gen. 1:26, about man's dominion over the earth.) "When you drink of clear water, must you foul the rest with your feet?" (Ezekial 34:18) "If you besiege a town for a long time, making war against it in order to take it, you must not destroy its trees by wielding an ax against them....Are trees in the field human beings that they should come under siege from you? (Deuteronomy 20:19) "You shall keep my statutes and my ordinances and commit none of these abominations...otherwise the land will vomit you out for defiling it, as it vomited out the nation that was before you." (Leviticus 18: 26, 28) "O Lord, how manifold are your works! In wisdom you have made them all; the earth is full of your creatures." (Psalm 104:24) "He gives to the animals their food, and to the young ravens when they cry." (Psalm 147:9)

By the 1980s and 1990s, the breadth of the Church's concern and that of other faiths—Judaism, Islam, Buddhism, Hinduism--was accelerating rapidly. In 1993, the U.S. Conference of Catholic Bishops (USCCB), the National Conference of Churches of Christ, the Evangelical Network, and the Coalition on the Environment and Jewish Life formed the National Religious Partnership for the Environment (NRPE). Among other initiatives, "the NRPE provides resources to our 135,000 congregations around the country on local environmental actions and ways to incorporate the theme of environmental responsibility into religious worship and study.""In March 2008, over 50 pastors and leaders from the Southern Baptist Convention released a call to action on the environment, declaring that 'it is time for individuals, churches, communities and governments to act.'" "On Earth Day 2009 (April 22), the [USCCB]and the Catholic Campaign on Climate Change announced a new wave of environmental initiatives related to climate change, including a proposal that each of the nation's 19,000 Catholic parishes undertake action and advocacy; the first step in that direction will be an assessment of the local carbon footprint of each parish.[39]

By 2012, at least 15 Christian denominations had web sites on environmental issues. The Presbyterian Church (U.S.A.), one of the more conservative of the mainstream U.S. Protestant denominations, had asked its 2.3 million members each to "make a bold witness by aspiring to carbon neutral lives." More concretely, at least 46 Presbyterian congregations had taken the Earth Care Pledge, which requires them to complete activities and projects in the fields of worship, education, facilities, and outreach. A Presbyterian Church (U.S.A.) Policy Brief states that "Presbyterian General Assemblies have been speaking on issues of environmental protection and justice since the late 1960s. Their witness ranges broadly from drinking water safety and acid rain, to protecting endangered species, to cleaning up dirty power plants, to climate change and U.S. energy policy."

The Episcopal Church was not far behind. The Church and its dioceses have been passing environmental resolutions since 1977, and increasingly to the present. These have included, for example, Response to Global Warming, Merciful and Human Treatment of God's Creatures, and Horizontal Hydraulic Fracturing (aka Fracking).

I asked Dean Lloyd about his own relations with nature. "Nature means a huge amount to me. I love to hike. Last summer I was hiking at 11,000 feet in the Rocky Mountains. Nature restores me.... I think of nature as sacred, a way to God, but not divine in itself."

Which brings the story back to me. Many Episcopal dioceses and parishes have embraced earth stewardship in their worship and other activities. Not least among these is the Washington National Cathedral, where my wife and I have been worshipping for several years. With its location in the Nation's Capital, its funeral services for Presidents, its celebration of national events, its conferences and services bringing together prominent members of different faiths, and its speakers drawn from Congress, the Federal Government, and the top echelons of journalism, it sees itself as the Nation's church. As such, its stance on care of the earth could have far-reaching influence.

For some time, the services have included prayers for earth stewardship and special attention to this on St. Francis Day and Earth Day. Speakers on the subject have come from various walks of life. The Harvard biologist E.O. Wilson, not himself a church-goer, talked about the need for the Church to join environmentalists in the push for conservation and a clean earth. There were Sunday Forums, in which the former Dean, Sam Lloyd, interviewed several environmental leaders among others in a series on the intersection of faith and public affairs. (These were streamed nationally.) The Earth Day program in 2012 featured Wendell Berry, author, poet, farmer, and Christian, and Matthew Sleeth, executive director of Blessed Earth, as well as an Earth Day pilgrimage hosted by the Cathedral Center for Prayer and Pilgrimage.

The Cathedral also has an environmental advocacy group, Earth Stewards, of which I am a member. Its mission is to increase awareness of environmental needs and involvement in caring for the earth by members of the Cathedral Congregation and visitors, and to identify things the Cathedral can do with respect to its facilities, grounds, and programs. I find in this group a powerful connection between faith and earth stewardship and feel pulled into this spiritual current. It causes me to think further about God and the earth, and my own spiritual journey.

I have been a member of an Episcopal parish since I was a child. In the early days I felt good when I came out of Sunday services, though I suspect this was partly relief at getting out of church as well as happiness at having been there. During adolescence, when the father who had been so important to me became alcoholic, I began thinking of God as my father. Since those years, I have thought frequently and sometimes deeply about religious faith.

One day in the 1990s I had a powerful spiritual experience, one whose significance and meaning I have been pondering ever since. It deepened my belief that there is a divine dimension—another reality—beneath everything. For various reasons I was feeling extremely low about myself as I drove through the hills of northern Alabama when all of a sudden the pastures around me seemed luminous and I felt what I could only call the presence of God. I seemed to have received a message—all is well--and I imagined myself giving it in a sermon to the people in my parish up in Washington: "Don't worry, folks. Everything is O.K." I felt an ecstasy that took two weeks to fade away.

So how do I answer the question, Is there a deity in the sacredness of nature? I'm a bit of a scientist, so I want to know where the universe came from. As I understand it, the mathematicians say the universe came from an infinitesimally small point having a value close to zero (and an infinite density in physical terms). A point, like a line, is then a mathematical concept that has no size or physical existence in the real world. So we might as well call the condition before the Big Bang zero—*nihilo*. The unimaginably large universe, even the coffee cup on my desk, I can't conceive of as coming from an infinitesimally small point, or zero. It's all a miracle to me. And unless science can sometime explain existence—why there is something and not nothing—which many scientists believe is impossible, I'll say it comes from God. But perhaps only the beginning, as the rest follows physical laws.

The mathematical physicist Paul Davies put it this way in his book, *The Mind of God*:

> ...in the end a rational explanation for the world in the sense of a closed and complete system of logical truths is almost certainly impossible. We are barred from ultimate knowledge, from ultimate explanation, by the very rules of reasoning that prompt us to seek such explanation in the first place. If we wish to progress beyond, we have to embrace a different concept of "understanding" from that of rational explanation. Possibly the mystical path is a way to such an understanding.[43]

Have I felt the presence of God in nature? The Alabama experience occurred in natural surroundings, but those surroundings had little to do with the experience. Other events were more relevant to the question. When I came out of the hospital from a mastoid operation at age twelve, the whole landscape—nature, buildings, everything—seemed miraculous, irradiant. When I walk along the tranquil C&O Canal at the end of a nice day, with the Potomac River flowing alongside and the sun setting, it seems a benediction. Sometimes flowers seem a gift from God. Twice in nature I have had a strong feeling of being one with the whole universe. Once this happened while I was canoeing late in the day on Lake Taneycomo in Missouri. Years later it happened while I was sitting on a hilltop in Joshua Tree National Monument in California in the evening, watching for coyotes. It was as if I had been living in a bubble, and now the bubble had burst. I was part of everything. In all these experiences there seemed to be an element of sacredness.

I think about the quote earlier from Thomas Keating (which Dean Lloyd's statement echoed): "...it is normal for someone who has taken the religious path to begin to perceive the wonders of God in nature as a further means of uniting with God." I think I have experienced this kind of union.

Of course, one can't make a definitive statement, "yes" or "no," about the question. It lies in the realm of faith, not science. But many people have answered in the affirmative.

I can say I am a part of nature and dependent on it, as everyone else is, whether they know it or not. I have love and reverence for nature. I am a conservationist. And I come down on the side of "yes."

17

Raising Earth Stewards

Helping children have experience with nature is important not only for their physical, emotional, and spiritual health. It is important, too, for the health of the earth. A childhood bond with nature should lead to an adult care for the earth.

Looking again at my own relationships with nature, I see first the excitement of exploring Glover-Archbold Park, then an intense interest in the many forms of life around me, and finally, continuing that interest, combining it with a moral, as well as practical, concern for the well-being of all life. I must admit I was somewhat ahead of the Church in care for the non-human part of the Creation, but behind it in care for the human part of it. I loved certain people, but took awhile to espouse the need for an *agape* form of love (love that expects nothing in return) for all people.

Returning to Stephen Kellert's valuations of nature, I can see myself as having all of them, beginning perhaps, with the *humanistic*, as expressed, for instance, in a love for dogs, especially my Irish terrier Teedo. By the age of six or seven I had a "*naturalistic* interest in experiencing direct contact with wildlife and the outdoors." By eight or ten I was developing "an *ecologistic and scientific* inclination to understand the biological functioning of organisms and their habitat." In my early teens I was shooting birds I considered harmful to other birds and killing a few mammals for one reason or another. This attitude about killing, which didn't last long, could be called *dominionistic*. In high school I painted many watercolors, among them wildlife and wild scenes, indicating "an *aesthetic* attraction for animals and nature." By the late teens I could be called a conservationist, who had a "*moralistic* concern for ethical relations with the natural world." I probably began having certain *negativistic* feelings about nature with my first case of poison ivy or bee sting. From then on I was from time to time reminded that nature could harm or kill me, especially when a grizzly bear tried to do me in. Along the way, I had to realize that a *utilitarian* attitude toward nature was necessary, since all the physical things we have or use come ultimately from nature. Like most people, I have practiced "a *symbolic* use of animals and nature for communication and thought," such as, "He's a rat."

Which of these valuations are most important for developing an environmental conscience? The *humanistic* and *naturalistic* lead one to an early love of nature; the *ecologistic and scientific* to an understanding of nature and our place in it; and the *moralistic* to a concern for the well-being of nature. These often happen as a child moves from five or six to ten or twelve and then the teenage years, beginning with the *humanistic* and arriving last at the *moralistic*. With a love and understanding of nature one can realize and hate what we are doing to it and what a threat this is to ourselves as well. The result, one hopes, is an active, voting environmentalist.

Two attributes of early childhood should be engaged by those introducing a child to nature. One is the sense of wonder. The other is the "bug stage," a fascination with things that creep and crawl.

Rachel Carson wrote eloquently about the importance of adults helping children use their innate sense of wonder to experience nature in its many forms. "If a child is to keep alive his inborn sense of wonder...he needs the companionship of at least one adult who can share it, rediscovering with him the joy, excitement, and mystery of the world we live in." [1]

Furthermore, experiencing these feelings should come before learning the facts of nature.

> I sincerely believe that for the child, and for the parent seeking to guide him, it is not half so important to *know* as to *feel*. If facts are the seeds that later produce knowledge and wisdom, then the emotions and the impressions of the senses are the fertile soil in which the seeds must grow. The years of early childhood are the time to prepare the soil. Once the emotions have been aroused...then we wish for knowledge about the object of our emotional response. Once found, it has lasting meaning. It is more important to pave the way for the child to want to know than to put him on a diet of facts he is not ready to assimilate. [2]

E. O. Wilson put it this way with regard to naturalists: "Most children have a bug period, and I never outgrew mine. Hands-on experience at the critical time, not systematic knowledge, is what counts in the making of a naturalist. Better to be an untutored savage for a while, not to know the names or anatomical detail. Better to spend long stretches of time just searching and dreaming.[3]

Two barriers to creating the child-nature bond are cultural changes that have occurred in recent decades: the fascination of electronic devices, including television, and the fear of parents that something will happen to their children if they go alone into the woods. A growing literature addresses the whole matter of establishing children's bonds with nature. Prominent in these writings is Richard Louv's book, *Last Child in the Woods: Saving Our Children from Nature-Deficit Disorder*.[4] He thoroughly presents the problems and possible solutions. I heartily agree with the *Boston Globe* reviewer who wrote: "This book is an absolute must-read for parents."

(On July 1, 2009 my wife and I heard Louv speak at the Chautauqua Institution in New York State. He humorously described his own passion for nature as a child: "Many children, like me, had a special place in nature they went to. I had some woods. When developers' stakes began appearing, I pulled them up. Some years later I told this to a developer, who said, 'You'd have been more effective if you had just moved the stakes.'")

How, I ask myself, have I influenccd the feelings about nature of my own children and grandchildren? I think I should have done more. Rather than deliberately teaching them, I've assumed or hoped they've gotten positive feelings by osmosis—by being with me and knowing my interests.

What has my record been? As for my three daughters, I've taken them camping and taught two of them such things as how to build a fire. I've taken them to national parks: Yellowstone; Great Smoky Mountains, horseback riding; Shenandoah; Isle Royale, camping, hiking, canoeing; Joshua Tree; several parks in South Africa and Kenya. We drew animals at the national zoo in Washington, walked and bicycled along the C&O Canal.

In later life two of them set up bird feeders, but none became serious birders or joined any conservation organizations. I think they all believe climate change is happening, but I don't know how they feel about nature in general—probably they do have positive feelings. Just a few minutes ago, on the phone, our oldest daughter Eleanor said she likes to look at birds, though she knows the names of only a few common ones. And she likes pictures with birds in them.

A New Year's Day tradition, walking along the C&O Canal
with our children

I painted this mural in the basement of our Ann Arbor home to illustrate
characters in my bedtime stories about Gug-a-rum, the bullfrog in the
Big Spring, Mount Vernon, Missouri

As for our five grandchildren, none have lived near us, so we see them only occasionally. Our youngest daughter Molly and her family recently moved to a house on six wooded acres in Michigan. She and her husband have become very interested in feeding birds, and when I was there I started a list of birds at the feeders and on their property, including wild turkeys that hang around. At Christmas I gave their nine-year-old son Carson a folder depicting animal tracks, and he liked looking for tracks in the snow. Our middle daughter Libby and her husband and three children used to live in Montreal. I took her two boys birdwatching there, and one in Switzerland, where they moved later. Now they live in California, where Libby likes to take them walking in nearby parks. Her oldest son, William, has volunteered with two organizations that rehabilitate injured wild animals and then entered the University of British Columbia, where he plans to major in biology. Andrew, his younger brother, has developed an interest in astrophysics and volunteers at a museum of astronomy.

So I have hope that one or two of my grandchildren will become earth stewards.

Today's children are the earth stewards of tomorrow. Today's adults must be stewards now. (If you don't understand the urgency, read Lester Brown's book, *World on the Edge*.) The word "green" is now in everyone's vocabulary, but everyone doesn't *act* green. It's a matter, as many have said, of cultural evolution. Let's hope that fear of what can happen to us, love of the earth that supports us, and guilt from degrading our natural home, will move that evolution fast enough. Then our children can keep the world on a healthy path.

Appendix

Other Children and Nature

Before and during my growing up, prominent people displayed the same passion for nature that I did. Here are the stories of a few who affected millions by their writings or actions.

John Burroughs (1837-1921)

The naturalist and writer John Burroughs grew up on a farm in the Catskills, on the slope of a mountain called "Old Clump." He called this "the mountain out of whose loins I sprang." [My father] "knew nothing of what we call love of nature....Probably I got my love for the contemplative life and for nature more through my mother...."[1]

But what sparked this love was simply his life on the farm and nearby environments. "The farm boy always has the whole of nature at his elbow and he is usually aware of it."

> Natural history was a subject unknown to me in my boyhood, and such a thing as nature study in the schools was of course unheard of. Our natural history we got unconsciously in the sport at noon time, or on our way to and from school or in the Sunday excursions to the streams and woods....I early became familiar with the songs and habits of all the common birds, and with field mice and the frogs, toads, lizards, and snakes. Also with the wild bees and wasps. One season I made a collection of bumble-bee honey, studying the habits of five or six different kinds and rifling their nests....I used to creep on my hands and knees through the woods to see the partridge in the act of drumming.[2]

He noted when flowers bloomed and birds came back in spring. On the way to school, "How the tracks in the snow—squirrels, hares, skunks, foxes—used to excite my curiosity."[3]

John of course hunted and fished like every farm boy. When twelve or thirteen he saw a hare huddled in snow between the roots of a maple tree. Taking up a large stone he hurled it at the hare but missed by a foot. The hare bounded off. Every animal was fair game. "This desire of the farm boy to slay every wild creature he saw was universal in my time."[4]

In spite of his love of nature, he had no compunctions about killing things. "A [pleasant] duty during those years was shooting chipmunks around the corn [which they pulled up and ate]....How remorselessly I used to kill them." Shooting matches were held. "A chipmunk's tail counted one, a red squirrel's three, a gray squirrel's still more. Hawks' heads and owls' heads counted as high as ten, I think. Crows' heads also counted pretty high." A man asked him to help him, offering "so much per unit....I found up in the sap bush a brood of young screech owls just out of the nest and I killed them all." "In those days the farmer's hand was against nearly every wild thing."[5] (The man never paid him.)

Burroughs' bond with nature seemed to come from something innate, perhaps with some genetic help from his mother, as he thought. And so did his desire to write, mostly about nature. "I had it in my blood, I guess."[6] But success was slow in coming, and his wife thought literary efforts not very important. To make a living, he tried many things: bank examiner, grape raising, school teaching, clerk in the U.S. Treasury Department. He wrote in his spare time. (And shot birds for his collection, to be mounted in glass cases—a popular thing to do in those days.) Among the 23 volumes of his work are *Wake Robin, Camping and Tramping with Roosevelt, Squirrels and other Fur-Bearers, John James Audubon,* and *Winter Sunshine.*

Gradually he gained a large readership and was able to build a house on the Hudson River across from Hyde Park. In the early 1890s he built a cabin two miles away that he called Slabsides, and here he did much of his best writing. My lasting image of John Burroughs is of a tall, slender man in a dark suit hunched over a writing desk in the parlor at Slabsides, his long white beard brushing the desk top. Outside, birds sing.

John Muir (1838-1914)

In his autobiography, John Muir wrote, "When I was a boy in Scotland, I was fond of everything that was wild, and all my life I've been growing fonder and fonder of wild places and wild creatures."[7] "He had no doubt that it was 'inherited wildness' that set him apart as a child from most of the adults he knew...."[8]

Muir's parents did not encourage his passion for nature. The only adult he mentions as someone who did was his grandfather Gilrye, a butcher. "My earliest recollections of the country were gained on short walks with my grandfather when I was perhaps not over three years old."[9]

When the family moved from Scotland to Wisconsin, young Muir found plenty of wildness—perhaps too much for his father, who never made a satisfactory living there. But John rejoiced in the "paradise of birds," especially the passenger pigeons whose hordes came through in spring and fall.

At the same time, Muir, like other boys of frontier Wisconsin, carried a gun and aimed "at whatever came into [their] sights." [10] He hunted deer, muskrats, raccoons, foxes, hares, and gophers. And ate pigeon pie, like all his neighbors. In later life he regretted the savagery his beloved wilderness had inspired, and "learned to practice a higher ethic toward other creatures."[11]

As he matured, Muir swung back and forth between work on the farm and activities elsewhere. At twenty-two he entered the University of Wisconsin in Madison. After completing two years there, he fled to the Canadian woods to escape conscription into the Union army, as his younger brother Dan had already done. John and his two brothers felt no special allegiance to the United States nor interest in any of the moral issues of the Civil War.

Muir spent two years in Canada collecting plant specimens and working in a woodworking factory. Then, the war having ended, he took a job in a large steam-powered factory making wagon parts in Indianapolis. Here he continued inventing machines and devices, something he had done for years, and felt himself becoming used to this sort of life. One night, as he was using a file, it slipped from his hand and flew up, piercing the cornea of his right eye. In a few days his left eye went blind "from sympathetic nervous shock."[12] Most of his sight and strength returned within a month. After a summer at home, he set out on a thousand-mile walk to the Gulf of Mexico, botanizing along the way, and thinking about his religious philosophy and future. By the end of this monumental trek Muir had cleansed his mind of his father's fierce Christianity—indeed Christianity in any form—and anchored his faith in God's nature.

Soon he was on his way to California, Yosemite Valley, and fame as an apostle of nature, a writer, and, eventually, father of preservationist conservation in America.

W. H. Hudson (1841-1922)

W. H. Hudson, the British naturalist and writer best known for his novel, *Green Mansions*, describes his childhood on the Argentine pampas in an enthralling memoir, *Far Away and Long Ago*. His parents had bought a ranch and raised sheep and cattle, which wandered freely over the pampas as other people's livestock did. Old trees surrounded the house, making an arboreal island in the vast grassland.

The young Hudson reveled in this environment.

> ...my memory takes me back to a time...when the delight I experienced in all natural things was purely physical. I rejoiced in colours, scents, sounds, in taste and touch: the blue of the sky...the sparkle of sunlight on water...the smell of dry or moist soil...of herbs and flowers...and there were certain colours in flowers, and in the plumage and eggs of birds...which intoxicated me with delight. When, riding on the plains I discovered a patch of scarlet verbenas in full bloom...I would throw myself from my pony with a cry of joy to lie on the turf among them and feast my sight on their brilliant colour."[13]

Around his eighth year,

> I began to be distinctly conscious of something more than this mere childish delight in nature....it was as if some hand had surreptitiously dropped something into the honeyed cup which gave it at certain times a new flavor. It gave me little thrills, often purely pleasurable, at other times startling, and there were occasions when it became so poignant as to frighten me. The sight of a magnificent sunset was sometimes almost more than I could endure and made me wish to hide myself away.[14]

This animism, as he called it, when "roused by the sight of a small and beautiful or singular object, such as a flower," simply intensified "the object's loveliness." Certain flowers aroused this feeling to a high degree, others less so. Trees evoked the feeling even more powerfully. He would go out in moonlight and gaze at "a group of large trees...." at such times the sense of mystery would grow until a sensation of delight would change to fear, and the fear increase until it was no longer to be borne, and I would hastily escape to recover the sense of reality and safety indoors, where there was light and company." Yet he would go out the next night...." the effect was strongest...among the large...white acacia trees" whose "featherly foliage on moonlight nights had a peculiar hoary aspect that made this tree seem more intensely alive than others, more conscious of my presence and watchful of me."

This sense of animism declined over the years, he says, but never entirely left him. "I can say of myself with regard to this primitive faculty and emotion—this sense of the supernatural in natural things, as I have called it—that...the feeling has never been wholly outlived."

The extraordinary intensity of Hudson's feelings about nature is stronger than that of anyone else I've read about. Perhaps John Muir comes closest. Hudson laments the fact that so many lose the attachment to nature that they felt for a while in childhood. This sounds similar to the loss of expression of E. O. Wilson's biophilia, which may be maintained only by exposure to natural environments and the encouragement of adults.

Theodore Roosevelt (1858-1919)

If he hadn't gone into politics, Theodore Roosevelt probably would have been a natural historian, and indeed was partly that throughout his life. Why? When someone asked him about this, in later life, he replied, "I can no more explain why I like natural history than why I like California canned peaches." Neither parent had a special interest in nature, though his father helped to found the American Museum of Natural History in New York. Theodore's Uncle Robert, who lived next door, wrote books about wildlife and might be expected to have encouraged him in this interest, but TR never acknowledged this. "Everything indicates that, in this matter, Theodore made his own decision, uninfluenced, at least to any conspicuous degree, by any other person."[15]

One must conclude that his love of and deep interest in nature was programmed in his genes.

At age seven, "Teedie," having acquired a seal's skull, started the "Roosevelt Museum of Natural History" with two of his cousins. At nine he produced a "Natural History on Insects." "…mostly," he wrote, "I have gained their habbits from observ-a-tion." After discussing and illustrating species of ants, spiders, lady-bugs, fire flies, horned "beetles," and dragonflies, he decides to include hawks, minnows, and crayfish as well.[16]

The Roosevelt home was in Manhattan, but beginning in 1863 the family spent four summers at their place in rural Madison, New Jersey, and after that they bought a country home at Barrytown-on-Hudson, New York. So from the age of five Teedie had rural landscapes to explore and in which to collect birds' nests and eggs, turtles, frogs, and whatever else he could find or capture. Many of these ended up in the Roosevelt Museum. Others seem to have lived elsewhere in the house. The washerwoman complained, "How can I do the laundry… with a snapping turtle tied to the legs of the sink."[17]

By age twelve he was recording his observations of birds by their scientific names (evidence of Kellert's *ecologistic and scientific* valuation of nature). At fourteen, wearing spectacles that allowed him to see even small birds, he "focused his general interest in animals to an almost total obsession with birds."[18] Having received a gun before the spectacles, he had been unable to hit any birds with it, but his bird collecting began in earnest while starting a cruise up the Nile, bespectacled, with his family. He shot a small warbler. By the end of the 1200-mile trip up and down the Nile, Teedie reckoned he had collected between one and two hundred birds.

After further travels in Europe, the Roosevelt children were placed with a family in Dresden, Germany, for daily studies, while their father attended to business in Vienna. During his time off, Teedie, now armed with a double-barreled shotgun his father had given him the preceding Christmas, "collected specimens industriously…hedgehogs and other small beasts and reptiles."[19]

In 1875 he collected specimens in the Adirondacks, Long Island, and New Jersey. During his years at Harvard, he kept animals in his room before skinning them; published his first printed book, *The Summer Birds of the Adirondacks*, and by 1877 had a collection of birds and skins numbering "well into the hundreds" that "was probably unequaled in variety and quality by any American of his age."[20]

By his junior year he still thought of becoming a natural historian, but certain developments changed his mind. Politics had strongly appealed to him, and one of his professors suggested that "the halls of American government were much more in need of idealistic young men than were zoological laboratories."[21] And Alice Lee, whom he desperately hoped to marry, was put off by all his collecting and didn't want to marry a zoologist. Though his natural history interests continued, he decided to get on the political track. As the first conservationist President, he was a major influence in turning the country toward a concern for conserving natural resources, and established many public lands to help achieve this.

While President his interest in natural history didn't fade. He kept a list of the birds he saw on the White House grounds. And after his presidency he collected large animal skins in Africa and helped to collect specimens in Brazil for the Smithsonian Institution. In E. O. Wilson's thinking, Teddy showed a lifelong expression of biophilia, something that can be shown by hunters.

Franklin Roosevelt (1882-1945)

At my parents' cocktail parties, where my father, a deep Republican, railed at the latest atrocities of Franklin Roosevelt, I was mainly interested in getting cherries from the guests' manhattans. If I had been sixteen or seventeen, I might have had a better opinion of Roosevelt than my father had, because in the 1930s his administration was introducing the most important conservation measures since the days of Theodore Roosevelt, 30 years earlier. Among these were the creation of the Civilian Conservation Corps, establishment of the Soil Conservation Service to restore badly eroded land, and the Tennessee Valley Authority to improve life in a degraded, poor region; and he greatly expanded the land in national forests, national parks, and national wildlife refuges.

As Philip Shabecoff wrote in *A Fierce Green Fire*, "the conservation ethic introduced as a central feature of federal policy by Theodore Roosevelt was carried a giant step forward by his cousin Franklin."[22]

All this might not have happened if Franklin Roosevelt had had a different kind of childhood. As it was, he grew up in an environment conducive to appreciation of nature, among people who encouraged that appreciation. That, it seems, made all the difference.

His home was at Hyde Park, New York, on the east bank of the

Hudson River, a few miles north of Poughkeepsie. His father, James, bought 110 acres here in 1867 and renamed the property Spring-wood. By the time Franklin was born, in January 1882, Springwood encompassed some 1,000 acres. Old-growth and virgin forest of hemlock, beech, and other trees covered the slope below the house leading toward the river. Other parts of the land were in hay, crops, woods, and pasture for James's dairy cows.

Though James called himself a farmer, he emulated the life of an English country gentleman, taking daily rides around his property to check on his workers, crops, and livestock. When Franklin was barely out of babyhood, he sat on his father's shoulder as he made the rounds, and when six accompanied him on his own pony.

James Roosevelt loved the outdoors, its plants and animals, and particularly its trees. He would not allow any to be cut unless dead or diseased. Franklin absorbed these loves on their many walks and rides, and learned from his father how to hunt, fish, row, sail, and, when the Hudson froze, how to skate and handle an ice boat.

Early on, Franklin became an almost obsessive collector. He collected books, prints and models of naval ships, family mementos, stamps, and birds. His bird collection—over 300 specimens—consists of skins in the Hyde Park museum and mounted birds in a case in the entrance hallway of the manor house. Franklin, like many boys at that time, had brought home bird nests and eggs when he was quite young, but decided when he was ten that he wanted to collect birds themselves—all those found in Dutchess County. This became possible the next year when his father gave him a small-caliber rifle, exacting the promise that he would shoot only one male and one female of each species, and not shoot any during the breeding season.

For three years, until he was thirteen, Franklin kept a bird diary (held in the Franklin D. Roosevelt Archives, Hyde Park), recording the birds he shot and those he just saw, as well as weather conditions and occasional mention of wildflowers. One day we also find: "Caught at Tuxedo a 1 ½ lb. land-locked salmon." Walking about the Springwood grounds today, one can imagine him shooting some of the mounted birds at the manor house: the Scarlet Tanager in the tall old trees below the house and the Lesser Yellowlegs, Spotted, Semipalmated, and Solitary Sandpipers down by the river or at the adjacent marsh. On the lawns and in the scattered trees around the buildings one can still see birds he frequently mentions in his diaries, such as bluebird, Chipping Sparrow, robin, phoebe, goldfinch.

It's very unlikely that he succeeded in collecting *all* the birds recorded in Dutchess County, but it was enough to impress his grandfather Warren Delano, who made him a life member of the New York Museum of Natural History, and Frank M. Chapman, curator of ornithology there, who offered him an associate membership in the American Ornithologists Union in exchange for the gift of ten Pine Grosbeak skins (a departure from the one male, one female rule); they were "very tame" he noted in his bird diary.

Franklin didn't just collect birds; he was very knowledgeable about them. At Campobella, where the family had a summer home, he gave a talk on ornithology to a nature class and parents. During the winter, when the family lived in New York City, he went to lectures about birds. It was an interest that diminished with time but never disappeared.

His love of trees and forests never diminished. He planted some 220,000 trees at Hyde Park. "When he was away from home, and reports of bad storms in Dutchess County reached him, his first comment was always 'I wonder what it did to the trees.'"[23]

Rexford Tugwell, a member of FDR's "brain trust," in his biography *The Democratic Roosevelt*, aptly describes Franklin's feelings about the American land:

> This [growing up at Hyde Park] was the first emergence... of his lifelong preoccupation with conservation. The earth and its inhabitants—plant and animal—he always treated as something especially precious....Trees and grass, well-tended crops, contented animals—these belonged to the round and rhythm of nature. His father had started him on this lesson. He developed it for himself, and its application was persistent. It was part and parcel of his religion.... Compromise and dissimulation were to be characteristic in his career. But about conservation there was something so special that when it was involved he seldom gave way to expediency.[24]

Rachel Carson (1907-1964)

Rachel Carson said once, "I can remember no time, even in earliest childhood, when I didn't assume I was going to be a writer. Also I can remember no time when I wasn't interested in the out-of-doors and the whole world of nature. Those interests, I know, I inherited from my mother and have always shared with her." On other occasions she added that among her earliest memories was a "feeling of absolute fascination for everything relating to the ocean."[25]

Maria Carson tried to pass on her love of and interest in nature to her children, taking them on long walks through the woods of the 64-acre Carson property, which sloped down from their hilltop house to the Allegheny River, sharing her knowledge of natural history--botany and birds especially. Neighbors believed that young Rachel's fascination with the ocean began, perhaps on one of these walks, when she discovered a large fossilized shell in a rock outcropping and wondered about the life and environment of the animal that had lived in it.

Maria's interest in nature was deepened by the teachings of the nature-study movement so popular from the 1870s until after World War I. Its aim, as Anna Botsford Comstock wrote in her *Handbook of Nature Study*, was to instill a "love of the beautiful," a "sense of companionship with life out-of-doors, and an abiding love of nature."[26] Furthermore, the movement taught that nature, the work of the Creator, was holy, and that the conservation movement was a religious crusade.

Rachel began writing as a child. A ten-page book, for her father, depicted animals she liked, and included a rhyming verse to go with each one. At about age eight she wrote "The Little Brown House," describing two wrens searching for and then finding a home. In fourth grade she wrote "A Sleeping Rabbit" and drew a cover illustration of a fat white rabbit sitting asleep beside a table on which lay a book entitled *Peter Rabbit*.

Recognition of genuine talent came when her story, "A Battle in the Clouds," was published in *St. Nicholas*, a magazine for children. The story was about the death of a Canadian pilot in combat over France during World War I, which her older brother Robert had described in a letter home. This was a real coup for an eleven-year-old. She won a silver badge for runner-up in the contest for best entry, and later a gold badge for another story, which put her in impressive company. Between 1907 and 1917 badge winners included William Faulkner, F. Scott Fitzgerald, S. Eliot Morison, Edna St. Vincent Millay, Stephen Vincent Benet, and E.B. White. When she was fourteen, Rachel was paid by *St. Nicholas* for a "publicity piece." She later said that was when she became a professional writer.

Rachel's determination to be a writer and her love for all of nature never dimmed, but how these would affect her life took several

twists and turns influenced by people important to her. At Pennsyl-
vania College for Women, in nearby Pittsburgh, she was required
to take a course in English composition, taught by Miss Grace Croff.
By spring of that first year, Miss Croff had become her friend and
mentor, and advised her to join the college newspaper and con-
tribute to its literary supplement. Her first piece was a short story
entitled "The Master of the Ship's Light." It vividly portrayed the
seacoast and ocean, a world she knew only through her reading
of great sea literature. Almost presciently, Miss Croff commented
about this story that "Your style is so good because you have made
what might be a relatively technical subject very intelligible to the
reader."[27]

In her sophomore year, Rachel took a year-long biology course
to fulfill the science requirement. The course was taught by Mary
Scott Skinker, who would change Rachel Carson's life. Tall, dynam-
ic, and glamorous, Miss Skinker taught biology from a deep fund
of knowledge and passion for the subject. Rachel was hooked. She
had been shown new and endless possibilities in scientific study of
the natural world.

During her junior year Carson's excitement about biology continued to grow. She had intended a writing career, "But by 1928
Mary Scott Skinker had replaced Maria Carson and Grace Croff as
Rachel's mentor....Skinker showed her that through the life sciences she might understand, rather than merely observe, the natural
world."[28] Rachel committed to science, changing her major from
English to biology in the spring of her junior year.

After graduation she spent a summer at the Marine Biological
Laboratory at Woods Hole, Massachusetts and finally could see
and study the ocean she had dreamed about for so many years. At
Johns Hopkins University in Baltimore, where she went for graduate work, money problems forced her to take a part-time job, which
stretched the time it took to get a Master's degree to three years.

She then tried to find a teaching job, but none was offered. Turning to writing for income, she revised some of her best college short
stories and poems and tried selling them to major magazines. They
were rejected, but in the process she experienced a reawakening of
her desire to write.

Providentially, someone appeared who would help Rachel Carson turn toward her true calling. In 1929, at the beginning of her
graduate studies, she had met Elmer Higgins, then the acting director of the U.S. Bureau of Fisheries, Division of Scientific Inquiry, in
the Department of Commerce. Higgins had suggested that govern-

ment science might be the best option for her. Now Miss Skinker, who was working and studying in the Washington-Baltimore area, persuaded Rachel to take examinations for federal jobs in biology, on which she did well, and to call again on Elmer Higgins, which she also did.

The upshot was that Higgins contracted with her to write fifty-two short radio programs on marine life. In July 1936 she took a job that had opened up—junior aquatic biologist in Higgins's Division of Scientific Inquiry. Besides analyzing data on Chesapeake Bay fish, the job entailed writing reports and producing brochures for the public on fish conservation.

Thus began a 15-year trajectory in which Carson combined work as a federal scientist and outside writing—writing that she hoped would become her sole work. In 1937 the *Atlantic Monthly* published her article, "Undersea," about sea creatures and the oceans that sustain them. She had reached the bigtime. From those four pages, she later said, "everything else followed."[29] In 1941, Simon and Schuster published her book, *Under the Sea Wind*. And in 1951, with the assistance of a literary agent, Marie Rodell, *The Sea Around Us* was published by the Oxford University Press. Helped by previous publication in *The New Yorker* of nine of the fourteen chapters of this book, its sales reached 250,000 by the end of 1952. With added income from a very successful republishing of *Under the Sea Wind*, Carson became financially independent and could devote herself entirely to her own writing.

She had at last realized her childhood dream. Her fame reached a peak with publication in 1962 of *Silent Spring*, about the alarming environmental effects of persistent pesticides, called by some the most important book of the 20th century. Sadly, she did not live to see the banning of long-lived pesticides in the U.S. and the surge in environmentalism that this book helped to cause. Cancer, and finally a heart attack, took her in 1964.

Thinking once again about the sources of her bond with nature and desire to write apparently were, as she said, genetic. Backing up this conclusion was the fact that her brother and sister also went on outdoor excursions with their mother, but developed no lasting interest in nature. Mentors certainly helped guide her toward the so successful blending of the two impulses. (Their guidance in effect was along the lines of advice I heard Robert Frost give aspiring writers in a lecture at Amherst College: "Don't take courses in writing; take courses in things you want to write about.") Her poetic but scientifically accurate evocation of the sea and nature, and her defense of nature, gave millions inspiration to love and defend what she loved.

Roger Tory Peterson (1908-1996)

Roger Peterson must have had a heavy dose of something like biophilia in his genes, for very few people have had such an intense, single-minded devotion to nature and its conservation. While one individual helped to trigger this obsession, once Peterson was on that track he ran down it full throttle the rest of his life, gaining ever-increasing success and fame.

Why and how did this happen to the person who was called by various people "the high priest of birdwatching," "the great man," "a genius," even "the father of the environmental movement?" As usual we have to look first at the early years.

Peterson described himself before the age of eleven as "rudderless." His biographers (and apparently Peterson himself) have said little about any interest in nature he might have had during those years. Instead, we get a picture of a rebellious child, often inattentive in school or absent, yearning to be free to do whatever he wanted to do. Ethnic prejudices where he lived, in Jamestown, New York, and a sometimes drunk, razor-strap-applying father didn't help.

Jamestown was founded by landed English gentry, who looked down on Swedes, who came next. Irish, and finally Italians, followed the Swedes and suffered the same discrimination in their turn. Roger, whose father was Swedish, more than once found himself in Swedish-Italian gang fights. Skinny but strong, he held his own. There was still discrimination against Swedes; signs said "No Dogs or Swedes Allowed," and "Only English Spoken Here." Such attitudes may have festered in Roger's subconscious and helped to fuel a determination to achieve eminence.

Roger, whom someone called "the mischievous boy of Bowen Street," frequently got in scrapes that prompted his father Charles's use of the razor strap. When Roger became obsessed with butterflies and then birds, Charles could not see any future in that and often said so. It was a very different relationship from the one that Franklin Roosevelt, for instance, enjoyed with his father. It is unfortunate that the young boy, apparently, did not know that "Charles was always extraordinarily proud of Roger, even if he could not understand him," as Charles's physician, Carl Hammerstrom, observed.[30]

Roger rebelled in school as well. For instance, instead of walking out of school two by two, as the students were required to do, he would go down the fire escape. Such behavior earned him a school record number of ruler whackings on his outstretched hands by the principal. In high school he often fell asleep in class, causing his classmates to call him "Sleeping Jesus." But this may have been due to his 3:00 a.m. waking to run his newspaper route, rather than disinterest in the subject at hand.

He did excel in certain subjects—art, history of art, mechanical drawing, and English composition. We see here a suggestion of the talents that later defined him—writing and painting. The subject matter to which these talents would be applied was beginning to appear.

Marlene Mudge, archivist at the Roger Tory Peterson Institute in Jamestown, said that Roger was collecting bugs, butterflies, and moths when he was seven or eight. Peterson's biographers describe this interest as beginning at a later age. In any case, it was a consuming interest that became life-long. Clarence Beal, a friend who sometimes went collecting with him, said, "Roger could spot a Cecropia, Polyphemous or Promethea cocoon with uncanny skill."[31]

"I had more than eight hundred caterpillars one year," Roger recalled.[32] Another time he fastened cocoons to his mother's lace curtains in the living room. The parlor coal stove heated the room so much the insects reacted as if it was summer. Soon gorgeous luna moths and others were flying all over, laying eggs on the piano as well as curtains. Only his mother was tolerant. Surprisingly, however, his father made mitered boxes and steel cabinets to house Roger's insects.

The central passion in Peterson's life—birds—was ignited when he was eleven. He already knew something about birds, but his knowledge and interest deepened when his seventh- grade teacher, Blanche Hornbeck, had her students join the Junior Audubon Club, which sent them ten leaflets describing ten birds. She also had them copy bird paintings (Roger chose the Blue Jay, a favorite of his), and took them on bird walks.

But one event helped to turn his interest into an obsession. He and a friend, Carl Hammerstrom (later his father's doctor), who had also been inspired by Ms. Hornbeck's enthusiasm for birds, took their first bird walk together on April 8, 1920 to the wooded Swede Hill. They saw a bird clinging to a tree. "It was a flicker," Peterson recalled, "tired from migration....I thought it was dead. I poked it with my finger; instantly, this inert thing jerked its head around, looked at me wildly, then took off in a flash of gold. It was like resurrection. What had seemed dead was very much alive. Ever since then, birds have seemed to me the most vivid expression of life."[33]

But Peterson's memories sometimes conflicted. He suggested that his total absorption in birds was not as sudden as the flicker incident. "It was while on one of my butterfly forays that I first met Clarence Beal who was to become my closest friend and field companion during my Jamestown years." Beal came along a fence row, looking at birds with opera glasses. "It was that chance encounter that brought me back to birds, which became an obsession from which I never freed myself."[34] (Beal, however, remembers first meeting Roger when out visiting his winter bird-feeding stations, and Roger for some reason washing Beal's face in the snow.)

Peterson, who as a boy had been so averse to discipline and so rebellious, once commented that if it hadn't been for birds he might have ended up in a reformatory.

Once hooked, Roger thought about birds night and day, and pursued them at every opportunity on the wooded hills and farms around Jamestown. On weekends he and Clarence Beal rode their bikes as far as Lake Erie, thirty miles away, returning well after dark. In winter they attended their many feeding stations. "Every other day," Peterson recounted, "when the four-o'clock bell concluded our studies, we would don our skis and start for the woods at the edge of town with a knapsack full of grain....With us, winter bird feeding was a passion. At one time we had twenty different feeding stations...."[35] Sometimes, when the thermometer dropped below zero, they returned with ice globules on their eyelashes and icicles dripping from their noses.

At other seasons, Clarence Beal remembered, he and Roger often "returned from some swamp or from climbing to an owl's nest—covered with mud or with our clothes half torn off—much to the amusement of other streetcar passengers."[36] Sometimes they slept out. They caught crabs and boiled them in tin cans.

Clarence, and Roger especially, were not unlike the "Two Little Savages" in Ernest Thompson Seton's book, one that Roger read until it was threadbare. The hero of this story, "twelve-year-old Yan, was also Swedish. He had difficulty in school, and his classmates, like Roger's, were older boys. Yan's father had little interest in his son's birding. Roger sympathized with Yan and understood his life, for Yan wanted to run away and be free, as did Roger."[37] It seems appropriate that one feature of this story so beloved by

Roger—Yan's drawing of ducks showing their chief identifying marks—planted the basic idea of the field guides that later made Peterson famous.

At sixteen Roger graduated from high school and took a job in Jamestown decorating furniture.

Peterson's subject matter was now fixed. He had been painting birds, and two—a kingbird and a Ruby-throated Hummingbird—were accepted for exhibit at a conference of the American Ornithologists Union at the American Museum of Natural History in New York. There he met Louis Agassiz Fuertes, then the country's top bird painter, who praised his art work. He also met prominent ornithologists, such as Ludlow Griscom and Frank M. Chapman from the ornithology department of the museum. He had been recognized as an up and coming bird artist and bird expert.

Roger's boss at the Jamestown furniture company had urged him to go to art school. This he did at nineteen, when he enrolled at the Art Students League in New York. From 1927 to 1931 he studied art here and then at the National Academy of Design, taking jobs refinishing and decorating furniture to pay for art classes. During holidays and weekends he chased birds with friends from the Bronx County Bird Club. Two members—Allen Cruikshank and Joseph Hickey—became especially close friends and associates. Cruikshank would work with him for many years at the National Audubon Society.

For five summers during this time, Roger was a nature counselor at Camp Chewonki in Maine. Clarence Allen, founder of the camp and director of the Rivers School in Brookline, Massachusetts, gave him a job at the school teaching natural history, drawing, and painting. While here he produced *A Field Guide to the Birds*, published in 1934, which revolutionized identification of birds in the field by the illustration of key features of each bird. This and subsequent field guides and other books recruited millions of new birdwatchers and natural history enthusiasts. Peterson was launched on a famous career as writer, bird illustrator and painter, lecturer, naturalist, and conservationist. He educated people about the natural world and inspired them to protect it.

With some support from his mother but opposition from his father, the rebellious boy from Jamestown had discovered his true path, to the benefit of the earth, its life, and its citizens.

References

Preface

1. Leopold, Aldo, *A Sand County Almanac*. New York: Oxford University Press: 1966, pp. 219-220.
2. Kellert, Stephen R. and Edward O. Wilson, eds. *The Biophilia Hypothesis*. Washington, D.C.: Island Press, 1993, p. 31.
3. Nabhan, Gary P. and Sarah St. Antoine, Loss of Floral and Faunal Story. In Kellert and Wilson, *The Biophilia Hypothesis*.
4. Louv, Richard, *Last Child in the Woods*, 2nd ed. Chapel Hill, NC: Algonguin Books of Chapel Hill, 2008, p. 7.
5. Louv, p. 36.
6. Kellert, Stephen R., *Kinship to Mastery: Biophilia in Human Evolution and Development*. Washington, D.C.: Island Press, p. 6.
7. *Ibid*, p. 164.
8. *Ibid*, pp. 166-167.

Chapter 3   Hooked on Birds

1. Lear, Linda, *Rachel Carson: Witness for Nature*. New York: Henry Holt and Company, 1997, p. 128.

Chapter 4   Ten to Thirteen

1. Halle, Louis, *Spring in Washington*. New York: William Sloane Associates, 1947.
2. Dove, Carla, et al, *The Auk*, 121 (4), p. 1282.
3. *Ibid*, p. 1284.
4. Gasset, Jose Ortega y., *Meditations on Hunting*. New York: Charles Scribner's Sons, 1972, p.15.
5. *Ibid*, p.31.

6. *Ibid*, p.118.
7. *Ibid*, p.129.
8. Thoreau, Henry David, *Walden*. Boston: Houghton Mifflin Co., 2004, p.168.
9. *Ibid*, p.168.
10. *Ibid*, p. 169.
11. *Ibid*, p. 169.
12. *Ibid*, p. 170.

Chapter 5   Fourteen to Eighteen: At School and Afar

1. Allen D. Cruickshank, *American Birds*, Vol. 28, No. 6, 1974, p. 970.

Chapter 6   Teenage Years with the Audubon Society of the D.C.

1. Barnes, Irston, Paul Bartsch—Part III. The Lebanon Years. *Atlantic Naturalist*, Vol. 9, No. 3, 1954, p. 117.
2. Peterson, Barbara. Roger Tory Peterson Institute archives, no date.
3. Devlin, John C. and Grace Naismith, *The World of Roger Tory Peterson: An Authorized Biography*. New York: New York Times Books, 1977, p. 109.
4. Vogt, William, *New York Times*. Quoted in Devlin and Naismith, p. 65-66.
5. Duffy, David C., William Vogt: a pilgrim on the road to survival. *American Birds*, Vol. 43, No. 45, 1989, p. 1257.
6. Peterson, Roger T., *The Wood Thrush*, Vol. 2, 1947, p. 47.
7. Carson, Rachel, *The Wood Thrush*, Nov.-Dec. 1948, pp. 75-76.
8. _____, Design for Nature Writing. *Atlantic Naturalist*, May-August, 1952.
9. _____, Lost Worlds: The Challenge of the Islands. *The Wood Thrush*, May-June, 1949.
10. Lear, p.141.
11. Rivinus, Edward and Shirley Briggs, The Audubon Naturalist Society—Past Achievements and Present Challenges, *Atlantic Naturalist*, Vol. 32, 1979, p.31.
12. *Ibid*, p.32.

Chapter 7   How Washington Remained Green

1. Bartsch, Paul, The Potomac River Marshes. *The Wood Thrush*, July, 1946, p. 21.
2. Rhodes, John, How Rock Creek Park was Established. *Atlantic Naturalist*, Oct.-Dec. 1957, p. 301.
3. Act of Congress, quoted in Thomas, Bill and Phyllis, *Natural Washington*, p. 36.
4. Taggart, Hugh, Report of Hugh H. Taggart, Special Counsel, on the Ownership of Lands and Riparian Rights Along the Anacostia River, in the District of Columbia. Washington, D.C.: Government Printing Office, 1910, pp. 2-3.
5. Caemmerer,H. Paul, *Washington: The National Capital*. Washington, D.C.: Government Printing Office, 1932
6. Brinkley, David, *Washington Goes to War*. New York: Alfred Knopf, 1988, p. xiv.
7. Passonneau, Joseph R., *Washington Through Two Centuries: A History in Maps and Images*. New York: Monacelli Press, 2004, p. 164.
8. Hennessee, Judith, *Washingtonian*, May 1968. Quoted in Passonneau, p. 197.
9. *Ibid*, p. 196.
10. Grant, U.S. III, Shall We Be the Destroyers? *Atlantic Naturalist* 9, March-April 1954, pp. 173-174.
11. Audubon Naturalist Society, Washington: City in the Woods. *Atlantic Naturalist*, Nov.-Dec. 1953, p. 17.
12. *Ibid*, pp. 17-18.
13. Barnes, Irston R., Conservation. *Atlantic Naturalist*, April-June 1960, p. 114.
14. Audubon Naturalist Society, *Washington: City in the Woods*, 1954, p. 40.
15. *Ibid*, p. 45.
16. *Ibid*, p.41.
17. *Ibid*, p. 43.
18. www.nps.gov/history/history on line.books/choh/admin__history/history 4.htm.
19. Stanton, Richard L., *Potomac Journey: Fairfax Stone to Tidewater*. Washington, D.C.: Smithsonian Institution Press, 1993, p. 156.
20. Coues, Elliott. Quoted in *Washington: City in the Woods*, pp. 20-21.
21. The Trust for Public Land, *2011 City Park Facts*, p. 10.
22. *The Washington Post*, 4/30/2010.

Chapter 12   Malaysia

1. Internet. World Wildlife Foundation—Sumatra—WWF, no date.
2. Stibig, H. J., Stolle, F., Dennis, R. and C. Feldkotter, Forest Cover Change in Southeast Asia: The Regional Pattern. JRC Scientific and Technical Reports, 2007, p.7.

Chapter 14   Turkey

1. Abdul-Matin, Ibrahim, *Green Deen: What Islam Teaches About Protecting the Planet.* San Francisco: Berrett-Koehler Publishers, p. 46.
2. Lewis, Bernard, *The Emergence of Modern Turkey*, 3rd ed. New York: Oxford University Press, 2002, pp. 438-439.
3. Wilson, E.O., *The Unity of Knowledge.* New York: Alfred A. Knopf, 1998, p.294.

Chapter 15   Azerbaijan

1. Shelton, Napier, Azerbaijan: Environmental Conditions and Outlook. *Ambio*, June 2003, pp. 302-306.
2. Keenan, Brigid, Oil's Boom and Bust. *Cornucopia* 45, 2011, p.41.

Chapter 16   Is Nature Sacred?

1. Diamond, Jared, New Guineans and Their World. In Kellert and Wilson, *The Biophilia Hypothesis.*
2. Nelson, Richard, Searching for the Lost Arrow: Physical and Spiritual Ecology in the Hunter's World. In Kellert and Wilson: *The Biophilia Hypothesis*, p. 212.
3. *Ibid*, p. 213.
4. *Ibid*, p.217.
5. *Ibid*, p. 223.
6. Wilson, Edward O., *Biophilia*. Cambridge, Mass.: Harvard University Press, 1984, p. 65.
7. *Ibid*, p. 185.
8. Leopold, Aldo, *A Sand County Almanac.* New York: Oxford University Press, 1966, p. 239.
9. *Ibid*, p. 225.
10. Gould, Stephen J. Quoted in David W. Orr, Love It or Lose It. In Kellert and Wilson, *The Biophilia Hypothesis.*
11. Kellert, Stephen, *The Value of Life.* Washington, D.C.: Island Press, 1996, p. 81.

12. _____ , *Building for Life: Designing and Understanding the Human-Nature Connection*. Washington, D.C.: Island Press, 2005, p. 76.
13. Soule, Michael, Biophilia: Unanswered Questions. In Kellert and Wilson, *The Biophilia Hypothesis*, p. 454.
14. Otto, Rudolph, *The Idea of the Holy*. London: Oxford University Press, 1958, pp. 149-150.
15. Benstein, Jeremy, Alma De'atei, The World That is Coming: Reflections on Power, Knowledge, Wisdom, and Progress. In Kellert, Stephen and Timothy Farnham, *The Good in Nature and Humanity: Connecting Science, Religion, and Spirituality with the Natural World*. Washington, D.C.: Island Press, 2002, p. 135.
16. Lear, Linda, *Rachel Carson, Witness for Nature*. New York: Henry Holt and Company, 1997, p. 227.
17. Gatta, John, *Making Nature Sacred: Literature, Religion and Environment in America from the Puritans to the Present*. New York: Oxford University Press, 2004, p. 7.
18. *Ibid*. Quote is from Linda Lear, ed. *Lost Woods: The Discovered Writing of Rachel Carson*. Boston: Beacon Press, 1998, p. 160.
19. Gatta, *Making Nature Sacred*. Quote is from *Always, Rachel: The Letters of Rachel Carson and Dorothy Freeman*, pp. 67-68.
20. Gatta, p. 171.
21. Peattie, Donald Culross, *The Road of a Naturalist*. Boston: Houghton Mifflin Co., 1941, p. 64.
22. *Ibid*, p. 315.
23. *Ibid*, pp. 176-177.
24. Schweitzer, Albert, *Out of My Life and Thought: An Autobiography*. New York: Henry Holt and Co., 1990, p. 155.
25. *Ibid*, pp. 157-158.
26. DuBos, Rene, *A God Within*. New York: Charles Scribner's Sons, 1972, pp. 33-34.
27. *Ibid*, p. 38
28. *Ibid*, p. 40.
29. *Ibid*, pp. 42-43.
30. *Ibid*, p. 45.
31. Emerson, Ralph Waldo, *The Complete Essays and Other Writings of Ralph Waldo Emerson*. New York: Random House, p. 6.
32. Worster, Donald, *A Passion for Nature: The Life of John Muir*. New York: Oxford University Press, 2008, p. 160.
33. *Ibid*, p. 8.
34. *Ibid*, pp. 374-375.
35. Gatta, *Making Nature Sacred*. pp. 149-150.

36. Worster, *A Passion for Nature*, p. 33.
37. Keating, Thomas. *The Better Part: Stages of Contemplative Living.* New York: Continuum International Publishing Group, 2000, pp. 106-107.
38. Quotation from Ellard, in Berry, Thomas, *Selected Writings on the Earth Community.* Maryknoll, NY: Orbis Books.
39. *Ibid*, p. 31.
40. *Ibid*, p. 107.
41. *Ibid*, P. 119.
42. DuBos, *A God Within*, p. 157.
43. Davies, Paul, *The Mind of God*, New York: Simon and Schuster, pp. 231-232.

Chapter 17   Raising Earth Stewards

1. Carson, Rachel, *The Sense of Wonder*, New York: Harper Collins, 1998, p. 55.
2. *Ibid*, p.56.
3. Wilson, Edward O., *Naturalist*, Washington, D.C.: Island Press, 2006, pp. 11-12.
4. Louv, *Last Child in the Woods*, 2nd ed., 2008.

Appendix: Other Children and Nature

1. Burroughs, John, *My Boyhood: With a Conclusion by His Son Julian Burroughs.* Garden City, NY: Doubleday, Page and Co., 1922, pp. 102-103.
2. *Ibid*, p. 48, pp. 91-92.
3. *Ibid*, p. 83.
4. *Ibid*, p. 84.
5. *Ibid*, pp. 50-52.
6. *Ibid*, p. 148.
7. Muir, John, *An Autobiography of John Muir*. Quoted in Worster, *A Passion for Nature*, p. 13.
8. Worster, *A Passion for Nature*, p. 30.
9. Muir, John, *My Boyhood and Youth.* Quoted in Worster, *A Passion for Nature*, p. 29.
10. Worster, *A Passion for Nature*, p. 51.
11. *Ibid*, p. 51.
12. Fox, Stephen, *John Muir and His Legacy: The American Conservation Movement.* Boston: Little, Brown and Company, 1981, p. 48.

13. Hudson, W. H., *Far Away and Long Ago: A History of My Early Life*. New York: AMS Press, 1968 (from the edition of 1923), p.238.
14. *Ibid*, p. 238-239.
15. Cutright, Paul Russell, *Theodore Roosevelt: The Making of a Conservationist*. Urbana: University of Illinois Press, 1985, p. 7.
16. Morris, Edmund, *The Rise of Theodore Roosevelt*. Modern Library Paperback Edition, 2001, p. 18.
17. *Ibid*, p. 19.
18. *Ibid*, p. 36.
19. *Ibid*, p. 45. Putnam, Carleton, *Theodore Roosevelt, Vol. I: The Formative Years, 1858-1886*. Scribner's, 1958. Quoted in Morris, *The Rise of Theodore Roosevelt*.
20. Morris, *The Rise of Theodore Roosevelt*.
21. *Ibid*, p. 87.
22. Shabecoff, Philip, *A Fierce Green Fire*. New York: Hill and Wang, p. 76.
23. Morgan, Ted, *FDR: A Biography*. New York: Simon and Schuster, p. 36.
24. Tugwell, Rexford G., *The Democratic Roosevelt: A Biography of Franklin D. Roosevelt*. Garden City, New York: Doubleday and Company, 1957, p. 45.
25. Lear, Linda, *Rachel Carson*. pp. 7-8.
26. Comstock, Anna Botsford, *Handbook of Nature Study*. Ithica, New York: Cornell University Press, 1911, 1970. Quoted in Lear, *Rachel Carson*, p. 14.
27. Lear, *Rachel Carson*. pp. 33-34.
28. *Ibid*, p.43.
29. *Ibid*, p. 88.
30. Devlin and Naismith, *The World of Roger Tory Peterson*. p. 13.
31. Beal, Clarence, My Recollections of Roger Tory Peterson. RTPI archives.
32. Devlin and Naismith, *The World of Roger Tory Peterson*. p. 19.
33. Rosenthal, Elizabeth J., *Birdwatcher: The Life of Roger Tory Peterson*. Guilford, Conn.: The Lyons Press, p. 6.
34. RTP papers at RTPI archives sent to Devlin.
35. Devlin and Naismith, *The World of Roger Tory Peterson*. p. 7.
36. Beal, Clarence, Letter to Edwin Way Teale, 3/2/49, RTPI archives.
37. Devlin and Naismith, p. 16.

Acknowledgements

I am deeply and most indebted to Kent and Marcia Minichiello for their extremely helpful readings of my drafts of this book. After reading my first draft, which carried my story to around age 20, they recommended that I extend it to the rest of my life, to show what the first part led to. So I did, and they both carefully read that draft as well, making numerous thoughtful suggestions and corrections throughout. This book is partly theirs.

The book is dedicated to my father. He must have passed on nature-loving genes to me, because I don't know any other reason for the origin of my interest. Thereafter, he always encouraged this love, giving me books about various facets of the natural world and binoculars to see it more clearly, introducing me to his friends with similar interests, and following my development as a writer. He was, among other professions, a journalist.

Donald Edward McHenry, first Chief Naturalist of the National Capital Parks and later of Yosemite National Park, was a mentor who got me involved as a Junior Member of the Audubon Society of the D.C., and, with his wife, Bona May McHenry, welcomed me to their lockhouse home on the C&O Canal, and later to their home in Yosemite valley, where he arranged summer jobs for me. His son Bruce was my best friend and observant companion on many canal walks and a hike along the John Muir Trail in California.

Other encouragers along the way included Paul Fundenberg, whose seashells from Florida started me collecting natural things; Charles Woodbury, a neighbor and early member of the Wilderness Society, who invited me to watch the many birds at his feeder; Alexander Wetmore and Roxie Collie Simpson at the Smithsonian Institution; and Millicent Todd Bingham, who hosted me at her summer cottage next to a National Audubon Society camp in Maine.

Ferdinand Ruge, a teacher at St. Albans School, taught me how to write "clear, correct, and reasonably graceful English." Shirley Briggs enlisted and helped me as a writer for publications of the Audubon Naturalist Society. Vincent Gleason, my boss in the National Park Service, gave me contracts to write several books for the NPS when I was a free-lancer.

Sam Lloyd, former dean of the Washington National Cathedral, helped me understand why the Church was slow to join the environmental movement, and described his own relationship with nature.

The staffs of the national parks I wrote about—Saguaro, Shenandoah, Isle Royale, Great Smoky Mountains, and C&O Canal, were all very helpful, as were the archivists at Franklin D. Roosevelt's home at Hyde Park, and at the Roger Tory Peterson Institute in Jamestown, NY

During my times abroad many people helped me with information and logistics: In Sarawak, Bernstein Daud Rajit, Bintulu Lumber Company; and Councillor Denis Mujang, chief of an Iban village. In Sabah, H.H. Bill and Albert Ganing, Weyerheuser. In Singapore, Chris Hails, University of Malaya. At Gunung Leuser National Park in Sumatra, Dr. Suharto Djojosudarmo, director of the Bohorok Orangutan Rehabilitation Centre, Nasori Djajalaksana, park warden, and Carel Van Schaik, Dutch researcher at the Ketembe Research Station. In Nigeria: J.S, Ibeun, superintendent, and Yusuf, guide at Kainji Lake National Park; Baba Grema, Senior Game Warden, Borno State; and Mark Boachi, my assistant from Ghana, who kept me out of trouble on our journeys around the country. In Turkey: The Society for the Protection of Nature in Turkey, especially Gernant Magnin, for information about migrating raptors, and Sunay Demircan, for explaining problems at the Kizilirmak Delta; Erdogan Kuknaroglu, at the U.S. consulate in Istanbul, who drove Elizabeth and me many places around the country; and Mustafa Sari, guide, who found Caucasian Black Grouse for me.

Moving on to Azerbaijan, ornithologist Dr. Elchin Sultanov offered his broad knowledge about the country's birds and conservation issues. Elnur, whose last name I forgot, drove me all over the country. And John Boit, editor of the English language newspaper in Baku, let me write a column about environmental problems, complete with an accompanying drawing of my wise countenance.

I thank the many authors listed in the references for supplying much of the informational foundation of this book.

Anna Lawton, Director of New Academia Publishing, has kindly answered my many questions about the publishing process, and her staff has done an excellent job of carrying out that process.

To my wife, Elizabeth, love and thanks for keeping me on the writing track when I considered more lucrative tracks.

To the (probably) many others who slipped through the cracks in my memory I offer my sincere apologies.